Pontiac 1946-1978

The Classic Postwar Years

Jan P. Norbye and Jim Dunne

Motorbooks International
Publishers & Wholesalers ®

This edition published in 1993 by Motorbooks International Publishers & Wholesalers, PO Box 2, 729 Prospect Avenue, Osceola, WI 54020 USA

© Jan P. Norbye and Jim Dunne, 1979, 1993

This is a reissue of the 1979 original edition with corrections and revisions added

Motorbooks International books are also available at discounts in bulk quantity for industrial or sales-promotional use. For details write to Special Sales Manager at the Publisher's address

Library of Congress Cataloging-in-Publication Data
Norbye, Jan P.
    [Pontiac]
    Pontiac, 1946-1978 : the classic postwar years / Jan P. Norbye, Jim Dunne.
        p.   cm.
    Originally published: Pontiac. 1979.
    Includes index.
    ISBN 0-87938-732-7
    1. Pontiac automobile—History.   I. Dunne, Jim.   II. Title.
TL215.P68N67   1993
629.222'0973'09045—dc20   92-33785

On the front cover: The 1955 Pontiac Star Chief Convertible owned by June Trombley. *Bud Juneau*

Printed and bound in the United States of America

Table of Contents

CHAPTER 1

Pontiac's Pedigree

WHAT WENT ON BEFORE 1945 has a bearing upon the postwar Pontiacs in several ways. Many of the major components in the 1946 models were put back into production without change from prewar specifications. The conditions under which the Pontiac marque was created explain to some extent why the product evolved the way it did, and how the division's status within the corporation was established. And the men who ran Pontiac in earlier times were responsible for setting traditions that were maintained long after their day was over. No book on Pontiac in the postwar years can be considered complete unless the salient points in Pontiac's prior history are presented.

Pontiac's pedigree as a make of car starts in 1926. It was then a product of Oakland Motor Company, division of General Motors, which was transformed into Pontiac Motor Company in 1932, after the Oakland car had been taken out of production. A year later, its title was changed to Pontiac Motor Division.

A word about the origin of the names of the cars: The Oakland factory was situated in Pontiac Township, Oakland County, Michigan. The township and the Pontiac car are both named after Pontiac, the cruel and cunning Ottawa chief.

The first Pontiac was a light six-cylinder car, built on a 110-inch wheelbase, available as a coupe weighing 2,320 pounds or as a coach weighing 2,400 pounds. Both had the same price of $825. That placed the Pontiac just about halfway between the Chevrolet, which was listed at $645, and the Oldsmobile, listed at $950. Since the Oakland was priced between the Oldsmobile and the Buick, it becomes clear that General Motors intended the Pontiac to play the same role for Oakland as the Essex did to the Hudson, the Erskine to the Studebaker and the Whippet to the Willys. However, the subsidiary makes of Hudson, Studebaker and Willys did not survive the depression, while in Pontiac's case, it was the lower-priced newcomer that displaced the senior member.

At this stage, it is vitally important to realize that the Pontiac was not created by Oakland. It was a creation of General Motors Corporation. Cadillac, Buick and Oldsmobile cars existed before there was a General Motors. So did the Oakland, but there was no Pontiac car when GM bought the Oakland Motor Company in 1909. Chevrolet was started later as a competitor to Ford (not by General Motors but by William C. Durant, founder and deposed president of General Motors) and later was incorporated into the corporation when Durant regained control. But the Pontiac was a GM project from the start, and the fact that it was given to Oakland was mainly due to the faltering sales of the Oakland car and the division's need for a new product.

1926 PONTIAC COACH

The first Pontiac had one of the most modern six-cylinder engines in the industry. It was built on a 110-inch wheelbase and had 20-inch wheels. Two models were built—this coach and a coupe.

7

The Pontiac car was born from a marketing philosophy that evolved at the very top of GM's management in the mid-twenties. And the Pontiac's success was due not only to its qualities as a car but also to the corporation's careful planning of its exact position in the market and the extreme emphasis on cost control in its production.

GM President Alfred P. Sloan had an overall marketing plan in which the corporation's makes were ranked by price class—Chevrolet at the bottom, Cadillac on top. But in 1924, when the concept of the car that became the Pontiac was formulated, the divisions did not overlap in price structures as they now do. Instead there were big gaps. And Sloan gave top priority to filling the gap between Chevrolet and Oldsmobile.

It was a totally new kind of project within General Motors, for up to this time the car divisions had been responsible for planning and developing new products. Now, suddenly, Sloan decided to bring into being a new car—not yet associated with any division—that would sell just above the Chevrolet in price.

Being a superb accountant and a shrewd economist, Sloan also realized that such a car would steal a certain business volume away from Chevrolet. This led him to the conclusion that the car must be designed in coordination with Chevrolet so as to benefit from the lower cost of mass-produced Chevrolet components, and at the same time avoid under-utilization of Chevrolet's manufacturing capacity.

Feasibility depended on the exact technical makeup of the car, and Sloan's next step was to discuss the idea with his technical advisor, Henry M. Crane, and the chief engineer of Chevrolet, Ormond E. Hunt. All were in agreement that the future lay with six- and eight-cylinder cars, so any thought of a four-cylinder engine was immediately dismissed.

Consequently, the Pontiac must have a six, it was determined. With almost equal alacrity, it was decided that it should be a new engine. Henry M. Crane had been working on a short-stroke L-head six since 1922, and was very eager to get it accepted for production. There was little or no opposition, for a suitable six did not exist. The Oakland six, new for 1925, was a big disappointment. And the Oldsmobile and Buick sixes then in production were considered too heavy or too powerful.

The next question was how to incorporate a maximum of Chevrolet body and chassis components into the new car. All Chevrolets used four-cylinder engines at the time, so the longer and heavier Pontiac engine would need a longer and deeper frame, a stronger front axle and a longer wheelbase. But the Chevrolet transmission and rear axle had adequate torque capacity, and Chevrolet body parts could be used to the extent they would not cause the Pontiac to look like a Chevrolet. For Sloan understood the importance of marque identity and individual design features for each make, and did not oppose spending when it would help the car look better. It was doubly important for the Pontiac to have its own look, since the concept was basically just a Chevrolet with a six-cylinder engine.

Sloan handed the concept over to the corporation's engineering committee for making up the detailed specifications and getting the car on the drawing board. While the Pontiac progressed through this stage, Oakland's general manager, George H. Hannum, requested that Sloan assign the development of the car to Oakland. But Sloan declined on the grounds that extensive use of Chevrolet parts made it imperative to have Chevrolet Engineering undertake the development.

The first Pontiac prototypes were built and tested at Chevrolet. Now Sloan and his advisors had to decide where to build it. The only logical solution was to give it to Oakland. The other divisions did not want it, for one reason or another. But Oakland welcomed it. Consequently, Sloan assigned the Pontiac project over from Chevrolet to Oakland for final development, production, distribution and sale.

The production design for the Pontiac was not executed by the Oakland engineering staff but by a new engineering team composed mainly of ex-Cadillac men. Pontiac's chief engineer was Benjamin H. Anibal, who also replaced Benjamin Jerome as chief engineer of Oakland in March 1925.

Anibal had been chief engineer of Cadillac from 1918 to 1921, held the same position at Peerless from 1921 to 1923, and was a consulting engineer to Studebaker when A. R. Glancy approached him about the new opportunity at General Motors in 1924. Born in Linden, Michigan, in 1886, Anibal held a degree in mechanical engineering from Michigan State University and began his career with Oldsmobile in 1909. He went to Cadillac in 1911, and learned to know and respect such outstanding engineers as Herman Schwarze, F. M. Holden and W. R. Milner. Schwarze had been at Cadillac since 1907 and had worked with Charles F. Kettering on the development of the electric self-starter that was adopted in 1911. In fact, Schwarze's name was to be linked with every important electrical development at General Motors up to the mid-thirties. He had accompanied Anibal to Peerless, and joined him in the Pontiac project in 1925. Fenn Holden and Roy Milner had also gone the Peerless route with Anibal, and Holden returned to GM in 1924 to serve as director of the Milford proving grounds before linking up with Anibal again as assistant chief engineer at Oakland in May 1925.

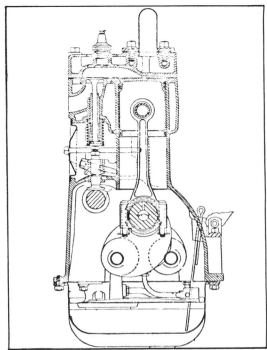

Left, idealized version of Chief Pontiac adorned magazine ads announcing the new make of GM car. Medallion bears Indian head, patterned after radiator ornament. Right, cross section of 1926 Pontiac engine shows simple side-valve gear and cylinder head design, with big-bore cylinders and short-throw cranks.

Holden had joined Cadillac as a research engineer in 1908 and was named chief research engineer in 1913. During World War I Cadillac loaned him to serve on the Collins Commission, investigating the aircraft industries in France, Italy and Great Britain for the U.S. government, which gave him intimate knowledge of advanced engineering in Europe, since it was the car companies that built most of the aircraft engines.

Milner did not come into Anibal's group until 1919 when he left Marmon, where he had worked for six years as body engineer and designer, and joined Cadillac in the same capacity. Prior to his Marmon experience, Milner had worked at Studebaker for a year. He became body engineer for the Pontiac project in 1925.

Responsibility for the Pontiac's chassis engineering was given to T. M. Mueller, a young man of considerable talent who was transferred from Chevrolet. Anibal himself took charge of developing Crane's

engine design. It was actually redesigned five times, but the principal features Crane had proposed were part of all versions including the final production engine. And it was a masterpiece. It became a technical trailblazer, making a clean break with current trends and setting an example that was to have tremendous influence on engine design for many years, not only within General Motors, but throughout the industry. Alongside the six-cylinder Chrysler, the 1926 Pontiac had one of the most modern engines in the industry.

Henry M. Crane was familiar with British scientific researcher Sir Harry Ricardo's work on controlled-turbulence L-head design, and combined these principles with a big-bore, short-stroke engine intended to develop peak power at relatively low rpm. With a bore of 3.25 inches and a stroke of 3.75 inches, the Pontiac engine had a displacement of 186.6 cubic inches, and put out 36 hp at 2400 rpm.

Compared with other small power units of the day, the contrast was striking. The Essex six had a 2.69-inch bore and a 4.25-inch stroke, and the Erskine six had cylinder dimensions of 2.625 by 4.50 inches. The Erskine peaked at 3000 rpm and the Essex at 3350 in 1926, and before they reached the end of their production life in the mid-thirties, they had been developed to reach 3400 and 3600 rpm respectively.

The Pontiac was smoother and quieter. Its high torque at low rpm reduced the need for frequent shifts, and made driving more restful. It ran with lower stress levels and gave longer bearing life. Its reduced piston speed resulted in lower wear rates. And it could be driven flat out for long distances without risk of failure.

Also, Henry M. Crane had a keen eye for manufacturing cost, and it was a most ingeniously inexpensive power unit to produce. The block was a one-piece grey iron casting, split below the crankshaft center line to provide a rigid crankcase. Water jackets surrounded the upper half of the cylinders only. Two identical cylinder heads were used, each covering three cylinders. The forged-steel crankshaft ran in three main bearings only (a Crane eccentricity from his Crane-Simplex days) and carried an internal pivoted-type harmonic balancer.

The use of a wide center bearing and one bearing at each end gave two crank throws with three crankpins each, and a rather weird shape on the outer webs due to the 120-degree firing intervals. This design did not in fact permit very high rotational speeds, due to excessive flexing when subjected to high bending loads as a result of torque fluctuations, and was soon to be modified.

The chain-driven camshaft was located in the side of the crankcase, with vertical valves opening into a cavity in the cylinder head. This cavity reached as far as the cylinder center, with a crevice to provide clearance for thermal expansion in the piston over the rest of the surface. Spark plugs were located in the high-turbulence area facing the intake valves and surrounded by coolant passages. Pistons were also of cast iron, with full skirts, and carried two compression rings on top and an oil control ring at the bottom.

In other respects, the engine made use of recent developments such as Kettering's new Delco ignition distributor. The Carter carburetor was of the updraft type, with fuel supplied via a vacuum tank, and feeding mixture into a large-diameter intake manifold bolted to the block above the exhaust manifold.

Apart from the power unit, the engineering of the 1926 Pontiac was a curious mixture of innovation and older practice. It had a three-speed gearbox (synchromesh was not yet invented), torque tube drive, and a rear axle with a final drive ratio of 4.18:1 (the faster-revving Oakland was geared at 4.70:1). The axle was of the new hypoid bevel type perfected by the Gleason Works and standardized the previous year by Packard. Front and rear suspension systems had elliptic leaf springs and no shock absorbers were fitted. Mechanical brakes acted on the rear wheels only. But the Pontiac chassis had a lower and more modern stance than the Oakland.

Responsibility for building and marketing the first Pontiac fell to Alfred R. Glancy, who had come to Oakland in 1924 as assistant general manager under George Hannum. Glancy acceded to the top post at Oakland in 1925 when Hannum left GM to take over the Lavine Gear Company in Milwaukee.

Glancy was anything but a car man. He was sort of a company doctor that the du Pont family called in to liquidate failing businesses or put troubled but meritorious ones back on their feet. Glancy closed down GM's Samson Tractor and Sheridan subsidiaries at minimal losses, and Sloan picked him to do his stuff at Oakland—aiming, naturally, for survival. The Pontiac car project was well along when Glancy took charge at Oakland. Having a cool sense of what is good business, he at once realized that a separate assembly plant would be needed for the Pontiac, and in 1925 the division purchased 246 acres of land on the northern edge of town. The total investment including buildings and equipment came to about seven and a half million dollars.

Setting up and running the plant became the responsibility of Oakland's brilliant production manager, P. H. MacGregor, a manufacturing expert who had been organizing and operating auto plants since 1903. He came to Oakland in 1922 and stayed for twenty years.

The first Pontiac came off the line in January 1926, and made its official debut at the New York Automobile Show that month. Selling the cars gave the general sales manager, William R. Tracy, a veteran who had started out in Oakland's sales department in 1912, less of a problem than he had anticipated. The Pontiac was a runaway success, and nearly 77,000 were sold that first year. Moreover, far from stealing sales from the Oakland, it helped boost Oakland's domestic deliveries from 35,000 to 50,000 cars.

While Sloan pressed the point in all discussions that the Pontiac should remain faithful to its original concept as a six-cylinder Chevrolet, Ben Anibal and his men were working very hard to upgrade

1927 PONTIAC LANDAU SEDAN

The 1927 Pontiac Landau sedan, left, boasted indirect lighting for the instrument panel and introduced the floor-mounted dimmer switch. Engine was carried on rubber block mounts to minimize vibration. Ben Anibal, right, was Pontiac's chief engineer from the start in 1926. He built a team of engineers from Cadillac and Peerless, but the Pontiac car was basically Chevrolet.

the Pontiac product. A little development work trimmed the weight of the 1927 Pontiac coach to 2,335 pounds, but no important changes were made that year. For 1928 the engine was given an AC mechanical fuel pump to replace the vacuum tank, and a thermostat was installed at the cylinder head outlet to control coolant flow to the radiator. The 1928 Pontiac also came with four-wheel brakes (mechanically operated). A redesigned body for that year raised the curb weight to 2,450 pounds.

Pontiac sales in 1927 soared to over 114,000 cars. Naturally, this was not a net gain for the division. The Pontiac had started as a companion car to the Oakland, but it was already the Oakland that was a companion car to the Pontiac. Oakland sales that year declined to below 43,000. The figure fell to 37,000 in 1928, while almost 184,000 Pontiacs were sold.

The 1929 Pontiac was virtually a new car. The engine received a new, balanced crankshaft and was enlarged to 200-cubic-inch displacement with 3.3125-inch bore and 3.875-inch stroke. Power output was raised to 57 hp at 3000 rpm. The chassis was redesigned with Hotchkiss drive (à la Cadillac) and four-wheel self-energizing brakes (Bendix duo-servo). All the GM divisions were getting quick benefits from the Art & Color section that Sloan inaugurated in 1927 and put under Harley Earl's command. The 1929 Pontiac was dressed up with a styling treatment that former Murphy designer W. Everitt

1928 PONTIAC TWO-DOOR SEDAN

Stylish 1928 Pontiac had four-wheel brakes and a revised engine with balanced crankshaft capable of higher rpm's. Wheelbase remained 110 inches.

Miller had intended for Vauxhall (a British car company that GM acquired in 1926). The coupe and coach continued, while a convertible coupe and a landau sedan were added. Though the coach weight increased to 2,840 pounds, the price was held at $845. The 1930 Pontiac was lightened to 2,702 pounds and received smaller wheels with fatter tires (5.00-19). The engine rating was 60 hp at 3000 rpm.

But sales for both Pontiac and Oakland had been falling. Only 158,000 new Pontiacs found buyers in 1929 and less than half that number were sold in 1930. As for the Oakland, it was headed for extinction, with sales of 32,000 in 1929 and less than 22,000 the following year.

Tracy resigned from Pontiac and went to Hudson, and William A. Blees was transferred from Chevrolet to head Pontiac's sales department. At this time, A. R. Glancy took five million dollars out of Pontiac earnings and put them into a new foundry. That was his last

major step in preparing for Pontiac's future, for Glancy left Oakland in 1931 and was replaced temporarily by Irving J. Reuter, who also ran Buick and Oldsmobile at the time. For eighteen months, Pontiac was merged with Buick and Oldsmobile, and their dealers handled all three divisions' products. During 1931, people bought six Pontiacs for every Oakland that was sold. Still, that meant less than 87,000 cars for the division.

The 1931 Pontiac had a new chassis with 112-inch wheelbase. It received a synchromesh transmission with helical-cut second-speed gears, a hand-me-down from Cadillac. It was also the first Pontiac to use a pressed-steel rear axle housing. In a separate move, the 1931 six-cylinder engine was equipped with electroplated cast iron pistons. The 1932-model six had connecting rods of uniform weight and center of gravity, and interchangeable steel-backed bearings. For 1932, wheelbase was increased to 114 inches for cars with six-cylinder engines.

There was also a Pontiac V-8, inherited from Oakland, where it had gone into production in 1930. Only a small number of Pontiac V-8's were built, and the engine is noteworthy mainly for being the lowest-cost eight-cylinder engine built by General Motors before Chevrolet began producing V-8's in 1955.

The Pontiac V-8 was rated at 85 hp at 3400 rpm, and ran with a 5.2:1 compression ratio. Oversquare—most unusual for its time—it had 3.438 by 3.375-inch bore and stroke, giving 251-cubic-inch displacement. It was a monobloc construction, with horizontal side valves operated from a single camshaft located in the valley between the banks. It was positioned too low to act directly against the valve stems, so a rocker arm arrangement was devised. Curiously, it had a flat (one-plane) crankshaft and was stabilized by a special link called a synchronizer. This sounds almost like a description of the Oldsmobile Viking V-8, but it was a different power unit, and each division in fact made its own.

Reuter overworked himself trying to assure the survival of three divisions. Finally he resigned from office to take care of his health. Pontiac had problems that did not affect Buick and Oldsmobile to the same extent, nor even in the same manner. The divisions in Flint and Lansing were long-established companies that were more comfortable the more autonomy they had. Pontiac's basic problem was that GM's top management, despite Sloan's shrewd insight and his committee system of setting policy, didn't know what to do with Pontiac. As for Glancy, still relatively young, he realized his dream of going into business for himself. He did well, and later was to serve as a

U.S. Army brigadier general of ordnance in World War II.

The resourceful corporate planning that had created the Pontiac seemed to have run dry. Corporate management undeniably fell short in giving guidance and support to the car divisions at this time. The general manager was left not only with running the division, but with shaping its future without much guidance as to what was the corporation's view of the Pontiac product and its role in the overall setup. As a matter of fact, Pontiac's survival, as a make of car and as a division, was quite insecure. There was lots of talk in the GM executive suite and the corridors about dropping the Pontiac. Sales had slumped to 48,000 cars in 1932. Blees left and was replaced by another draftee from Chevrolet, Robert K. White.

After a period of observation and consternation, GM Executive Vice President William S. Knudsen and President Alfred P. Sloan agreed to fight for the survival of the Pontiac car. Sloan's ideas again prevailed. A plan was adopted by which Pontiac's manufacturing operations were to be more closely integrated with Chevrolet's in order to benefit from the lower unit cost of high-volume components. The outcome of this was that Knudsen himself added the general management of Pontiac to his other duties, on a temporary basis, to turn the division around. One of his major tasks was to pick the man who could run Pontiac when Knudsen moved up the corporate ladder. He found him in the person of Harry J. Klingler, general sales manager at Chevrolet.

With Klingler's arrival began a new era at Pontiac; an era of active salesmanship. And the engineering department had new products ready for him to sell. What Pontiac did for 1933 was no less sensational than the making of the low-priced six-cylinder Pontiac for 1926. By 1933, the six was no longer in production, and all Pontiacs came with an in-line L-head eight-cylinder engine. It was the industry's lowest-priced eight.

Layout and dimensions of the Pontiac in-line eight were derived from the six, with a bore and stroke of 3.188 by 3.50 inches, giving 223.4-cubic-inch displacement. Power output was 75 hp at 3600 rpm. The new eight had a new type of cylinder head known as GMR (GM Research), for it had been developed by Kettering's engine group at the Research Laboratories. One of the special features of the cylinder head consisted of gas flow guide ridges on the surface above the valves. They served the dual purpose of setting up a swirl in the gas flow and simultaneously cooling the exhaust valve heads by directing the fresh charge over them.

All 1933 models were built on a 115-inch wheelbase. And in 1933 sales nearly doubled, to 85,000 units—far below capacity, but an encouraging step towards recovery. It was in the 1933 models, with

1932 PONTIAC TWO-DOOR SEDAN

A V-8 became available for the 1932 Pontiac. Sixes were built on a 114-inch wheelbase, eight-cylinder models had 117-inch wheelbase. The six-cylinder two-door sedan weighed 2,963 pounds, the V-8 coupe 3,180 pounds.

new styling and the backing of Klingler's salesmanship, that Pontiac's image was born. The styling story alone is worth relating, for it was to influence future thinking about design and marketing not only at Pontiac, but throughout General Motors.

Frank Hershey became chief designer of the Pontiac studio at the GM Art & Color section in 1931. When he arrived, the 1933 models were more than halfway finished. He felt terribly dejected at what he saw, for the so-called new model could hardly be told apart from the old one. He had visions of a totally new Pontiac style, and was full of enthusiasm in his hope of endowing the cars with *his* own look. Reuter agreed with the desirability of a dramatic change in appearance, though he could hardly have understood what Pontiac was in for. And Hershey's hopes were dashed to the ground when he was told that he had only two weeks to do it.

1934 PONTIAC FOUR-DOOR SEDAN

1935 PONTIAC SIX 4-DOOR TOURING SEDAN

Knee-action independent front suspension became available on the 1934 Pontiac, and the division claimed to be the world's largest builder of straight-eight engines.

First with the Silver Streak was the 1935 model, which also introduced Fisher Body Division's 'turret-top' steel roof. A new six became the base engine for cars built on a 112-inch wheelbase. Eights had 116.6-inch wheelbase.

He took his inspiration from the Bentley, recently taken over by Rolls-Royce, and tried to combine a Bentley grille with the Chevrolet body sheet metal. Part of the credit for how well it was accomplished must go to Roy Milner, chief body engineer. Hershey and Milner were to become close friends, and they spurred each other on to make the Pontiac an evermore distinctive-looking car. The Fisher 'no-draft' ventilation system was introduced on the 1933 bodies. This consisted of vent windows in the front doors, hinged on a vertical axis, swinging in at the front and out at the back, to create a low mass airflow in and out of the passenger compartment.

Like his boss, Harley J. Earl, who brought styling to GM, Frank Hershey came from California. From childhood he was a car 'nut' who filled copybook after copybook with drawings of high-style automobiles. Hershey designed many cars for Murphy from 1928 to 1931. Then Murphy went under, and Hershey went to Detroit to look

for work. He was hired by Frank S. Spring, styling director at Hudson, whom he had come to know while Spring was general manager of Murphy.

One day in 1932 the phone rang in Hershey's office at Hudson, and it was Howard O'Leary at the other end of the line. O'Leary was Harley Earl's assistant, and he told Hershey that they were looking for a new project designer for the Pontiac studio. He jumped at the chance, for Pontiac was obviously in need of help in that area, and he had found working conditions at Hudson less than ideal, because Spring had the final word on everything and a natural predilection to vote his own designs the best.

However hurriedly the 1933 models were designed, they marked a new departure for Pontiac. All of a sudden the GM fledgling, now in its eighth year, acquired an image. Without departing from the low-cost construction principles laid down by Sloan, Pontiac in 1933 placed before the public a low-priced eight-cylinder car with all the flair, all the aplomb, all the panache of far more expensive automobiles, such as the Chrysler Imperial, Studebaker President or Auburn 8-105.

It wasn't the same kind of car, but the reality of that fact became subordinate to the image. And that image was to propel Pontiac to new heights of success during the years that followed.

In Pontiac's engineering department, sweeping changes were in the works for 1934. Wheelbase went up to 117.25 inches, and the weight increased from 3,020 pounds to 3,325. As in earlier years, Pontiac used the Chevrolet frame and many Chevrolet body parts. The 1934 models used a beefed-up version of Chevrolet's transmission, and a Chevrolet rear axle.

The 1934 Pontiac eight gained 7 hp due to improvements in the GMR head. The block had wide bore-spacing, with coolant passages of unusually generous dimensions. The five-main-bearing crankshaft was line-bored and featured full-pressure lubrication. Connecting rods were rifle-drilled to provide positive wrist pin lubrication. Pistons, however, were still of cast iron. The cylinder block was deep, extending about 2½ inches below the crankshaft center line, for extra rigidity.

General Motors had two systems of independent front suspension in 1934, both advertised under the Knee-Action label. One was developed by Cadillac; the other was a unique case of GM's going overboard on an NIH (not invented here) development, the Dubonnet system. Andre Dubonnet was a French inventor and racing driver, whose fortune was built on an *apéritif* wine. Chevrolet and Pontiac used the Dubonnet; Oldsmobile and Buick got the Cadillac system.

Regrettably for Chevrolet and Pontiac, field experience was to prove that the Dubonnet system was unripe for mass production. It needed frequent attention, for it was essential that its cylinder be filled to the top with oil. When neglected, it was unreliable in operation, with unpredictable behavior, as well as being difficult to service and repair. It was discarded during the 1936 model year.

Chevrolet reverted to an I-beam front axle and semi-elliptic leaf springs, while Pontiac was allowed to use the Cadillac system with double A-arms and coil springs. Originally designed for Cadillac by Maurice Olley, it was adapted to the Pontiac by Robert R. Hutchinson, who had replaced Mueller as chassis engineer. This system became standard on the 1937 Pontiac. By that time the sales picture was positively rosy, with registrations of over 140,000 Pontiacs in 1935 and nearly 172,000 in 1936.

Klingler was so confident in his knowledge of what would and would not sell that he never hesitated to play a leading part in Pontiac's product planning. Despite the favorable reception of the all-eight line in 1933, he immediately decided to bring back the six. Of course, Anibal did not bring back Crane's old six, but designed a completely new engine. It was another L-head unit, somewhat bigger, with 3.375-inch bore and 3.875-inch stroke, giving 208-cubic-

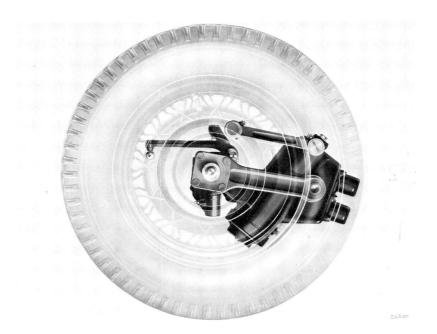

Dubonnet-type front suspension system, optional on 1934-36 Pontiacs, carried the wheel hub on a single control arm. A spur on the arm acted on the spring, which was enclosed in the casing that also embodied a hydraulic shock absorber.

inch displacement. The crankshaft ran in four main bearings and was fully counterweighted. It could tolerate high rpm, and the engine was set to reach its peak power output of 80 hp at 3600 rpm. It went into production in time for the 1935 models.

For the 1937 models, the six-cylinder engine was enlarged to 222.7 cubic inches by boring out the cylinder to 3.4375 inches and lengthening the stroke to a full four inches. It was rated as delivering 85 hp at 3520 rpm.

Pontiac's in-line eight had been developed to deliver 84 hp at 3600 rpm in 1935. The following year it was enlarged to 232.3 cubic inches, with 3.25 inches bore by 3.50 inches stroke, giving a peak

1938 PONTIAC SIX 4-DOOR SEDAN

Pontiac's 1938 models adopted gear-shift on the steering column and pistol-grip handbrake under the cowl. Tires were 6.00-16 on new-type pressed-steel disc wheels.

output of 87 hp at 3800 rpm. The 1936 eight-cylinder engine also had a sealed pressure cooling system, and the carburetor was equipped with an anti-percolator valve. For 1937 the eight-cylinder engine displacement reached its ultimate 248.9 cubic inches by adopting the bore and stroke of the original Pontiac six (3.25 by 3.75 inches). This boosted its output to 100 hp at 3800 rpm.

The engineering department had undergone a period of hectic activity, and was not to be allowed to rest on its laurels. This period was also not without tragedy. It was a sad shock when Anibal had to find a replacement for Herman Schwarze, who had suffered two strokes and was felled by a third one while working in his home near Pontiac one day in 1934. His replacement as electrical engineer of Pontiac was George Delaney, who came from Graham-Paige.

Throughout this period, Pontiac styling—and the marque image— were dominant factors in the division's fortunes. And foremost among

Pontiac's symbols was the Silver Streak. The first of the Silver Streak Pontiacs went into production in the fall of 1934, as a 1935 model. The inspiration for the Silver Streak came from a picture Frank Hershey had seen in a French magazine of an old racing Napier which had a bright aluminum oil cooler protruding through the top of the hood.

The Fisher A-body was all-new for 1935, with a 'turret top' all-steel roof, slanting windshield and sloping rear end. Strangely, the front doors, which had always been hinged at the cowl end, now were hinged on the B-post so that they opened forward. This was not well received, for two reasons that GM had not thought of until the car was already in production. First, the safety angle. If a passing car hit the open door as the driver was alighting, the door would break his legs, at best, or cut them off. Secondly, ladies found it awkward to make an elegant exit, even with long skirts. The 1936 models reverted to the conventional door arrangement, with the front doors hinged on the A-post and the rear doors on the C-post.

As early as 1934 Klingler had said he wanted a new body plant for Pontiac, and prevailed upon William S. Knudsen to instruct Fisher Body Division to put up a complete factory adjacent to Pontiac's assembly plant. This was completed in 1935, but unexpected bottlenecks appeared in getting the body shells out of the Fisher plant and into the Pontiac works. Klingler felt these problems could best be met by by-passing them, and in 1936 he approved construction of an overhead conveyor between the Pontiac assembly plant and the adjacent Fisher Body stamping and body-welding plant. In 1937 Pontiac also built a new axle plant and started an apprentice school to train future skilled craftsmen.

Frank Hershey, however, left Pontiac at the end of 1935. Hershey's last design for Pontiac was the 1937 model. Frank then went to Buick, and after a while was assigned to the newly established overseas studio. His first job there was the 1939 Opel Kapitän. Virgil Exner, who later served as vice president for styling at Chrysler Corporation from 1953 to 1961, replaced Hershey as head of the Pontiac studio. Exner was responsible for the 1938 Pontiac, and then left General Motors to join Raymond Loewy Associates who were then designing the Studebaker Champion for 1939.

For 1937 Pontiac dropped the small Chevrolet A-body and acquired the Fisher B-body that was also used by Oldsmobile and Buick. Other GM cars that year had their headlamps carried as ears on either side of the grille. But Pontiac was different. The lamps were mounted on top of short pods extending from the fenders. Wheelbase was increased from 112 to 117 inches for the six-cylinder cars and from

116.625 to 122 inches for the Pontiac eight. But some weight savings were made at the same time, the six scaling 3,249 pounds and the eight 3,380 (for the two-door sedans).

Pontiac added a convertible sedan in 1937. It was called Streamline and used the same fastback design that was offered on the smallest Buick. This was the first use of a term that was to become a separate series some years later. It was in 1941 that Pontiac began building a spectacular fastback in the Torpedo series, which the public spontaneously and unanimously, dubbed 'streamliner.' Acting with surprising speed Pontiac officially adopted Streamliner as the series identification for both sixes and eights with that body style. Up to that time, Pontiac's model designations were copied on Chevrolet's, showing an incredible lack of imagination, especially in view of everything that was being done to build up the Pontiac image.

In 1936 Pontiac's line consisted of the Deluxe Six, Master Six and Deluxe Eight. In 1937 and 1938 they were simply called Six and Eight (two series). For 1939 Pontiac buyers had a choice of the Quality Six, Deluxe Six and Deluxe Eight.

A Torpedo Eight was added to this lineup for 1940, and in 1941 the Pontiac range included the Deluxe Torpedo Six and Eight, Custom Six and Eight, Streamliner Six and Eight and Super Streamliner Six and Eight. The line was cut back to six series for 1942 by dropping the Super Streamliners and Customs, but adding Chieftain Streamliner Six and Eight models.

Klingler's bet on the revived six was proving out to be a good one. The Pontiac six was playing an increasingly vital part in the division's recovery and growth. Pontiac built 137,515 sixes and 38,755 eights in 1936. The following year the sixes climbed to 179,244 and the eights to 56,945. The depressed market of 1938 pushed Pontiac's production rates down. That year only 77,713 sixes and 19,426 eights were produced, but by 1939 the assembly lines were moving normally, with an output of 109,568 sixes and 34,774 eights. In 1940 Pontiac built 165,344 sixes and 51,657 eights.

The shape of Pontiac cars was changing faster than technical progress was being made. The 1937 models sported a new frame with cross-bracing and a divided propeller shaft. For 1938, Pontiac went to the steering column gearshift and at the same time added a booster for the clutch pedal. The 1939 models had revised front and rear suspension systems, with link-parallelogram steering and Duflex rear springs with parabolic-section leaves.

On Klingler's orders, in 1939 Pontiac produced a price-leader Deluxe Six on a 115-inch wheelbase sharing the A-body with Chevrolet. All other models with six- and eight-cylinder engines had

For 1939 most sixes were built on the 120-inch wheelbase of the Pontiac eight, others on a 115-inch wheelbase. Duflex rear springs with parabolic-section leaves were new this year. Headlamps were mounted on the fenders for the first time on a Pontiac.

the same 120-inch wheelbase and shared the new B-body with Oldsmobile and Buick. For 1940, the price-leader, now named Special Six, went to a 116.5-inch wheelbase. The DeLuxe Six and DeLuxe Eight were built on a 120.5-inch wheelbase, and the new Torpedo Eight was on a 121.5-inch wheelbase.

Power output from the 222.7-cubic-inch six increased to 87 hp at 3500 rpm for the 1940 models. Then the engine was bored out to 3.56 inches, giving a displacement of 239.2 cubic inches. The 1941 Pontiac six delivered 90 hp at 3200 rpm and output from the 1941-model eight was boosted to 103 hp at 3500 rpm.

The 1941–42 models were developed under the direction of Forrest H. Kane, who became executive engineer of Pontiac in 1940. He was formerly assistant chief engineer and is credited with introducing the vacuum-assisted gearshift on the 1941 models. Two wheelbases

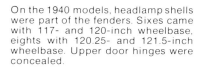

1940 PONTIAC DELUXE 4-DOOR TOURING SEDAN

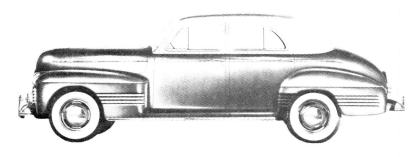

1941 PONTIAC CUSTOM TORPEDO 4-DOOR SEDAN

On the 1940 models, headlamp shells were part of the fenders. Sixes came with 117- and 120-inch wheelbase, eights with 120.25- and 121.5-inch wheelbase. Upper door hinges were concealed.

For 1941 Pontiac offered six- or eight-cylinder engines in the same chassis, with a choice of 119- or 122-inch wheelbase. Vacuum-assisted column shift was adopted.

were used for the 1941 models: 119 and 122 inches, and buyers had a choice of six- or eight-cylinder power in either size car. The 1941 Custom series shared the C-body with Cadillac, Buick and Oldsmobile. Pontiac had never before had a C-body car and was never to have one again.

Vincent D. Kaptur took over from Exner as chief designer of the Pontiac studio in 1938, with Bob Lauer and Joe Schemansky as his assistants. They were responsible for all Pontiac exterior designs from 1939 through 1942. Frank Hershey came back from Europe and replaced Kaptur in 1940, but the 1941–42 designs were frozen then, and he had little or no influence on their appearance. Interestingly, some Lincoln-Zephyr influence showed up in the 1940–41 Pontiacs, as the grilles got lower and wider, and the headlamps gradually vanished into the fenders.

Pontiac's 1942 models went into production on September 4, 1941, and civilian production ceased on January 30, 1942. By that time, Pontiac was already knee-deep in defense work. A booklet issued to celebrate the twenty-fifth anniversary of the Pontiac car in 1951 stated, "Pontiac was at war nine months before Pearl Harbor." Here's how that came about: On March 6, 1941, Pontiac received the official order to produce the Oerlikon 20 mm anti-aircraft cannon for the U.S. Navy. This order came after months-long preparation and study of ordnance-making machinery, planning and experimental installation at Pontiac.

The second war-materiel production assignment received by Pontiac was an order from the U.S. Army for Bofors automatic field guns. To meet this order, Pontiac cleared more than 200,000 square feet of floor space in the sheet-metal plant and installed high-precision machinery for producing the Swedish-designed weapons.

On the military vehicle front, Pontiac participated by manufacturing the front axle for the M-5 high-speed tank developed by Cadillac and produced for the U.S. Army. Pontiac also manufactured parts for large Detroit Diesel two-stroke diesel engines, which were in great demand for both stationary and marine purposes by the Army as well as the Navy. To meet these orders, Pontiac's engine plant was retooled to machine diesel engine parts, and the foundry was used to make castings for truck engines. To complete the list of Pontiac's contributions to the war production effort, the division also made aircraft-launched torpedoes for the U.S. Navy.

Defense contracts were canceled, one by one, as the end of the war drew near, and Pontiac began making plans for its return to civilian production. Reconverting its manufacturing facilities in the shortest possible time was the most pressing objective. Beyond that Klingler instituted a vast expansion program that would increase production capacity by fifty percent. He was aiming at the half-million cars a year mark. To achieve this, he ordered a great enlargement of Pontiac's iron foundry, and the layout of the engine plant was revised to admit a greater number of machines and speed up the flow of materials. This would take time to complete, he knew. The essential thing was to get an early start. And Pontiac, with a pedigree that evolved from design and engineering work dating back over many years, would be ready for the waiting market in 1946.

1942 PONTIAC TORPEDO 4-DOOR SEDAN

Front fenders were stretched into the doors on the 1942-model Pontiac. All door hinges were concealed. Rear springs were equipped with wood liners.

CHAPTER 2

Traditions Honored

REALITIES AND IMPRESSIONS rarely conform, but in the case of Pontiac cars in 1946, the two were closely related. People thought of the Pontiac as reliable and durable family transportation and little else.

Generally, they were right. The Pontiac cars were capable of extremely long and faithful service, with modest upkeep and running costs, to justify the premium purchase price (compared with Chevrolet). Pontiac's image was bland, dulled by the close technical relationship between its products and those of Chevrolet. Pontiac was thought of as a 'hand-me-down' division, using low-cost components from Chevrolet, taking certain ingredients from other divisions, and manufacturing little other than its own engines.

No one at that time thought of Pontiac as an innovator in either engineering or styling, but those were indeed the qualities that had helped Pontiac survive the Great Depression of the thirties and assume a respected fifth place in domestic sales in 1940–41.

The Pontiac car, in 1946, was no more old-fashioned than other General Motors cars at the time. And when the 1946 Pontiac first appeared in the showrooms, most people who saw it thought it was beautiful. In truth, it was a good-looking car, but people also said the Dodge, Hudson, Buick, Studebaker, Lincoln and Packard were beautiful. The nation was car-starved, after four years during which the

auto industry had been busy turning out war materiel, and people were not going to be critical of any car that was absolutely, totally *new*. When a market that's used to absorbing more than five million cars a year is deprived of new cars for such a long time, the consequences are pervasive and far-reaching. Inevitably, the promise of an early return to peacetime production engendered certain expectations in people's minds.

We all had visions of shiny, modern cars that would be faster, quieter, more comfortable and longer lasting than the old crates we were still running around in. And despite the fact that the new cars, when they came, were basically unchanged from the last of the prewar models, we were not disappointed. We hailed them all with the same enthusiasm.

Pontiac's sister divisions at General Motors were building cars that were mildly modified 1942 models. Ford slapped a new grille on what was the 1942 body. Plymouth, Dodge and De Soto had no sheet metal changes from 1942. Studebaker built a lot of Champions that were virtually unchanged from the last ones built before the war, while tooling up for the new Loewy designs. Hudson dusted off the Commodore Six and Eight from 1942 and got the assembly lines running again, while Nash revived its prewar 600 and Ambassador Six. Packard made no significant changes in its Clipper series. Only Willys-

1946 PONTIAC STREAMLINER SEDAN COUPE

Sedan coupe was Pontiac's name for the fastback two-door Streamliner in 1946. Among available colors was Catalina Cream—first appearance of the name that was to be used for a future series.

The 1946 Streamliner four-door sedan was built on a 122-inch wheelbase and was 210.25 inches long overall. Postwar restyling of 1942 body was directed by Bob Lauer.

Overland had a new car, and it was a civilian edition of the wartime Jeep.

Visible changes on the 1946 Pontiac from the 1942 look were limited to cosmetic items such as the grille and body moldings. The central part of the grille was retained, and only the vertical slots that extended the grille into the fenders were changed to a horizontal theme. The chrome molding along the beltline disappeared and was replaced by a small identification dart on the sides of the hood, back near the cowl.

The Silver Streak continued unchanged, with the same proud Indian head as a hood ornament. Because of the shortage of whitewall tires, a number of cars were sold with plastic rim inserts that, when new, resembled whitewalls. But with time they yellowed and warped, making the whole car look shabby. Most buyers preferred plain blackwall tires until the shortage ended, about 1949.

Of course, Pontiac's 1942 models had not been all-new either. The body was a facelifted version of the 1941 model, with certain sheet metal changes, such as pulling the front fender skirts back into the doors.

Pontiac's body designs were mainly due to Vincent D. Kaptur, Robert J. Lauer and Joseph R. Schemansky, young enthusiasts who had been hired by Harley J. Earl, head of GM Styling, in the mid-thirties. These three men formed a progressive team that developed the Pontiac look for the 1939 through 1942 models. In 1944, Bob Lauer was named chief designer of the Pontiac studio, and the 1946-model exterior styling evolved under his direction.

When Pontiac resumed civilian production in 1946, shortages restricted the model range to one single body style, the two-door Streamliner fastback sedan. Later, a four-door Streamliner sedan and a second series, the Torpedo, with notchback body styles for both two- and four-door models, were added. Both series shared the Fisher B-body with Oldsmobile and Buick. This body sharing refers to the main structure or underbody, not the outer sheet metal. Each division in those days still had its own hood and fenders, for instance.

Sharing major components was a great way to cut costs, and it was part of the Pontiac formula. But at times the need to share must have been a brake on technical progress. On that subject, Robert H. Knickerbocker, who joined Pontiac in 1951 as a project engineer in the experimental department, had this to say: "I felt that we were reasonably independent—let's say in those days we shared a lot of body panels and a lot of body trim—which is not unlike the situation today. The front and rear suspension systems on the Pontiac were unique, designed and built by Pontiac. The power train, except for the transmission, was unique. The only things we shared with Chevrolet in the chassis were steering gear and transmissions."

The 1946 Torpedo was built on a 119-inch wheelbase and had an overall length of 204.5 inches. The Streamliner was 210.25 inches long, with a 122-inch wheelbase. Four-door and two-door models were available in both series. The four-door sedans had four side windows: The front door windows had vent panes, and there were fixed rear quarter windows in the sail panels. On the two-door models, the rear side windows were extended forward to the B-post.

Fisher body structures for the 1946 Pontiacs were identical with those used in the 1942 models. A steel floor, ribbed and braced, was fused solidly with the cowl and side panels. The steel cowl and dash were heavily braced. The all-steel 'turret top' roof was supported by steel corner pillars and center posts and included U-profile steel roof bows.

All models used a cross-braced frame with the side members running like two straight rails as wide apart as possible, coming in at the front end to form a cradle for the engine, and bending up over the rear axle to slope down over the fuel tank. A front cross-member provided a base for engine mounts and carried the front suspension. Another cross-member supported the engine at the clutch housing. A third cross-member connected the side members at the highest point of the rear axle kickup, and a fourth ran across the frame at the tail end. This frame design was new in 1937. It was a cantilevered X-frame, replacing the massive K-Y frame used since 1934.

All 1946 Pontiacs had independent front suspension. The basic design was the same as first used on the 1937 models (and derived from the system introduced on the 1934 Cadillac). Briefly described, it consisted of double A-arms, one above the other, at each front wheel. The upper arms were short, and the lower ones long. The splayed ends were attached to pivot shafts anchored on the frame, and the pointed ends linked to the top and bottom ends of the kingpins. A single vertical coil spring stood on the bar of the lower A-arm, working against a hooded abutment extending from the front cross-member outboard of the chassis frame. The lower control arms were connected via a stabilizer bar—a thin spring-steel rod (torsion bar) that seems puny in comparison with those adopted in recent times.

Hotchkiss drive was used at the rear end, which means that the axle was supported by semi-elliptic leaf springs that not only carried the load but also served to locate the axle relative to the frame. Pontiac had long used Hotchkiss drive, and the 1946 design differed from the 1936 model only in detail specifications.

On the 1942 models, Pontiac had introduced wood liners to limit inter-leaf friction in the rear springs. The same design was revived for the 1946 models. Delco-Lovejoy hydraulic shock absorbers were used all around. Ring gear and pinion were made with hypoid drive, combined with a semi-floating rear axle. The propeller shaft was a one-piece design, running straight through the center of the frame cross-bracing.

Standard final drive ratio was 4.10:1 for the Torpedo and 4.30:1 for the Streamliner. For both series, an 'economy' axle with a 3.90:1 or a 'mountain' axle with a 4.55:1 ratio was offered at no extra cost. The transmission was a simple three-speed gearbox with synchromesh on second and third. The column shift linkage was vacuum-assisted to reduce the muscle effort needed to shift gears. The clutch was 9.5 inches in diameter, single dry plate, with ball-bearing release.

Power units were the same prewar engines dusted off and put back in production. The smaller one was a 239-cubic-inch-displacement

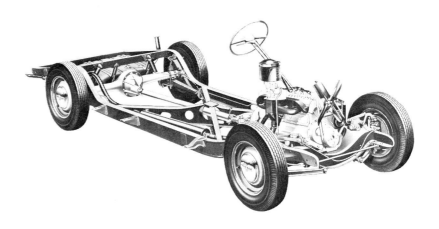

Cross-braced ladder-type frame used for 1946 models dated back to the 1930's. Of similar vintage were the coil-spring front suspension, Hotchkiss drive, and hypoid bevel rear axle.

side-valve six and the larger one a 249-cubic-inch-displacement side-valve eight-in-line. They were far from new. The eight originated in 1932 (for the 1933 models) and had not been modified except for detail improvements since 1937. The six dated from 1934 (for the 1935 models) and was last updated for 1941.

The six came with 3.56-inch bore and 4.00-inch stroke, giving a 1.12 stroke/bore ratio, very close to the industry average for the time. Chrysler and Chevrolet used shorter strokes; Buick, Packard and Studebaker, longer.

The Pontiac eight had 3.25-inch bore and 3.75-inch stroke, giving a stroke/bore ratio of 1.15 in spite of actually having a shorter stroke. With L-head design, the Pontiac engines might be thought obsolete, but it should be remembered that all American car engines in 1946—

with the notable exception of Chevrolet and Buick—were still using side valves. Chrysler sixes and eights had side valves, and so did Packard's. Ford and Cadillac V-8's used L-heads, too.

Pontiac's design had a camshaft located low on the right side of the block, chain-driven from the crankshaft. Valve lifters were solid, with single valve springs on the stems.

The six had an intake valve head diameter of 1.59 inches and an exhaust valve head diameter of 1.47 inches. That means the intake valve head was 44.6 percent of the bore, and the exhaust valve 41.3 percent of the bore, compared with an industry norm of about forty-five percent for the intake valves and forty percent for the exhaust valves. The eight had an intake valve head diameter of 1.46 inches and an exhaust valve diameter of 1.34 inches. That gives 44.9 percent of the bore for the intake valves and 41.2 percent for the exhaust valves.

Both engines had crankshafts made of forged steel, weighing 86.83 pounds for the six and 81.4 pounds for the eight. Curiously, the longer crankshaft for the eight-cylinder engine was lighter than that for the shorter six. This was due to the shorter firing intervals in the eight (ninety degrees versus 120 in the six) which lowered the need for mass in the counterweights, and the eight-cylinder crankshaft used only eight counterweights, compared with nine for the six-cylinder crankshaft. Both crankshafts carried harmonic vibration dampers at the front ends.

The six-cylinder crankshaft ran in four main bearings, while the eight-cylinder crankshaft had five mains. In the six, bearing diameters varied from 2.50 inches on the front one to 2.63 inches on the rear one, growing progressively fatter towards the rear, with 2.53-inch diameter on the second main, and 2.59-inch diameter on the third. Bearing widths varied also, from 1.12 inches on the third main to 1.56 inches on the rearmost one. The front main had 1.25-inch diameter and the second had 1.19-inch diameter. End thrust was taken by the next-to-last main bearing and total projected bearing area was calculated as being only 13.1 square inches.

Crankpin bearing diameter on the six was 2.13 inches, which for a stroke of 4.00 inches gave an overlap from 0.315 to 0.38 inches. Crankpin bearing width was 1.28 inches.

The eight-cylinder engine had a five-main-bearing crankshaft with eight counterweights. Main bearing diameters ranged from 2.38 inches at the front end to 2.63 inches at the rear. End thrust was taken by the next-to-last main, which was 2.47 inches in diameter. The second and third mains were 2.41 and 2.44 inches in diameter, respectively. Main bearing width was 1.12 inches on the end-thrust bearing, but

1.56 inches on the rear bearing. The front main was 1.25 inches wide, the second 1.19 inches wide. The center bearing had a width of 1.44 inches.

On the eight-cylinder engine, crankpins were two inches in diameter, so that the overlap ranged from 1.315 to 1.44 inches with a stroke of 3.75 inches. Crankpin bearing shells were only 1.06 inches wide.

Rods were also forged steel with a center-to-center length of 7.562 inches, weighing 36.9 ounces, including bushings, for the six. In the straight-eight, connecting rods were 7.562 inches long (center to center) and weighed 31.8 ounces including bushings.

Connecting rods were rifle-drilled to provide positive wrist pin lubrication. The blocks had wide bore spacing which permitted uncommonly generous coolant passage dimensions. The blocks were also quite deep, extending 2½ inches below the crankshaft center line, for extra rigidity.

New technical details in the 1946 models included shot-peened wrist pins and an aluminized tail pipe. Shot-peening hardens the surface and improves the wear resistance. Aluminizing exhaust system parts reduces the effects of corrosion and lengthens exhaust pipe life. New long-life mufflers featured a shell of thicker-gauge steel and heavier internal parts. The baffles were developed for improved silencing at certain critical speeds.

The intake and exhaust manifolds were placed one on top of the other on the right-hand side of the block, with the carburetor towering above the intake manifold. Sixes had one-barrel carburetors, but all eights came with two-barrel carburetors. That was done to assure greater uniformity of the air/fuel ratio going to the cylinders located the farthest from the carburetor compared with those closest to the carburetor. That's a big difficulty on eight-in-line engines, while the six, because it is shorter, has no great problems of disparity in air/fuel ratios from cylinder to cylinder. All carburetors had automatic chokes.

Neither the six nor the eight was designed for or geared for drag-strip acceleration. The 1946 Torpedo Eight sedan would reach 60 mph from standstill in 15.5 seconds. First gear was a real stump-puller, capable of jerking the car into motion like a kangaroo, but then the engine would run out of revs, and one had to shift into second at about 22 mph. But second was good for nearly 50 mph, and third would take the car above 90 mph. To reach 90 from standstill would take about thirty-six seconds. The important thing for Pontiac at that time was not the all-out accelerative capability of the car, but flexibility and tractability. One could easily start in second, for instance,

Genuine wood panels were used for the 1946 Pontiac station wagons and served to emphasize Silver Streaks repeated on fender skirts. With eight-cylinder engines, three-barrel carburetors were standard. Sixes had one-barrel carburetors.

with the engine idling, on level ground. And it would pull smoothly in top gear from about 9 mph. That made for easy, restful motoring. In suburban driving, one did not need to shift gears at all, except for traffic lights and stop signs. Even in the city, the car could be driven in top gear most of the way, with only occasional use of second. First gear was rarely needed.

The six was even less lively, but possessed the same virtues: smoothness, high torque at low speeds, and fine top-gear performance. If one could speed up from 20 to 40 mph in top gear in eight seconds, it seemed kind of pointless to change down to second and do it in six (plus the time for downchanging after making the decision —instead of just stepping on the gas and leaving the gearshift alone). In straight-line acceleration from standstill the 1946 Streamliner Six needed eighteen seconds to reach 60 mph—just about the same as the Chevrolet Master 85, but faster than Dodge and DeSoto.

The six-cylinder car cruised quietly at 50–55 mph, but became noisy at higher speeds. This is largely explained by the gearing, which gave it exceptional top-gear performance. One could leave it in third

gear right down to 15 mph and accelerate smoothly by merely stepping on the gas. The standard axle ratio did not make for good high-speed fuel economy, but it certainly made for simple and restful city and suburban driving. The eight was even smoother at low speeds, but gave no real improvement in high-speed noise levels.

Fuel economy was remarkably good in both sixes and eights. In normal driving the six would give 21 mpg and the eight, 18 mpg. Strangely, it was almost impossible to gain further mileage by particularly careful driving. On the other hand, in hard driving, with a lot of wide-open-throttle acceleration, even the eight rarely returned less than 15 mpg, or the six less than 17 mpg. The Pontiac engines had a reputation for being easy on oil, and if a complaint about excessive oil consumption came up, it was usually due to outside sources, such as neglect or abuse.

Driving the 1946 Pontiac was an experience forcibly colored by what cars the driver was used to. A Ford driver would have been impressed with the ride, first of all, and a Buick driver would have found the Pontiac nimbler and easier-handling. A Plymouth driver would have found it more sure-footed and enjoyed the better visibility of the Pontiac. The owner of a Nash Eight would have found the Pontiac Eight quieter but lacking in power, while a Packard customer would have found the Pontiac noisier and lacking in refinement. Coming out of a Studebaker Champion, one would no doubt have been more impressed with the Pontiac Six in every way, while the Hudson owner trying out a Pontiac would have missed the acceleration but found the steering precision better in the Pontiac.

The bench seat was of chair height, giving an upright driving thirty-five degrees from vertical, so that the driver could use some muscle on it without going into any unusual action with his arms. Not that the steering was particularly hard, but the effort needed for parking, for instance, was quite high, and the resistance got stronger the tighter the turn. It was somewhat slow-geared at 19:1 but not sloppy. The car could be placed fairly accurately in its lane and did not wander.

The steering geometry was called Tru-Arc in Pontiac's publicity, and its principles were not in any way new—it was just a specific combination of static alignment, linkage and relative steering angles. A worm-and-roller steering gear operated a parallelogram linkage with an idler arm anchored in the chassis and equal-length drag links bolted into the eyes of steering arms extending backwards from the front wheel hubs.

Rather front-heavy, the car tended to understeer, but could be forced around curves under full control despite strong body roll and, usually, loud squeals from the tires. Springs were quite soft, and the front end would dive under braking. On bad roads, the car would rock and pitch at low frequency, calling for such unfavorable comments as likening the motion to a boat ride. It could cause seasickness in certain people at times, but the 1946 model was relatively solid compared to the Pontiacs that were to be built ten years later.

The 1946 Pontiac steering wheel design was reminiscent of an airplane silhouette, with the three spokes forming the wings and tail. Silver Streak elements on the side-to-side spokes reinforced the aircraft impression. An ivory-white rim was of eighteen-inch diameter and surrounded a full-circle horn ring.

The small speedometer was circular in shape and set right in front, with smaller instruments on both sides. A dash clock was mounted in the glovebox lid, and the space between the instruments and the glovebox was taken up by a radio with a Silver Streak theme covering the loudspeaker and, below that, heater controls.

The pedals were big and trucklike, well spaced out and with tall arms standing up from the floor in an arc, giving long pedal travel. The gearshift was on the steering column, consisting of a delicate-looking lever that operated a vacuum-assisted linkage. It had short, sure motions, and was fully satisfactory. The three-speed transmission itself was quiet, and the synchromesh on second and top gears was faultless. But the first gear had no synchromesh, and would often engage with a *clunk*. So would reverse.

The view over the hood was dominated by the Silver Streak with the Indian head at the front edge. A tall driver could see the top of the left fender, but the right front fender was lost from view for *any* driver. The split windshield gave adequate corner vision, and the rearview mirror on the divider bar was well placed for getting the maximum picture through the one-piece rear window. Wipers were vacuum-operated, which usually meant that they would slow down or stop when one floored the accelerator to gain speed—conditions when the wipers are desperately needed—while they would flap happily across the glass when the car was coasting or idling. Wiper arms were cowl-mounted and cleaned all the essential area.

The alligator hood was hinged at the cowl end, and released by a button under the dash. Except for making valve adjustments, engine accessibility for servicing or repairs was excellent. The engines were narrow, and the accessories sensibly located. But the valves were hard to get at, despite a removable panel on the inside of the fender. Some mechanics preferred taking off the whole fender.

The four-wheel duo-servo brakes were generally adequate. The term duo-servo means that the two brake shoes forming a pair are linked at the ends opposite the wheel cylinder by a floating pivot, so that the leading shoe can transfer self-energizing effect to the trailing shoe. The car had ten-inch drums on all four wheels, operated by a single hydraulic circuit without power assist. For normal use, the brakes were smooth in action and easy to modulate. And they had enough fade resistance for its performance, and for the driving conditions and traffic patterns of its day.

It was common to call family sedans six-seaters at the time and, of course, there was enough room for six persons to sit in the car. The front seat, though a bench-type, was not truly intended for more than two people. Three could be squeezed in, but the driver would suffer from lack of elbow room on the right.

In the four-door models, back seat room was excellent, though the transmission tunnel in the floor necessitated a hump that could inconvenience the middle passenger if sitting three abreast. On two-door models, the back seat was less comfortable. Even though the coupe was built on the same wheelbase as the sedan, the back seat was positioned farther forward, restricting both knee room and leg room. It had no great benefit in terms of larger trunk space, but served only to allow a sportier roofline without losing too much head room for the back-seat riders.

The 1946 Pontiac landed on a seller's market, and it was obvious that Pontiac dealers could sell every single car Pontiac could produce. Then General Motors plants were hit by strikes on November 21, 1945. Other strikes followed, and 1946 became a year of labor unrest. Mining, steel production, railroads, trucking, shipping—all vital functions to the auto industry—were curtailed. Pontiac's output was seriously affected, though the selling effort continued at an unabated pace.

Pontiac advertisements stressed such features as "pre-war quality and value" and "pre-war safety and sturdiness," rather than beauty, power and performance. Pontiac was not out to attract customers who might buy its cars for the wrong reasons. Pontiac was not going to change—it promised to continue to deliver "extra values of the type which influenced buyers to select Pontiac in years past."

This attachment to the past is not difficult to understand. A top Pontiac engineer, now retired, Edmund L. Windeler recalls: "The car was then advertised as 'built to last a hundred thousand miles.' We used to test things for ages before we ever put anything into production. We had to make sure it was at least as durable as what we had got." Its traditions were honored.

Harry J. Klingler was general manager of Pontiac in 1946, having held that office since 1933. He had a strong background in sales.

CHAPTER 3

Preparation for Greatness

PONTIAC PROSPERED IN the postwar era. Its leadership was perhaps conservative in many ways, but the division was turning out a quality product and experimenting with radical new cars.

The fact that Pontiac cars sold well in the late forties and early fifties, and that the division was able to increase production enough to maintain fifth place in the sales race through 1953, may have masked Pontiac's real problems during this period. Basically, Pontiac lacked direction. By that we do not mean day-to-day management, but an idea of where it was heading.

At the divisional level, Pontiac must be said to have been well managed, but the general manager had neither the vision nor the personal force needed to map out the succession of Pontiac cars for more than a short-term future.

Corporate plans involving Pontiac were also weak and not well defined in the years that Charles E. Wilson ('Engine Charlie') was president of General Motors (1941–1953). Though Sloan still held office as chairman of the board, he was far removed now from taking an interest in the detailed plans of each car division. The result was that Pontiac was allowed to drift. Too many things just happened that way—propelled by circumstance rather than by intent. Due to Pontiac's

dependence on Chevrolet, however, product planning and evolution went ahead in great style, as if nothing were amiss.

What the division really lacked was a determined management team with a firm plan for Pontiac's future. That was to come later. In the meantime, the division underwent a period of slow progress, carried forward by the efforts and foresight of many good men in vital positions.

With 113,109 new car sales in 1946, Pontiac accounted for 6.23 percent of the market (in which General Motors held only a thirty-eight-percent share). Chevrolet led Ford and Plymouth, and Pontiac followed behind Buick and Dodge to occupy sixth place, ahead of Oldsmobile, Mercury, Nash and Chrysler. Pontiac almost doubled its sales in 1947, with registrations of 206,411 new cars. Since the entire industry was getting back into stride, Pontiac's market penetration did not advance much: from 6.23 to 6.52 percent. General Motors boosted its share of the market to forty-two percent, and the ranking list did not change above Pontiac's level.

Much of the credit for Pontiac's growing sales was given to its new general sales manager, L. W. Ward, who immediately set out to strengthen the sales organization in both the wholesale and retail

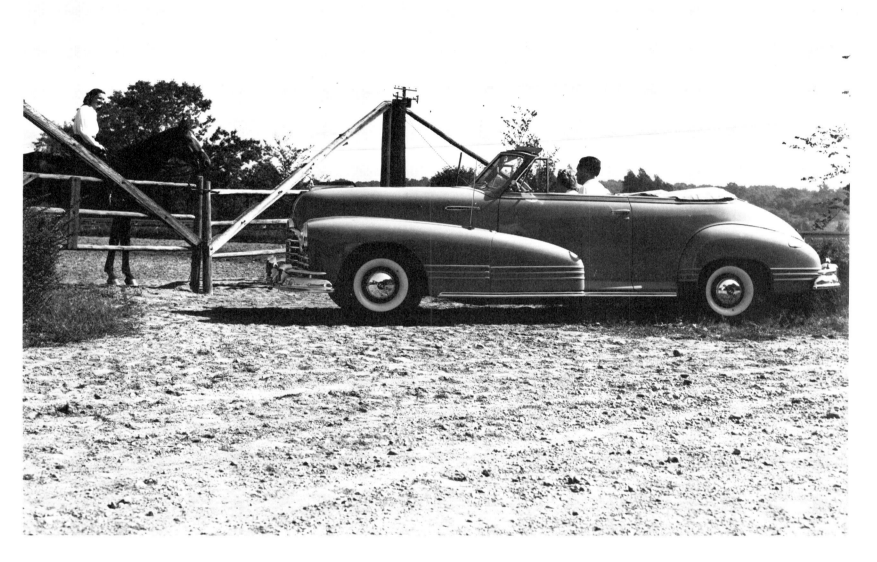

Torpedo convertible from 1947 was built on a 119-inch wheelbase. Buyers had choice of 87.5-hp six-cylinder and 101.5-hp eight-cylinder engines. Ragtop was manually operated. Brake drums sported triple sealing that year.

1947 PONTIAC TORPEDO 4-DOOR SEDAN

Two-door Streamliner coupe heads 1947 array of Pontiacs in factory hall reserved for adjustments, changes and rectifications to be made after final assembly. A business coupe is visible behind it.

The 1947 Torpedo four-door sedan was built on a 119-inch wheelbase. Options included outside mirror, back-up light and trunk light. Dash-controlled hood lock was standard.

fields. At the outset Pontiac's real competitors were the Mercury, Dodge and DeSoto, cars of similar type selling in the same price bracket. Pontiac was far more successful, however, and soon began thinking of Oldsmobile and Buick as competitors rather than fellow stablemates on the same team.

Pontiac's general manager was Harry J. Klingler, who had held that post since 1933. The chief engineer was Benjamin H. Anibal, who had led the design team that created the first Pontiac in 1926. Both were approaching retirement age.

Klingler was not known as a business administrator but as a salesman. He was general manager of Chevrolet before GM President Alfred P. Sloan and Executive Vice President William S. Knudsen picked him to run Pontiac. Klingler had made himself a hero at General Motors by setting sales records for Chevrolet in years when the whole industry was in trouble. His appointment signified a new direction at

Pontiac—selling. Until his arrival, selling had been a passive mode at Pontiac—more or less a matter of taking orders.

Now selling became a major activity, with market research, advertising and sales promotion programs to support the effort. None of this would have worked unless the product had been brought along to match the trends in demand. And though Madison Avenue had not yet discovered the term, 'image' is what the public demanded from Pontiac—and it's what they got. As chief engineer, Ben Anibal was running the entire product end of the business, from planning to production, and in the early years he concentrated on simply improving the quality of its engineering design and materials.

Later he allowed himself to get fancy, and his Pontiac eight, for instance, was justly regarded as an engineering masterpiece. Anibal was a former chief engineer of Cadillac and had experience from Peerless and Studebaker. After the war, he could look back on a very distinguished career, and wanted to take life easy. He applied for early retirement at age sixty, left Pontiac in 1947, and lived for another thirty years.

In his place, Klingler appointed fifty-two-year-old George Delaney, who had been assistant chief engineer since 1939. Joining Pontiac as electrical engineer in 1934, Delaney came from Graham-Paige, where

1948 PONTIAC DELUXE TORPEDO 4-DOOR SEDAN

he had gone in 1920 as an experimental engineer, later becoming electrical engineer and assistant chief engineer. He hailed from Missouri, and had graduated from the University of Missouri in 1917 with a degree in electrical engineering.

At the same time, Klingler began to think about his own retirement, and realized he ought to groom a successor to his post. In 1947 he named Arnold Lenz as executive assistant to the general manager. Lenz served as Klingler's right-hand man and moved up to the top job when Klingler was appointed to higher office in 1951.

By that time, Pontiac's status at the corporate level had been somewhat modified. Pontiac began building cars again in 1946. But the division was no longer alone in producing Pontiacs, for General Motors had established a new organization to assemble Pontiac, Oldsmobile and Buick cars on the same lines in a variety of locations throughout the United States. Thus, by 1947, Pontiacs were also built in Linden, New Jersey; South Gate, California; Atlanta, Georgia; Arlington, Texas; Kansas City, Kansas; and Wilmington, Delaware.

On the product front, there was nothing new of substance in the 1947 models. But work of vast consequence was going on in the engineering department. At a time when automatic transmissions were taking the industry—and the public—by storm, Anibal and Klingler had resisted making use of the HydraMatic that Oldsmobile and

Two-door Streamliner coupe was basically unchanged for 1948. Model year is identified by grille treatment and revised side chrome strips. HydraMatic transmission was offered as an extra-cost option on all models.

Styling mockup for the 1948 model was photographed on January 8, 1946. Proposed fender line had to wait till 1949, and the drop-center grille theme proved abortive. Bob Lauer was chief designer of the Pontiac studio.

Automatic transmission and two-tone color schemes were offered for all 1948 Pontiacs. Writing on the cowl reads "Silver Streak." Picture shows the 1948 Deluxe Torpedo four-door sedan.

Pontiac station wagon for 1948 continued as a true woodie. Instrument panel, windshield and window moldings had a quarter-sawed mahogany finish, and steering column, gearshift and handbrake were color-matched in brown.

Height was reduced 2½ inches for the 1949 Pontiacs. Wheelbase was standardized at 120 inches for all models, with an overall length of 202½ inches. Track was 58 inches in front and 59 inches in the rear.

Cadillac had pioneered. Delaney understood the competitive advantage a good automatic transmission would give Pontiac in the market place, and the HydraMatic became optional on all of Pontiac's 1948 models. There's no doubt that Delaney was more progressive than Anibal in every area. Bob Knickerbocker summed up his view: "Delaney I think was responsible for pulling the technical engineering thing up. But I don't think he changed the image much."

The 1948 cars also had oil-filled, hermetically sealed ignition coils. Increased coolant capacity was a feature of the six-cylinder engines. Neoprene-jacketed ignition cables were used to prevent leakage, and plug leads ended in molded rubber caps to seal the contact. The 1948 bodies retained the same sheet metal but received completely new redecorating, with different grille, bumpers and chrome moldings.

Many innovations that followed in the years up to 1955 were due to Robert R. Hutchinson, a veteran engineer who had joined Pontiac at the age of forty-five in 1935 and worked in a wide variety of assignments. Anibal had named him assistant chief engineer, and he became an unofficial director of advanced projects for Delaney. Hutchinson retired in 1955 but loved cars too much to quit the business, so he signed up as an engineering consultant to Opel.

Pontiac also had its own little exclusivities. Russ Gee, until recently assistant chief engineer of Pontiac, described it this way: "We had sophistication in unfashionable values—primarily in durability and reliability. I believe Pontiac was the only car maker that wrapped up the rear springs—we had steel covers on them to keep them lubricated and prevent noise from interleaf rubbing."

Pontiac had a decent year in 1948. It was still a seller's market, with a ready buyer for every car that could be produced anywhere in the country. A total of 228,939 new Pontiacs were registered in 1948, which boosted the division to fifth place in the sales race, relegating Dodge to sixth position.

Pontiac's market share in 1948 was still only 6.56 percent. Chevrolet alone held over twenty percent, and General Motors as a whole took better than forty percent. Such was the situation when General Motors was preparing its first truly postwar cars: the 1949 models.

"Great style" are two words which in a way sum up the 1949 Pontiacs with their all-new Fisher bodies. Effective with production of the 1949 models, Pontiac reverted to sharing the A-body with Chevrolet. Use of this A-body was in fact extended even to the more

Rarest model in Pontiac's 1949 lineup was the sedan delivery, sharing the sheet metal of the new all-steel station wagon (though woodies continued in production). Delivery belonged in Streamliner series, and was built in standard trim only.

prestigious divisions, as Oldsmobile had it on the 1949 Series 76 and 88, and Buick on the new Special in 1950. What typified all the new models that year was a lower, wider, longer look.

Overall length for the 1949 models was stretched to 202.5 inches for both the Chieftain (the Torpedo name was dropped) and Streamliner series. The Chieftain label had been used briefly for a 1942 model and was now revived to stress Pontiac's Indian identification.

Height was reduced by 2.5 inches and ranged from 61.75 inches for the convertible to 63.25 inches for the four-door sedan. Though interiors were wider, overall width was actually reduced from 76.75 inches to 73.875. The Chieftain inherited the notchback body style from the Torpedo, and the Streamliner continued with its fastback design. Both series had the same chassis, with a 120-inch wheelbase.

What made the styling so outstanding was, above all, its newness. The public had seen new styles appear on Kaiser and Frazer cars, Studebakers and, perhaps most dramatically, Hudsons. But the Big Three (General Motors Corporation, Ford Motor Company and Chrysler Corporation) perpetuated the use of their prewar body shells

through the 1948 model year. It gave the appearance of an all-new Pontiac. And yet the engines were the same trusty old power units of prewar vintage, and engineering improvements in other areas did not break with the design principles used in the preceding models.

Engineering news for 1949 included a redesigned cross-braced frame, of the cantilevered type, with straight side-members. The six-cylinder engine was moved four inches forward in the chassis, and an additional cross-member was installed to support the radiator. At the same time, the synchromesh gearbox was extended to match the HydraMatic's length, so that the same propeller shaft could be used regardless of which transmission was fitted. A larger-diameter fan with reduced pitch was introduced for both sixes and eights. It was mounted directly on the water pump shaft instead of on the pump pulley flange as before.

Butyl rubber radiator hoses were adopted, and the accessory fuse panel was moved from under the hood to a place below the instrument panel. Fiber-core ignition cables came into use on the 1950 models. A new steering system was adopted, to be marketed with the label Tru-Arc Safety Steering. It had the pitman arm pointing down, and all arms running parallel across the chassis to the steering arms, which pointed straight back from the lower end of the kingpins.

Telescopic shock absorbers in the rear suspension were mounted inside of the frame and straddle-mounted to control crosswise body quiver. At the time, Pontiac also claimed this type of mounting worked against sideway, but of course that's not true. Shock absorbers are simply a brake on spring deflections, and cannot play any part in adding to roll stiffness.

A totally new profile was the first thing that struck people who looked at the new Pontiac. Though the windshield angle had hardly changed at all, it looked as if it had a sharper rake, due to the sweeping rooflines and tailend design. Rear overhang was considerably greater than on the 1948 models, and even front overhang was increased, but not quite so readily visible. There was no pretense of having separate front fenders. They blended into the body sides, forming a beltline that reached into the rear fender area. The beginning of the rear fenders was marked by a bulb-type swelling in the panels.

From the front, all eyes naturally tended to focus on the grille, so low that it did not even reach up to headlamp level, and it was hooded by a chrome-plated arch. A winglike horizontal bar filled the center of the air intake, supported by short vertical pontoons. The Silver Streak was there, running from the Pontiac emblem on the front of the hood, providing a platform for the Indian-head ornament, and interrupting itself at the windshield base. It resumed on the deck lid and ran all the way down to the combined lock and trunk handle.

Curved windshield and backlight glass was used for the first time on a Pontiac. The windshield was not yet made in one piece, but the center divider bar was much more discreet and less structural in appearance than it had been on the 1948 models. Parking lights were convertible to dual duty as directional indicators, encased in rectangular frames in front and round ones at the rear.

Both the Streamliner and Chieftain were offered in two trim levels, standard and deluxe. Chieftain body styles included four-door sedan, two-door sedan, sedan coupe, convertible, business coupe (standard trim only) and taxicab; while the Streamliners were available as four-door sedan, sedan coupe, wood-panel station wagon, all-metal wagon, and sedan delivery (panel van).

All doors were hinged at the leading edge, front doors on the A-post and rear doors on the B-post. Four-door models had vent windows in all doors, while two-door models had plain rear side windows. None of the body styles had sail-panel side windows in the 1949 A-body. Wood-panel station wagons were built through 1949. The 1950 lineup shows an all-metal wagon only.

Both the A and B bodies had been created under the direction of Harley J. Earl, director of GM Styling. Bob Lauer and Joe Schemansky in the Pontiac studio worked independently of Clare MacKichan in the Chevrolet studio, but there was full coordination on basic dimensions and at the engineering level.

The man who directed the adaptation of the new Fisher A-body to the Pontiac chassis was Herman Kaiser. He had joined Pontiac in 1928 as a chassis designer, and was to work on chassis design for Pontiac until 1942. In 1943 Kaiser was transferred to Fisher Body Division, where he served as a power-plant project engineer. Fisher was then tooling up to build Allison aircraft engines. He returned to Pontiac in 1945 as chief body draftsman, and played a major part in engineering the 1949 A-body in its Pontiac version.

Compared with the 1948 model, the 1949 Pontiac had a decidedly softer ride, but was well balanced. The combination of coil springs in front and leaf springs in the rear was good enough for Cadillac, so Pontiac had no excuses to make for its suspension systems. But the shock damping was inadequate, for the springs would continue to flex in repeated cycles from a single bump. This worked well on rough roads, driven at low speeds, but on good roads it could lead to motion sickness in passengers. The steering was slow, the worm-and-roller steering gear having a ratio of 22.25:1, but the large eighteen-inch steering wheel provided a good grip and plenty of leverage, so that the steering effort was quite moderate.

Response to the helm was predictable, but delayed partly by initial understeer and partly by the need for cranking the wheel so much for an ordinary curve. Body roll on curves was a weak point, too, for the chassis did not provide much roll resistance. On sharp turns, tire squeal was inevitable at anything above horse-and-wagon speed. Yet on long curves, the car was very stable, especially as long as the driver avoided braking. Stepping on the brake after beginning the turn could result in axle hop and tailwagging, even on dry pavement. Nosedive under braking was accepted in those days, and the Pontiac did a lot of it.

The sedans gave ample seating for six, though the hump over the propeller shaft was even higher than it had been in the 1941–48

Arnold Lenz, left, worked for years as Klingler's understudy, but was killed in a car/train crash less than a year after taking over as general manager of Pontiac. Robert Critchfield, middle, started as an electrician and worked most of his career at Delco-Remy. He ran Pontiac from 1952 to 1956. George Delaney, right, became chief engineer of Pontiac when Ben Anibal retired. He directed development work on the V-8 and put automatic transmissions into Pontiac cars.

1950 Streamliner two-door fastback was named Sedan Coupe in Pontiac sales literature. Sheet metal was largely unchanged, but a new grille used heavy vertical bars to link the three main horizontal members.

The eight got bigger for 1950, offering power outputs of 108 and 113 hp. The six remained at 90 hp. Hydra-Matic transmission was available for all models, with either engine. Fingertip starter button was standard throughout.

1951 PONTIAC DE LUXE CHIEFTAIN 4-DOOR SEDAN

Catalina coupe introduced hardtop styling to Pontiac for 1950. It belonged in the Chieftain series and was offered in Deluxe and Super Deluxe trim, with two-tone paint in such combinations as San Pedro Ivory below the beltline and Sierra Rust for the roof.

For 1951 Pontiac continued to offer America's lowest-priced straight-eight, delivering a maximum of 106 hp from 268.4 cubic inches. Standard compression ratio was 6.5:1 and 7.5:1 optional (with no change in hp rating).

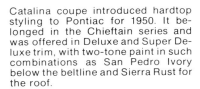

models. Doors were high enough and opened wide enough to make it easy to get in and out.

Visibility over the hood, which seemed longer than ever from behind the wheel, was actually improved, for the cowl had been lowered to meet the top of the fenders. And the fenders had been raised, so that both could be seen, making it easier to maneuver the car in tight places. The C-posts inevitably caused blind spots in the rearview mirror, but the backlight was wide, with a low base, so that traffic coming up from behind could be seen clearly.

And it's probably true that drivers of 1949 Pontiacs were passed on the road more than they passed other cars. The six was less than brilliant in terms of performance even with the three-speed synchromesh, and became downright sluggish when combined with the HydraMatic. For manual-transmission cars, Pontiac had abandoned the vacuum shift, and the 1949 model had a simple mechanical linkage to the column-mounted lever. Its motion was precise enough, but the throws were extremely long, so that gearshifts tended to become slow.

The eight-cylinder engine did not have much more pep, nor was it smoother or more silent to any degree that mattered to the average owner. Both engines were developed for tractability and long life, not for sprint starts and speed records.

Pontiac made its three-millionth car in February 1949, and a new production record of 336,000 cars was set that year. Pontiac registrations soared to 321,033 cars, but Pontiac's market penetration was nearly static, now at 6.63 percent. As the market went in 1949,

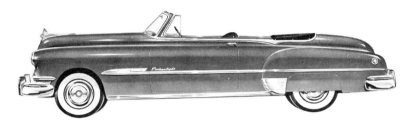

The 1951 Chieftain Deluxe four-door sedan. Options, as on all Silver Anniversary Pontiacs, included either the six- or eight-cylinder engine. Restyled grille had vertical bars cut in half and new V-shape setting off Indian-head medallion in center.

On the 1951 Chieftain convertible, new Pontiac Eight lettering on the door replaced the former Silver Streak lettering on the front fender. Six-cylinder engines were, of course, still available in convertibles, and identified as such on the doors.

the division should have done better. Chevrolet went ahead to 21.3 percent and General Motors took forty-three percent of the market. It was said at the corporate level that Pontiac wasn't pulling its weight.

"I remember the words of some of our general managers," said a long-time Pontiac engineer. "The key word was to have good solid transportation, and not cars aimed at attracting people who were interested in particular innovation. Back in those days, for one reason or another, Oldsmobile was known as being a pretty gutsy organization, but it wasn't all their own work. Some developments from outside just happened to be introduced on their vehicles. I am not so confident that Oldsmobile developed its own automatic transmission, for instance. Sure, they did a high-compression V-8 engine before Pontiac, no doubt about that, but some of the other factors I'm not so sure of."

From those remarks, we get the idea that Pontiac could have done much more to keep abreast without actually having to undertake all its own research and development. The corporation had research facilities, engineering resources and supplier divisions ready to fill

the car divisions' demands. But Pontiac made little use of what the corporation offered, while Oldsmobile reaped the benefit of several avant-garde developments.

Could the 1950 models bring Pontiac better results? The most significant event that year was the introduction of the Catalina hardtop coupe, which marks the first use of that name, taken from an island resort off southern California and made famous by a World War II flying boat. It also introduced the two-door hardtop (with assistance from Fisher Body and shared with Oldsmobile and Cadillac) into the Pontiac model lineup.

Pontiac six for 1951 remained faithful to original design but benefited from years of development work. All parts display the same basic simplicity that was the secret of Pontiac's quality and longevity.

inset between the bumper and the main grille bar. The Indian-head medallion above the grille grew to twice its former size, and the hood ornament was streamlined to look more modern.

In the spring of 1950 the division had 16,000 workers in its home plant in Pontiac, Michigan, and 21,000 nationwide. Pontiac did not know exactly what its production capacity was, partly because of the B-O-P (Buick-Oldsmobile-Pontiac) assembly plants, and partly because of the remodeling and improvements that were constantly going on in the home plants. In any case, a new production record was set in 1950 when Pontiac turned out over 450,000 cars in one year. A year earlier, that would have been enough to overtake Buick, but the Flint-based division also raised its output and sales enough to stay in fourth place, keeping Pontiac in what was fast becoming its usual number five position. Buick stretched its lead over Pontiac from 50,000 to 95,000 cars. And Oldsmobile was threatening from behind. So were Dodge and Mercury. Pontiac's market share that year was 6.96 percent—just a shade better than its standing in 1940.

For 1951 the Pontiac straight-eight was enlarged to 268.4-cubic-inch displacement and delivered 116 hp in the 1951 models. And it was still the lowest-priced straight-eight in America. Ford's V-8 had undersold it for many, many years, and the industry was turning increasingly to V-8's, which made the merit of the straight-eight somewhat open to question.

Both Pontiac engines were offered with optional high-compression cylinder heads from 1949 through 1954. On the 1951 engines, standard compression ratio was 6.5:1 throughout, and the optional heads raised it to 7.5:1. It had a minor effect on power output, as this table shows:

	Standard Six	Hi-Comp. Six
Hp at rpm	96 @ 3400	100 @ 3400
Torque at rpm	191 @ 1200	195 @ 1200
	Standard Eight	Hi-Comp. Eight
Hp at rpm	116 @ 3600	120 @ 3600
Torque at rpm	220 @ 2000	225 @ 2000

Chrome-nickel iron pistons were still used in 1951 but they now had tin plating for less wear. One piston weighed 26.7 ounces. The major news in chassis engineering was a six-inch lengthening of the rear leaf springs, which led the sales department to coin for its rear suspension system the name 'Travelux ride.'

Not unnaturally, this gave the axle even more freedom to move in planes not intended, which resulted in making the car's handling characteristics, never more than average, even worse. As the weight of the car increased year by year, the front suspension became

Except for the wood-panel station wagon, all the other body styles from the year before were continued. No sheet metal changes were made, and the major alteration was a revised grille. The main grille bar was extended to wrap around the front fenders. All three horizontal grille members were made heavier, for what the Pontiac literature claimed as "a more massive beauty."

The air intake louvers were marked by five enlarged vertical teeth and the parking lamps were moved up, directly below the headlights,

sloppier, and the steering more and more vague. The Pontiac car was degenerating from an automobile with an esteemed image to just a piece of 'Detroit iron.' Undue emphasis was placed on appearance and gimmicks, and not enough on real engineering.

A new grille marked the 1951 models, using a wing-formed main bumper bar rising from the center of the bumper to the level of the Indian-head medallion and then extending horizontally to either side. Above it was an arc-shaped chrome bar reaching to the Pontiac label which marked the start of the Silver Streak. The Streamliner fastbacks were phased out at the end of the 1951 model run, and the name disappeared from the lineup.

In parallel with the technical and styling changes in Pontiac cars, a series of management changes were soon to occur at the division— some voluntary, others involuntary. In 1951 Klingler left Pontiac to accept a new position as vice president in charge of vehicle production for General Motors. He was succeeded by Arnold Lenz, who was not given time to prove his worth at the head of Pontiac, for he was killed in a car/train crash in 1952. His place was soon filled by a veteran engineer and administrator named Robert M. Critchfield, who had joined General Motors in 1921 as an engineer with Remy Electric Division in Anderson, Indiana. Born in Columbus, Indiana, in 1894, he had gone to school there and in 1916 graduated from Ohio State University with a bachelor's degree in electrical engineering. He had worked his way through college, running more or less simultaneously a bookstore and an instrument repair service.

His first job as an engineer was with Westinghouse in Pittsburgh, where he stayed for one year. Then came two years in the Navy, after which he joined Owen-Dyneto in Syracuse, as assistant chief engineer. Going to Remy two years later, he was named assistant chief engineer of Delco-Remy in 1933 and chief engineer in 1936. From 1947 to 1951 he was Delco-Remy's factory manager, and then served one year as assistant general manager of Allison in Indianapolis before coming to Pontiac.

Critchfield was a man of considerable vision and optimistic outlook. He embarked on the most extensive expansion and modernization program that had taken place at Pontiac since 1927.

Straight-eight engine in 1951 version has carburetor towering above the cylinder head and manifold, with an air cleaner designed for a hood line leaving plenty of free space inside.

CHAPTER 4

The Motorama Years

CRITCHFIELD'S ATTITUDE HAD a lot to do with his success. He was in control at Pontiac, and he felt it. He knew what was going on inside the division, and he was aware of what was going on in the world outside. His optimism made it easy for him to make brave decisions without worrying and vacillating.

Under Critchfield, Delaney and the engineering staff found it easier to get approval for new projects and funds to try new things. Technical trends at the time were focused on V-8 engines and automatic transmissions. Pontiac already had one of the best of the latter and was going to get one of the most interesting of the former.

Automatic transmissions were finding a steadily higher acceptance rate among customers, and the HydraMatic had an outstanding reliability record. The brilliant English engineering consultant Reid Railton described the HydraMatic in 1951 as a "mechanism of excellent overall efficiency, slightly marred by the fact that it operates in stages which can be felt as slight jerks, and by the fact that the car-performance it provides is not quite as good as can be obtained by a skilled driver with a conventional box." But the HydraMatic engineers had not been idle, and were developing new ideas in collaboration with the power-train engineers at the car divisions.

Around 1950 a trend towards larger-displacement engines with a flatter torque curve emerged, and HydraMatic engineers concluded

that a 3.96:1 overall reduction ratio was more than adequate for all general driving requirements. But that was still too high numerically to give the best fuel economy and the lowest noise level possible for a given car-and-engine combination. In a quest for lower final drive ratios, HydraMatic and the GM car divisions jointly came up with the idea of providing a performance drive range, which in practice ended up being nothing more than a block to prevent the transmission from automatically upshifting from third to fourth. Even with final drive ratios as low as 3.07:1, this would provide overall gearing of 4.40:1— high enough to give extra acceleration, improved gradeability and better downhill engine-braking characteristics.

The new Dual-Range HydraMatic became available on Pontiac cars in 1952. What was so different in that? Just a modification in the shift-control mechanism, related to overall gearing. As in the 1948–51 transmissions, the Dual-Range HydraMatic consisted of a two-element fluid coupling mounted in front of three planetary gear trains giving four forward speeds and reverse.

By selection of D or D1 the driver could control whether to remain in third gear through traffic and on winding roads, or to move through the lower gears into top for maximum fuel economy and quieter running. The driver could shift from one range to the other any time, at any speed. This was done by moving the selector lever from one

Catalina two-door hardtop showed minor refinements for 1952. This is the Super Deluxe version. Two-tone paint combinations included Sea Mist green below the beltline and a Belfast green roof. Chrome use was relatively restrained.

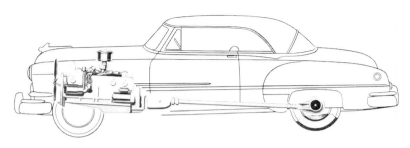

Semicircular speedometer was placed at the center of the instrument cluster on the 1952 Pontiac. A huge dash clock was placed above the radio. Indicator on steering wheel hub shows shift pattern for Dual-Range HydraMatic.

The 1952 Pontiac introduced Dual-Range HydraMatic transmission, which enabled the car to use a final drive ratio as low as 3.08:1, lowest in the industry that year.

side of the Drive slot to the other (the shift pattern was Neutral-Drive-Low-Reverse). Since the worst shock this could provide was stepping down from top to third (by locking out top gear), stress levels came well within the margin provided for normal operation.

In 1952 Pontiacs with synchromesh transmission, the six had a final drive ratio of 4.1:1 while the eight used a 3.9:1 axle as standard. Cars with HydraMatic had a 3.08:1 final drive ratio.

Pontiac customers who bought the new automatic drive felt an effect very similar to that of overdrive. In the open-road driving range, the engine turned fifteen percent slower than with the old gearing,

which reduced engine wear, noise and fuel consumption. The owner's manual also encouraged shifting to the 'performance' range when going downhill, to save the brakes.

"In our new Dual-Range HydraMatic cars introduced for 1952 we have given particular emphasis to this function," Chief Engineer George Delaney stated in a press release. "When the engine takes up a major portion of the braking duties on long, steep hills, brake lining life is immeasurably prolonged and furthermore both brakes and tires remain cooler. It must be remembered that foot brakes accomplish their purpose by converting the energy in the moving vehicle into heat. This heat is produced by friction between the brake lining and the brake drum. The heat must then be dissipated into the air.

"Naturally, in the process of developing friction and heat, the temperature of the brake drums, wheels and tires rise to a considerable degree. While brake linings and tires are capable of withstanding a tremendous amount of this strenuous duty, wear inevitably takes place. On the other hand, when the engine is used as a brake, the energy of the moving car is simply utilized to operate the engine as a compressor or pump. Since the car is equipped with a complete heat dissipation system provided through the radiator, there is no problem involved, and wear is negligible."

It wasn't only to save the customer the wear on the brakes and the cost of frequent relining that was behind Pontiac's insistence upon this engine-braking feature.

Chieftain four-door sedan for 1952 continued a strong Silver Streak styling theme, with a streamlined but still prominent Indian head. Grille with center medallion was inherited from the 1951 models; grooved-disc hub caps were new.

For 1953 the wheelbase for the Pontiac Chieftain station wagon was increased to 122 inches. All wagons were now all-metal, the last woodie dating from 1950. Tailgates were a two-piece design, split at the beltline.

Cars were becoming bigger and heavier, and Pontiac had several models with curb weights above 3,500 pounds. That meant many Pontiac drivers were moving 4,000 pounds or more down the road, at all sorts of speeds and on all sorts of roads. Ironically, cars were to get even bigger and heavier before anything dramatic was done to give them better brakes.

The four-millionth Pontiac was built in July 1951, and the five-millionth Pontiac in June 1954. What happened to Pontiac sales between those dates is not a true reflection of the free market forces at work, but a picture distorted by *force majeure*. All car makers curtailed auto production during 1951, as defense work for the war in Korea laid claim to many of their manufacturing facilities and much of their raw materials. Pontiac dealers sold 337,821 cars that year and the division held on to its fifth place, though its market share slipped back to 6.68 percent.

In 1952 auto production was just loafing along, and Pontiac registrations were only 266,351 cars that year. It was enough to hold on to fifth place, but Dodge was only 20,000 units behind, and the gap between Pontiac and Oldsmobile had closed to 42,000 cars. Pontiac's penetration receded to 6.41 percent, in a year when Chevrolet maintained its market share at 20.5 percent and General Motors took 41.75 percent of the car market.

Defense contracts were canceled when the Korean war ended, and the auto industry soon found that all material shortages had evaporated. At the same time the demand for new cars revived, and the factories geared up for new production records. Pontiac's sales in 1953 totaled 385,692 cars and its market share climbed to 6.72 percent. The division was nearly 100,000 cars ahead of Dodge, in the Chrysler camp, as well as Mercury in the Ford camp. But Pontiac was not keeping pace with Chevrolet and Buick, whose growth boosted GM's market share to forty-five percent for the first time since 1941.

While all other GM divisions increased their sales in 1954, Pontiac alone experienced a decline. Sales dipped to 358,167 cars and the market share to 6.47 percent. How was Pontiac's ranking affected? It dropped one place, because Oldsmobile sold 407,150 cars, and was making waves. The traditional order was considerably upset that year, and the list of the top ten now read Chevrolet—Ford—Buick—Oldsmobile—Plymouth—Pontiac—Mercury—Dodge—Cadillac—Chrysler. However, the cars that Pontiac built during this period remained true to their traditions.

Side view of 1953 Pontiac four-door sedan shows projecting headlamps. Rear fender sculpture fills most of rear door panel, while front fender blends into beltline.

Power steering became optional on the 1953 Pontiac. The system was made by Saginaw Division, and used an engine-driven pump.

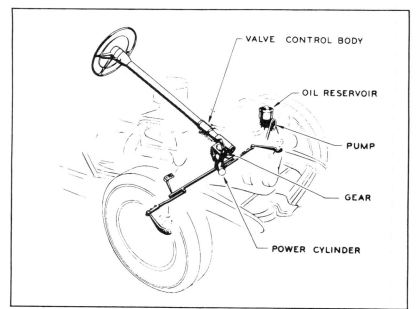

Delaney coordinated vehicle development with the demands of the divisional sales department and the corporate dictates as relayed through the general manager, Critchfield. A high-ranking member of the engineering staff explained the situation in a few concise words: "Klingler retired. Lenz was a factory man, not innovative. Critchfield was an electrical guy from Delco. None of these guys really knew cars."

Still, Pontiac had a big engineering story to tell when the 1953 models were announced. The cars had a completely new front suspension system, though the new design also worked with A-arms and coil springs. Upper control arms were lengthened to reduce positive camber on the outside wheel in a turn and simultaneously obtain less negative camber on the inside front wheel. The new suspension had a higher roll center and correspondingly higher roll stiffness. This was advertised as the Curve Control suspension.

"At that time, Pontiac was organized in such a way that they had staff and design engineers, while all the development and test work was done through the experimental department," Bob Knickerbocker explained. He was then in the experimental department, and "I had a good share of the chassis area in 1951," he recalls.

Springing and shock absorber valve characteristics were modified to improve the ride comfort. Changes made in the static suspension geometry were supplemented by a deepening of the spring seats in the lower control arms, so as to permit the use of longer coil springs with reduced spring rates. The longer coil permitted extra-cold working in the fabrication of the spring, which added to its life and reduced its tendency to sag after a certain time in service.

A revised Tru-Arc steering system was adopted. And Saginaw power steering became an extra-cost option. At the same time, the non-assisted steering ratio was slowed down from 22:1 to 25:1. That did reduce the steering effort, but negotiating a street corner needed so much work with the wheel that it turned out to be a great

advertisement for power steering, even as an extra-cost option at $177.40.

Pontiac increased the wheelbase on all models from 120 inches to 122. Curb weight was fast approaching 4,000 pounds. And the eleven-inch-diameter cast-iron drums were hard-put to handle any sustained braking without fade. Pontiac tried to improve brake cooling by using steel-shell drums with cast-iron inserts. Steel has better conductivity, but cast iron is a better heat sink. In overall brake performance, it was no improvement.

The most noteworthy engine modification for 1953 was that the six went to aluminum pistons, while the eight continued with iron pistons. The new light alloy piston for the six weighed only 1.23 pounds, while the smaller eight-cylinder piston weighed 1.71 pounds.

Pontiac also adopted two-barrel carburetors for the six-cylinder engine, and a revision in the intake manifolding followed to exploit the increase in breathing capacity. A new high-speed camshaft gave longer valve opening durations and increased overlap. On the 1953 engine, intake valves remained open for 245 degrees of crankshaft

New Dual Streak Chieftain styling features for 1953 included one-piece curved windshield, entirely new grille without vertical bars, different chrome treatment consisting of two groups of bands running up the center of hood and deck. Embryonic tailfins are also evident. Shown is a Custom Catalina two-door hardtop.

rotation, instead of 224 degrees as in 1952. The exhaust valve opening duration was fifteen degrees longer, stretched from 230 degrees to 245.

Ed Windeler was proud of the last of the side-valve sixes: "Lots of customers ran them 100,000 miles or more. In those days that was not so common as today. Very few cars at the time would run that long without trouble."

Oil pump capacity was increased on both engines to provide greater oil flow and assure extra durability. The oil pump received a new larger body as well as enlarged gears, and was able to deliver 3.3 gallons per minute at a car speed of sixty miles per hour. Fuel tank capacity was increased from 17.5 to twenty gallons.

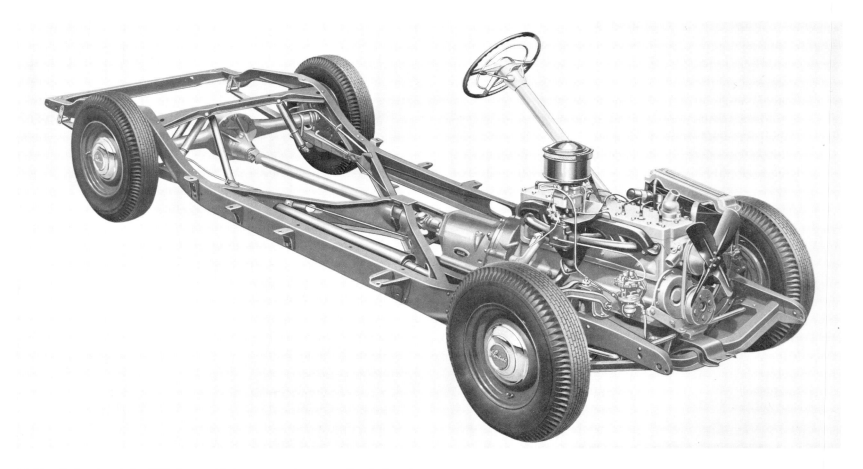

Eight-cylinder chassis for 1953 shows wide frame, one-piece propeller shaft, and Dual-Range HydraMatic transmission. Front suspension and steering linkage details were new that year.

A lot of electrical modifications were made, such as a new generator with cut-in at lower rpm and higher low-speed output so as to balance current delivery with electric energy requirements at a lower car speed than before. The 1953 models also had a dash ground strap (introduced in the latter part of 1952-model production) to assure lower resistance between generator and regulator, and a ground lead from the ignition warning light was added.

Increasing numbers of Pontiac buyers decided they had the extra cash needed for the HydraMatic and the order books were full when the HydraMatic plant at Livonia burned down in 1953, leaving Pontiac without a supplier of automatic transmissions. Chevrolet came to its aid with an offer of the two-speed Powerglide. This was a very different type of transmission, based on Buick's Dynaflow. It combined a five-element torque converter with a two-speed planetary gearset.

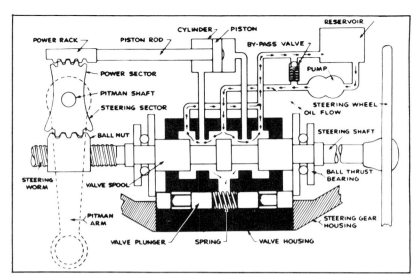

Front suspension system was redesigned for 1953, with new geometry involving control-arm lengths and pivot axis locations. It did not restrict roll, but reduced roll camber. The 1952 car is on top, a 1953 model is on the bottom.

Power steering system for the 1953 Pontiac had a hydraulically controlled power rack working on the pitman arm shaft.

With this transmission Pontiac had to outfit its automatic-drive vehicles with a 3.70:1 final drive ratio.

Dual-Range HydraMatic deliveries did not resume until operations had been moved to Willow Run. General Motors purchased this huge plant from Kaiser-Frazer, who had bought it from Ford, who had built it as an assembly plant for the B-24 Liberator bomber. It was not until the 1954-model Pontiacs were coming off the line that HydraMatic supplies were again coming in regularly.

On getting behind the wheel of the 1953 Chieftain, one was struck by the glittery instrument panel—this design used a lot of chrome and was more reminiscent of a Wurlitzer organ than of an aircraft cockpit. A semicircular speedometer dominated the design straight ahead of the driver, with four gauges below it. On the right, a small panel contained the heater controls and radio. The design ended left of the glovebox with a circular frame containing a large dish with a small clock, covering a radio speaker.

The cars did not steer or stop well, and in the opinion of most drivers, even lacked the power to provide competitive performance. Yet a test report in *Motor Trend* stated the Pontiac had more than adequate acceleration at both low and high speeds. *Motor Trend*'s eight-cylinder 1953 Pontiac was equipped with the Dual-Range

Star Chief series was introduced for 1954, a new top-of-the-line car built on a 124-inch wheelbase. After using a dual Silver Streak in 1953, Pontiac reverted to a solid band on all 1954 models.

The 1954 models blended carry-over styling from Raoul J. Pepin's time as head of the Pontiac studio with influences from new chief designer Paul W. Gillan. Pepin led the studio from 1951 to 1953.

HydraMatic and accelerated from standstill to 60 mph in 17.9 seconds (in D). This time was cut to 13.9 seconds by running in D1.

A "DriveReport" by Ken Gross, published in *Special-Interest Autos* No. 32, featured a 1953 Pontiac Model 27 Chieftain Custom Catalina and listed its top speed as 95 mph. The 268.4-cubic-inch displacement eight-cylinder engine was matched with a HydraMatic transmission and a 3.08:1 final drive ratio. The report gave 0–60 mph acceleration as taking 18.8 seconds.

There is a difference between adequate and competitive. The Pontiac eight could not keep up with a Cadillac or an Oldsmobile, with their high-compression V-8's, nor with the hemi-head Chrysler V-8. But the Pontiac could hold its own against a Mercury with its old L-head V-8, and even a Packard, with its L-head straight-eight.

In the world of the sixes, the Pontiac was a good match for the Dodges and Plymouths of the time, but was often bested by Studebakers and Kaiser Manhattans in terms of both performance and economy. And it could not touch a well-tuned Hudson or Nash. Even the Chevrolet six was an overhead-valve engine that breathed better and could run with higher compression ratios than the side-valve Pontiac unit. But Pontiac never redesigned the six. Bob Knickerbocker explains: "In the early fifties, I think, Pontiac had a different marketing strategy than Chevrolet. Our theme was a dreary, reliable, comfortable, family automobile. But of course it wasn't advertised that way."

The 1953 models were the first to be designed under the direction of Raoul Pepin, who had replaced Bob Lauer as chief designer of the Pontiac studio in 1951. Body changes for 1953 were slight, with sheet metal changes through the outer skin. Fender designs were modernized, and a high-contour deck provided a fresh rear-end appearance. The cars received a one-piece curved-glass windshield and wraparound backlights. There was a new spear-type side molding, and dual-streak decoration was adopted. This dual streak consisted of having two narrow parallel Silver Streaks instead of a single wide one. All Pontiacs were Chieftains that year, split into three sub-series: Special, Deluxe and Custom.

The grille arch was flattened a little and the center bar retouched, but the overall aspect was one of staid continuity. What had been novel in 1949 had become trite in 1953. People were disappointed in Pontiac. It was as if the average buyer could sense the aimlessness of the product policy and reacted by looking elsewhere. Two arch-competitors, Dodge and Mercury, made great progress in 1953.

Pontiac had a lot at stake with its 1954 models, introducing an entirely new car line: Star Chief. The Star Chief had three stars on the rear fender fins and a star-studded oval frame in the center of the grille with the usual arch on top. The Pontiac medallion above it now sported wings, and the dual streak had become united again.

Electric power windows became optional on the 1954 Pontiac. Air conditioning was also made optional in 1954. The instrument panel on cars with A/C equipment had three cool-air outlets.

The 1954 model year was to be the last for eight-in-line engine production. It was replaced the following year by an overhead-valve V-8. The side-valve straight-eight had been developed to its final peak. As a Pontiac engineer explained: "It was obvious that our straight-eight was not as suitable for high compression ratios as the more compact and rigid V-8. Of course, then the trend was towards higher compression—towards overhead-valve engines that breathe better and produce higher specific output." The story of how Pontiac built its V-8 is told in the next chapter.

Reporting on the 1954 Pontiac Chieftain in *True's Automotive Year Book*, Tom McCahill stated that "oddly enough Pontiacs are rarely discussed as high-performance cars and in my book they are real sleepers in this department." The test car reached 60 mph from standstill in fifteen seconds flat, and had a top speed of 90 mph.

It remains a fact that engineers who were working at Pontiac at the time felt a certain shame at the lack of 'guts' in their engines. Said one: "We felt that our straight-eight was becoming outdated by the more modern overhead-valve V-8's then coming out all around us." Another put it more simply: "We were dogs on the road."

Before Pontiac got its V-8 engine into production, the division built a number of prototypes that were not the usual experimental models, kept as secret as possible, but specifically intended for showing to the public.

Cars of the future held everybody's interest, and General Motors pioneered the public showing of futuristic cars to test public reaction, under the pretext of offering the world a view of how its designers "explore new horizons." It all started with Harley Earl's Buick-based Y-job in 1938, and continued with the XP-300 and LeSabre in 1951.

Pontiac's five-millionth car was a Star Chief Custom Catalina two-door hardtop produced on June 18, 1954. Robert Critchfield (left) hands the milestone car over to sales manager H. E. Crawford.

Two years later all GM divisions released styling prototypes for public display.

General Motors chose the name Motorama for a combined show of dream cars (as they were often called) from all its car divisions. The first Motorama was held at New York City's Waldorf-Astoria Hotel on Park Avenue in February 1953.

Pontiac was represented by one car, called the Parisienne, and it used a styling theme that was originally derived from horsedrawn carriages and came into automobiles designated 'coupe de ville.' The chauffeur had no roof at all, though a retractable plexiglass dome could be moved out to provide shelter from the rain. A formal,

Parisienne was the first in a series of
experimental vehicles Pontiac built
and displayed to test public reaction
to ideas for future production cars.
The Parisienne had a standard 1953
Pontiac chassis.

wheelbase and had a standard Pontiac engine. With its seven-inch
ground clearance, it stood fifty-six inches high.

The other divisions all chose convertibles, which were usually seen
only with the top down. Cadillac called its sleek two-seater Le Mans,
a name which had some meaning for that division, since two Cadillacs
took part in the twenty-four-hour race there in 1950, finishing tenth
and eleventh. But Cadillac decided that the name did not have
favorable connotations for its traditional American clientele, and
rejected it for use on a production car.

It was to be Pontiac that, many years later, would revive the name
completely out of context. No Pontiac or Oakland had ever run at
Le Mans. Of the other 1953 dream cars, Oldsmobile used the name
Starfire and Buick introduced the Wildcat, while Chevrolet called its
roadster Corvette. These names were all to be used on production
models from the divisions that first adopted them in 1953. Later,
Pontiac also made use of the Parisienne name, but only for cars made
in Canada.

The following year Pontiac had two dream cars which contained
some interesting ideas with potential application in production cars.
Both had fiberglass-reinforced plastic bodies. They were the Strato-
Streak and Bonneville Special. The Strato-Streak was a full-size sedan
built on the 124-inch-wheelbase Star Chief chassis, and the Bonneville
Special was a two-seater sports coupe, related in concept to
Chevrolet's Corvette. This marked the first use by Pontiac of the
Bonneville name and, unlike Le Mans, it was a name to which Pontiac
could lay some claim, because of Eddie Miller's Pontiac-powered
lakester that ran on the Bonneville Salt Flats in 1950.

The Strato-Streak four-door sedan was built as a hardtop type of
design inspired by the two-door Catalina models. It was unusual in its
door arrangement. The front door was hinged in front and the rear
door at the back, in the manner of prewar sedans. But the B-post was
missing. The doors latched into the sill and roof. This configuration had
been used on European production cars (Fiat in 1935, Lancia in 1937)
but those bodies were of much smaller size than the Strato-Streak,
and perhaps it was wise of Pontiac never to adopt this feature for a
production model.

Eventually some styling influences from the Strato-Steak definitely
did show up in production models, such as the wraparound windshield
with the 'dogleg' A-post, and the ultra-low build of the passenger
compartment. The use of a fiberglass-reinforced plastic body has not
resulted in production-model applications at Pontiac, however. The
idea of making the two bucket-type front seats swivel at right angles
to the sides for easier entry and exit, first used on the Strato-Streak,

hooded roof covered the back seat area. This was intended to convey
the idea of privacy and intimacy, assisted by the Parisienne name to
evoke an image of luxurious night life and romance.

But in a total clash with the concept that the car was created to
cater to the passengers' comfort and convenience, Pontiac made it
a two-door, so that the dignitaries it was to transport had to contort
themselves in motions that were singularly lacking in elegance in
order to reach their seats! Naturally, the chauffeur would stand outside
and hold the door open for the Baron and his Lady, and then watch
them scramble through the narrow passage, leaning over the folding
front seat backrest, and then turning around before crouching into
their seated positions. The Parisienne was built on a 122-inch

Bonneville Special was Pontiac's answer to the Chevrolet Corvette, but never went into production. Built on a 100-inch wheelbase, it was only 48.5 inches high. A special straight-eight engine was the power plant.

was used as an option on the 1973–75 LeMans, but was dropped due to lack of demand.

Strato-Streak styling features included Silver Streak ribbons on top of both front fenders and a low, wide grille with no top bar. The bumper formed the lower bar. The rear window glass wrapped around to the sides, with a backwards-tilting C-post behind the vent window in the rear door. Rear fenders were rounded off and ended in an airplane-fuselage silhouette.

The Strato-Streak was 8.7 inches lower than the 1953 production cars. Its overall height was 54.7 inches, which compared with 56.6 inches for the low-slung 1959 model Catalina. It had an overall length of 214.3 inches and an overall width of 74.5 inches.

While the Chevrolet Corvette was inspired by the Jaguar XK-120, partly in production form and partly as the C-type that ran at Le Mans in 1951, Pontiac's Bonneville Special took part of its styling theme from the Cunningham cars that also raced at Le Mans. It took the idea for

its gullwing side window arrangement from the Mercedes-Benz 300 SL, and the fender lines from a variety of speed-record cars. The main fender line was perfectly horizontal, but was broken by kickups for both front and rear wheels.

On speed-record cars large wheels were a necessity—to reduce the rotational speed of the tires—which made the wheels the tallest parts of the chassis; therefore the bodies came to contain lumps to cover the wheels while deviating as little as possible from the theoretically 'ideal' teardrop or bullet shape. On the Bonneville Special these lumps emphasized the wheel size and stressed the high-speed purpose of this model. There was no grille, just an opening in the sheet metal that separated the two protruding front fenders. It also had dual Silver

Strato Chief was a four-door hardtop in the truest sense, with no center pillar (B-post). Swivel-type bucket seats were used in front. The car pioneered panoramic windshield and had curved-glass rear quarter lights.

Strato Star coupe was notable for its 'greenhouse' styling. Its many other experimental styling touches have, in one form or another, showed up on production cars, but not always for long enough to become part of Pontiac's styling continuity.

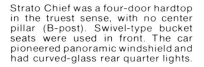

Streaks on the hood, sweeping up from the air intake and ending in functional NACA (National Advisory Committee on Aeronautics) ducts in the cowl structure that admitted ventilation air into the interior. Its fiberglass-reinforced plastic body was finished in metallic red. The passenger compartment was enclosed by a transparent plexiglass canopy. Hinged at the center, each part opened gullwing-fashion, counterbalanced by a spring arrangement similar to that used with alligator-hood hinge mechanisms. Doors could then be opened from the inside. There were no exterior door handles.

Built on a one-hundred-inch wheelbase, the Bonneville Special was 158.3 inches long and 48.5 inches high. It was powered by a special version of the straight-eight engine equipped with four two-barrel carburetors. Its HydraMatic transmission selector was mounted on the console in imitation of a genuine stickshift sports car.

The Strato Chief appeared in 1955. It was a two-door six-seater coupe with a greenhouse-type passenger compartment. All roof support posts were extremely thin airfoil-section pillars, and almost the entire surface above the beltline was glass. It had no Silver Streak and no Indian head, and was not easily identifiable as a Pontiac project.

This shows that the Pontiac studio under Raoul J. Pepin, as well as the Advanced Design Group working directly under Harley Earl, was groping for new identification marks for Pontiac. In fact the Strato Chief was too *outré* to seriously offer any suggestions. It had a grille that closely resembled the production-model Chevrolet of the same year. Protruding headlamps had fairings made to simulate fanjet air intakes, and the front bumper had a lowered center section, bending up on both sides of the grille. The front fenders were hollowed out aft of the wheels—a gimmick borrowed from a Bertone-bodied Abarth designed by Franco Scaglione in 1951. The Strato Chief stood only fifty-three inches high and, to permit easier access to the passenger compartment, hinged panels in the roof were raised automatically when the doors were opened.

The Safari name was first used for a Pontiac station wagon in January 1955. It was built as a special show car to participate as an exhibit in the 1955 General Motors Motorama. It was fifty-nine inches high, and was claimed to be the designers' interpretation of a dream car for the family. The Safari was a two-door hardtop station wagon, and Critchfield revealed "it was scheduled to go into production soon." In the spring of 1955 it became part of the regular production lineup as a model in the Star Chief series.

Pontiac had been building station wagons since 1937 but had never been an important factor in the wagon market. It was not for lack of trying, for by 1953 Pontiac offered no less than twelve different wagons, from all-metal utility versions to business-type sedan deliveries and wood-paneled luxury models. The Safari represented an attempt to reach a new type of station wagon buyer, whose needs were not satisfied by any wagon then in production. Today, we would call it a sports-wagon concept. The idea was borrowed from the 1954 Chevrolet Nomad show car, which was based on the Corvette chassis and body. The design was credited to Carl Renner of the Advanced Styling Studio.

Among its most notable styling features was the grooved roof—which stemmed from the realization that when cars get that low, a lot of pedestrians will be looking down at the roof—and a new dimension in styling was opened. The sharply raked tailgate also helped set the Safari sports-wagon apart from Pontiac's conventional wagons. The Safari remains unique among Pontiac's dream cars in having spawned a whole generation of production cars. More about them later.

No doubt the best known of all Pontiac dream cars, the 1956 Club de Mer, never produced a spinoff in actual production. The Club de Mer, promptly dubbed 'Mal de Mer' by some unenthusiastic rival, had other merits, however. It was far more than a styling exercise, for it proposed major engineering innovations, such as De Dion rear suspension and a transaxle, providing a clue to the origins of some features used in the 1961 Tempest chassis.

A De Dion axle is a type of semi-independent suspension, with a drop-center beam axle connecting the two driving wheels aft of the open, double-jointed drive shafts, and separate from the final drive unit, which is attached to the chassis frame and carried as unsprung weight. A transaxle is a combination of the final drive unit with the transmission, located between the driving wheels. It separates the transmission from the engine, moving a significant weight mass towards the rear, and thereby evening out the weight distribution.

The Club de Mer power plant was a special version of Pontiac's new V-8, which had been introduced the year before. It was equipped with twin four-barrel carburetors, and Pontiac claimed a maximum power output of 300 hp for it.

Built on a 104-inch wheelbase, the Club de Mer was 180.06 inches long overall. Height to the top of the windshield was 38.4 inches. There was no windshield in the usual sense, but twin bubble-type glass covers, one in front of each seat. Nor was there a grille. The front air intake was an open crescent below a clamshell-type nosepiece that carried the concealed headlight units. Two dual Silver Streaks, for good measure, ran from the nosepiece to air scoops on the cowl,

Club de Mer body design features included simulated gas-turbine waste gate in doors, single central tailfin, and bubble-type windshields. Air intake included a set of concealed headlights.

which served as inlets for ventilation air. Sweeping up from the rear deck was a single central tailfin intended to serve as an aerodynamic stabilizer. Wheel covers had a turbojet look to them with protruding hubs.

The Club de Mer was gleaming Cerulean blue, made of anodized brushed aluminum panels. A terrific attention-getter, but no more. Its styling theme was judged too radical, and none of its design elements found their way into a production-model Pontiac. Its engineering features may have played a part in certain technical solutions used in later years, but nothing from the Club de Mer chassis was adopted in its original form. The Club de Mer also ended the series of Pontiac dream cars.

CHAPTER 5

The Way to Power

FOR PONTIAC, THE WAY to power was spelled V-8. It went into production in September 1954, for the 1955 models, replacing both sixes and in-line eights. The change could not have been more total. In its initial form, the Pontiac V-8 was an oversquare design of 287-cubic-inch displacement, giving a seven-percent increase over the 268 cubic inches of the old in-line eight. It was notable for having a short, stiff crankshaft and lightweight overhead-valve gear with ball-stud-mounted rocker arms.

A two-barrel carburetor was used with both standard and high-compression cylinder heads. The base engine had a compression ratio of 7.4:1 and delivered 173 SAE gross hp at 4400 rpm, with a maximum torque of 256 pounds-feet at 2400 rpm. The high-compression (8.0:1) engine delivered 180 SAE gross hp at 4600 rpm, with a maximum torque of 264 pounds-feet at 2400 rpm. This version was used in all cars equipped with HydraMatic transmission. Later in the first model year, Pontiac released a still more powerful version outfitted with a four-barrel carburetor, raising the power output to 200 SAE gross hp. Along with the carburetor came a heavy-duty air cleaner and a low-restriction intake manifold.

The engine had been a long time a-borning. Why did it take so long? Nobody at Pontiac had much sense of urgency. It was always intended for some undefined future model, never for next year. And then George Delaney, the chief engineer, was a conservative man. Ed Windeler, who worked on the V-8 engine as a design engineer, elaborated this point: "The whole outfit was conservative, not just the chief engineer. It was the organization. The chief engineer ranked second to the general manager. And Klingler had been there a long time. He probably inherited the conservatism, and he never got around to changing it. He kept it going as long as he was there."

Windeler was an engineer whose outlook and temperament were well suited for the division's top technical post, but whose promotions came to him late in life. He was to progress to the level of assistant chief engineer at an age when younger men were being picked as chief engineers. Ed Windeler came from Brooklyn, New York, where he was born in 1913 and he held an engineering degree from Virginia Polytechnic Institute. Coming to Pontiac in 1936, Windeler first worked as a driver at the proving grounds. He stayed at the proving grounds until 1943, having risen to the rank of project engineer. He worked at Fisher Body for two years along the way, and returned to Pontiac in 1945 as a supervisor of technical data. In 1948 he was named senior project engineer, and in 1954 experimental engineer.

Pontiac had begun a research program on V-8 engines as early as 1946, because it became evident that future styling requirements would demand shorter and lighter installation packages than were

V-8 engine began life with Strato Streak label, turned into Tempest, and later became Trophy. Basic design remained unaltered for 21 years.

possible with the division's existing power units. Unlike his predecessor, Anibal, George Delaney was not a specialist on engines. It was Mark Frank, staff engineer on engines, who really fathered the V-8. He had two assistants working closely with him, Clayton B. Leach and Edmund L. Windeler. Others who played key roles were George Roberts as project engineer for the V-8, and Malcolm R. McKellar as the designer who did most of the detail work on the drawing board.

'Mac' McKellar remembers: "Our first effort was an L-head V-8 because an L-head was thought to be less expensive to manufacture than an overhead-valve V-8. There are more parts in overhead-valve engines. Different casting processes are involved. An L-head is very simple to make—there's almost nothing to it. It was really the breathing characteristics that made us change to overhead valves—even though there were some novel approaches taken to try to make the L-head V-8 breathe better at high compression ratios. The overhead-valve gave better breathing characteristics, plus it had the advantage of a more compact combustion chamber, which gave higher thermal efficiency because there wasn't so much area to cause heat losses."

Delaney recalled the growth of the six and the straight-eight over the years, and instructed the design engineers to make room for displacement increases without major tooling changes and without compromising basic engineering functions. He also demanded overall simplicity of design for control of manufacturing cost, ease of quality control, and to facilitate service and repair.

James C. Kaufeld, who worked on straight-eight engine development at Pontiac right through to the end in 1954, pointed out: "Basically the V-8 is more expensive to produce than a straight-eight. There are more parts involved, and the castings—by the standards of those days—were considered to be more complicated. As it turned out, with the innovations we were able to effect, it wound up being very simple to cast.

"We did spend a lot of time developing much simpler coring of the casting in both the cylinder block and cylinder heads to make them easier to manufacture, also to make more precise castings because of the reduction in the number of cores that was used compared with Oldsmobile and Cadillac V-8 engines. That was one thing that demanded a lot of time and attention."

The overall layout for the Pontiac V-8 was similar to that of the Cadillac, Oldsmobile and Buick engines which had gone into production earlier. This common approach comprised a monobloc structure with ninety degrees between the banks, and a single chain-driven central camshaft operating a pushrod and rocker-arm type of valve gear to each bank. Cylinder heads were of the crossflow type, with the intake manifold between the banks and exhausts on both outside flanks.

By 1948 Clayton Leach had invented a new type of overhead-valve gear that eliminated the rocker arm shaft. Leach had come to Pontiac in 1937 as an engineering graduate of GM Institute and worked in various assignments before he was given the title of assistant chassis engineer. He was also fascinated with the machinery of engines, and experimented with his ideas for a simplified valve train in his basement workshop at home, in his spare time. His invention not only worked, it worked very well.

Each rocker arm was individually mounted on a ball pivot mounted on a stud extending from the cylinder head. He took it to the engine designers, who saw the beauty of the thing and wanted to try it out in a real engine. It was tested and tested again in various experimental engines over the years, and always proved quite successful. In the first production V-8, the ball contacted the inner surface of the rocker arm. Rocker arm flanges were raised in a bridge-like structure to enable the arm to carry the valve-gear load. Positive lubrication was provided by letting pressurized oil from the gallery in the cylinder head mount through a drilled hole in the stud and enter the ball.

The studs were pressed into the cylinder head, with the ball bolted on. Stamped steel rocker arms were cyanide-hardened before being mounted on the ball pivots. By alignment with the pushrod, the rocker arm was able to square itself on the end of the valve stem. Thus, misalignment of the rocker arm relative to pushrod and valve stem was eliminated automatically. The design also minimized any tendency towards valve cocking. All moving parts were arranged in a single plane for geometrically correct valve movement, without lateral bending loads on the rocker arm.

Several Pontiac engineers have stressed the thoroughness of Pontiac's testing, not only in developing the V-8 and its valve gear, but in every area of engineering. And this is a direct reflection on the philosophy of the chief engineer. Ed Windeler recalls one of them: "Delaney was a very patient man, and he was very careful. I can remember one time we had flywheels coming loose on the six-cylinder engine. Every month we would get some of those out in the field. They would rattle around and make a lot of noise. We searched for about three months for a solution to that thing. And we'd test some and say okay, we've got it! Delaney would say, 'Well, are you sure?' We'd test some more, and some more, and some more, and say 'yeah we've got it.' And eventually we had him convinced that the fix was real, and then he would go into production. But he never would go into production with anything that he wasn't absolutely sure was proper. He never panicked. Never panicked. No matter what the problem was, he took it very seriously. He wouldn't ever let us try some fly-by-night thing."

With the arrival of Buick's V-8 in 1953, Pontiac and Chevrolet were the only GM divisions that still did not have V-8 power. A Chevrolet V-8 engine was being designed by an engineering team led by Ed Cole, future president of the corporation (who was killed when, flying his own plane, he crashed in poor-visibility weather in 1976, shortly after his retirement). Cole wanted the Pontiac rocker-arm for his engine, and Pontiac generously acceded to his request. Normally within GM, whenever a car division originates a new technical improvement, it has the novelty as its own exclusive advance for one year before the sister divisions are allowed to share it.

Throughout the design and development stage, Delaney chaired monthly meetings on the V-8 program. "These meetings were instituted," recalled Russell Gee, assistant chief engineer of Pontiac, "because we were going into something completely new and were in the early learning stage of modern engine technology."

At the start of 1951, the engine was scheduled for 1953 model-year production, but it was postponed partly because of design and production problems, and partly for economic reasons. So it had to wait till 1955. Explains Mac McKellar: "We could have brought it out sooner, but the feeling was that we had to produce an engine that was economical to build and try to be competitive on price in our segment of the market as it was viewed at that time."

In common with Ed Cole, who had designed Cadillac's first overhead-valve high-compression V–8 before going to Chevrolet, Gil Burrell, who created the Rocket V–8 at Oldsmobile, and Joe Turlay, mastermind behind Buick's V–8, Mark Frank also chose a wide bore and a short stroke. The 3.75-inch bore assured ample valve head size, and the short 3.25-inch stroke reduced friction losses. Piston speed was kept low, which meant low stress levels and reduced cylinder wear. And the big bore gave the engineers greater freedom to choose combustion chamber configuration. Increased piston area translated into higher specific power output.

In contrast with the deep-block in-line sixes and eights, the V-8 block was split at the crankshaft centerline. The Pontiac engineers felt that the block's basic rigidity was so great that the opportunity to save weight by pulling the block structure out of the lower crankcase area could be taken without risk, and should be taken. It was taken.

As was common throughout the industry, the engine block was designed with ample room for enlarging its displacement, so as to be

Cross section of the 1955-model V-8 engine shows valve gear with stamped rocker arms and ball-stud mounting instead of rocker shafts. It was Pontiac's first overhead-valve engine, and its first to use hydraulic valve lifters.

ready with a more powerful unit whenever required, without having to make big changes in the tooling.

The size of the water jackets shows that a lot of room existed for expansion in terms of bore size. Cylinder heads were bolted down by four half-inch bolts per cylinder, tied directly into the walls of the block. These bolts were well separated from the cylinder bores to assure freedom from distortion due to tightening. Tin-plated slipper-type aluminum-alloy pistons with steel struts were chosen. Three piston rings were fitted and the top compression ring had a chrome-plated surface. The second ring was lubrite-coated. Finally, the oil control ring was a four-element, chrome-plated steel rail. The crankshaft was made of forged steel and ran in five main bearings with a diameter of 2.5 inches. With a crankpin diameter of 2.25 inches and a stroke of 3.25 inches, overlap was a healthy 0.76 inches. The five main bearings were supported by rigid caps, doweled in position, and attached to ribbed bulkheads in the cylinder block. A sprocket on the front of the crankshaft drove the timing chain for the single, central camshaft, which was supported by five bearings.

Hydraulic valve lifters were chosen to give quiet running under all conditions without compromising valve timing for peak power output or strong mid-range torque. Hollow pushrods, cyanide-hardened, were lubricated at both ends by oil from the hydraulic valve lifters. Spark plugs were inserted on the outside of the vee, above the exhaust manifolds, which were purposely kept low to facilitate spark plug replacement. Keeping the exhaust system at low height also minimized the risk of heating up the underhood air being drawn into the air cleaner.

One unusual design element in the Pontiac V-8 was the arrangement of the right bank of cylinders slightly forward of the left bank. This was done to permit installation of the distributor on the right side of the engine, so that the force of the camshaft drive gear on the distributor gear was directed upward. That assured better lubrication and simplified the distributor mounting.

The ignition distributor was positioned at the back of the engine, standing straight up like a tower in the valley, behind the air cleaner. This was good for protection from water intrusion, but not the best for easy adjustment or repair.

The fuel pump was driven by a rocker arm operated by a special cam at the nose of the camshaft. Also, the fuel pump was installed on the left side, as far as possible away from the heat of the exhaust pipe and in the middle of the wash of cooling air from the fan, so as to minimize the risk of vapor lock. The generator was positioned on top of the engine, between the cylinder heads, where it was well separated from exhaust heat and easily accessible.

The space available between the banks made intake manifold design easy, even with an exhaust gas crossover. The distance from the centerline of the crankshaft to the top surface of the intake manifold was only 13.9 inches. In combination with a carburetor height of five inches, this gave an installation package lower than what was absolutely necessary in the vehicles planned for the mid-fifties.

Pontiac engineers designed a special reverse-flow gusher cooling system for the V-8 engine. The system directed the water from the radiator to the cylinder heads, forcing the coolest water straight to the hottest parts of the engine.

The engine was thoroughly tested by the time it went into production. "Over three million miles have been run on experimental installations to test its new features," Critchfield claimed, "The engine was subjected to continuous grueling road tests at the GM proving grounds in Michigan and Arizona. In addition, destructive laboratory tests, precise dynamometer checks at Pontiac and GM Research Staff have aided Pontiac's engineers in perfecting our new Strato-Streak engine."

The switch to V-8 engine production was accomplished without disruption, but not without drama. James C. Kaufeld tells how it came about: "Our basic engine manufacturing plant here was the so-called Plant Nine, and of course, that's where we wanted to build the V-8. But it was also the place where the straight-eight was built. So they tore down the complete straight-eight facility and moved that whole engine line to a building at the north end of our complex here that had been used for making defense materiel. This caused us a materials-flow headache, for there was no conveyor system to or from that area. The engines had to be carried by truck to the assembly line, while we were tooling up for the V-8 in Plant Nine."

At first, Critchfield and Delaney had the intention of continuing production of the six-cylinder engine, letting the V-8 replace only the straight-eight. But as they interpreted the engineering trends, there was no future for the six in big, heavy cars like the Pontiac, and they coolly decided to make the V-8 standard across the board for 1955. "Tests indicated it will be the most economical V-8 engine on the market," said Critchfield when announcing the 1955 models on October 26, 1954.

The V-8 engine was not all that was new for 1955. Pontiac also had a completely new body. In fact, the 1955 had more changes than any single new model since the first Pontiac was introduced in 1926. No

Star Chief hardtop coupe from 1955 was built on a 124-inch wheelbase and was 210 inches long. Panoramic windshield and wraparound rear window added to impression of open-air motoring.

less than 109 new features were incorporated in the 1955 models.

Appearance changes, were, of course, the most visible and the most dramatic. A-, B- and C-bodies were totally renewed that year. Harley Earl had directed the styling of a new three-box shape, with a low, wide, flat hood in front and a matching deck lid in the rear. All GM cars that year had the same look. Paul Gillan, who had replaced Pepin as chief designer of the Pontiac studio at the beginning of 1953, needed all his imagination to make his car look different from an Olds or a Buick whose B-body it now shared. The 1955 Pontiac was 2.75 inches lower in overall height than the 1954 model, and the hood line was lowered 3.75 inches, so that the fenders came right up to hood level.

Then there was the panoramic windshield, which was bent around at the corners to meet a near-vertical A-post. Pontiac claimed it had twenty-six percent more glass area, and gave fourteen percent better forward visibility. The backlite also wrapped around, to meet very thin C-posts. On four-door sedans, rear quarter windows were brought back. Considerable progress had been made in space utilization. Although the overall width had been reduced by 1.25 inches, the front seat was actually three inches wider than on the 1954 model.

The front bumpers had bright, massive dual impact bars and a connecting arched grille bar. There was no real grille, but an aircraft-inspired air intake. The nonfunctional fanjet-type crescents above the headlamps, as used on the Strato-Streak and Strato-Star show cars, were also part of the production-model design. Dual Silver Streaks, adopted from the Bonneville Special show car, started at the grille arch and ran to the cowl, and were repeated on the deck lid. Rear fenders had longer fins, rising from the tail end of the skirts. A cowl-wide air intake was designed to ensure a continuous flow of fresh air from a high level for interior ventilation.

Two-tone paint jobs also helped stress the newness of the 1955 Pontiac. The roof color extended down towards the middle of the front doors, sweeping back across the fenders and rear deck. The lower parts, hood, cowl and front fenders were painted in the main body color.

Four-door Chieftain sedan from 1955 shows roof color extended downwards from beltline aft of the windshield and air-intake-type grille integral with the front bumper structure.

General Motors did not undertake the same kind of market research as Ford, for instance, with private previews of possible future designs and first-hand interviews with thousands of people. But GM still tested public reaction, and questionnaires on its dream cars were part of that effort. Exaggerating its importance, General Sales Manager H. E. Crawford told the press at the launching of the 1955 models: "These cars were in effect designed by the American public. In our careful efforts to give the public what it wants in a car, we studied their reactions to our famous 'dream cars' which were shown at the GM Motoramas and other auto shows during the past several years. The American public helped us determine what features they wanted most. We made practical adaptations of the most widely accepted designs in the Bonneville Special, the Strato-Streak and the Parisienne and put them into the 1955 Pontiacs."

On the engineering front, a modified frame with straight side members and cross-bracing was adapted to carry the V-8 engine and match up with new front and rear suspension systems. At the front end was a new design with vertical kingpins, coil springs and A-arms, combined with a new recirculating-ball steering gear and parallelogram linkage. At the rear end, leaf springs were longer, with fewer leaves, and mounted 3.25 inches farther apart for a wider, more stable base. Front brake drums grew to twelve-inch diameter, but the rear ones remained at eleven inches. Tubeless tires were made standard on all models, and all had twelve-volt electrical systems.

The lineup consisted of two series, Star Chief on a 124-inch wheelbase and Chieftain on a 122-inch wheelbase. Both series had two-door and four-door sedans and station wagons. A convertible was included in the Star Chief series, and the Catalina coupe was a Chieftain while the Custom Catalina coupe was a Star Chief.

The four-barrel version of the high-compression engine was offered at the very low premium price of thirty dollars. *Motor Trend* made a comparison test between two similar cars, one with the 180 hp engine and the other powered by the optional 200 hp mill. The latter shaved over a second off the zero-to-sixty mph acceleration time, doing it in 12.7 seconds, compared with 13.8 for the former. Both were equipped with Dual-Range HydraMatic, and note should be taken of the hot-rod shifting methods of the test drivers, not likely to be duplicated in everyday traffic.

Remember, this was a transmission with four-speed mechanical gearing. Moving the selector lever to D1 assured that first gear would be engaged for jerking the car off the line. At about 44 mph, when the upshift to second was made automatically, the driver would move the selector to Lo position, thereby preventing the transmission from going into third. He would hold second until the engine ran out of revs, and then move back to D1 for third gear. Leaving the lever in the normal D position meant starting in second, with earlier upshifts depending on throttle position, and engaging direct drive for best fuel economy.

On the road, the 1955 Chieftain was generally a comfortable car. On smooth roads, it could cruise straight and level, but uneven road surfaces would show up an exaggerated softness in the springs, paired with insufficient shock damping. The car nosedived on hard braking and squatted on full-bore acceleration. Body roll on curves was pronounced, but no worse than the typical GM car of its time. Steering was slow-geared but the response tended to be a little bit quicker than most drivers would expect from a car in its weight class having a definite forward bias in weight distribution. A determined driver could make good time even on winding roads, but his passengers would be thrown about by the heaving and rolling of the softly sprung body. The much advertised ride comfort was conditional upon finding good roads or, failing that, keeping the speed down.

The power was great for pulling out of turns, but the brakes were not meant for repeatedly bringing the car down to decent cornering speed right after speeding along a short straight on a switchback road. They would fade badly, though giving the driver plenty of warning through a rise in pedal effort and a strong odor of overheated brake linings.

In the market place, the 1955 Pontiac was quite a hit. And Pontiac needed an upswing after its poor sales in 1954. The publicity around the V-8 and the new-found performance boosted Pontiac's popularity so strongly that 530,007 cars were sold in 1955. But the total market had expanded from 5.5 to 7.2 million, so its market share did not increase as much as expected, although it had been knocked out of its static pattern, with a nice jump to 7.4 percent. Yet Buick and Oldsmobile, both with higher prices, outsold Pontiac.

It is not known what contribution was made by the trite, prosaic slogan for the year: 'Dollar for dollar, you can't beat a Pontiac,' but the low prices must have had a great deal to do with the success in the showroom. Prices started at $1,917.45 for the Chieftain two-door sedan and ran to $2,462 for the Star Chief convertible. Pontiac had made its five-millionth car in June 1954 and reached the six-million mark in August 1956.

Despite its best calculations, Pontiac seems to have failed to make much of a profit through its policy of setting prices low to build up trading volume. A man who was on the inside of the organization revealed: "Pontiac apparently had a very poor return on investment during those years, and it led to a change of management at the division." That did not happen till 1956–57, however, and the Pontiac product actually had bigger changes from 1954 to 1955 than in any model year up to 1959.

The morale was high at Pontiac when the 1955 sales results were announced, and Pontiac's executives went into 1956 full of optimism. They expected a repeat and received a shock when sales began to stumble. The general sales manager, Howard E. Crawford, went into the field to find out why. What he reported was that despite all the product development undertaken for 1956, the Pontiac image had not changed. The public still regarded the Pontiac as an 'old man's car.'

The design and engineering news for 1956 came out of Critchfield's reasoning that if the changes for 1955 had been great, more of the same would make 1956 even greater. That meant, first and foremost, more power. The V-8 engine had been enlarged and was now rated at 205 hp for the Chieftain series and at 227 hp for the Star Chief. All

Mockup built in the Pontiac styling studio in the fall of 1954 represents a proposal for facelifting the 1956 models. Front end shows Packard, Buick and Chrysler influence.

1956 models had a V-8 engine bored out to give 317-cubic-inch displacement.

With the stronger torque of the new engine, it became more important to assure drivetrain smoothness, and HydraMatic was ready with a new transmission. Design work on the 1956 HydraMatic had been going on since 1952. The fundamental principles remained the same. The new transmission continued to use a fluid coupling with three planetary gear sets providing four even-stepped forward gears and reverse. The Dual-Range principle that had found such favor on the 1952 models was also retained, along with the split-torque hookup which improved the transmission's good economy characteristics.

But for 1956 the methods of obtaining the gear ratios had been completely revised. Almost every part in the transmission was redesigned. The key element in the 1956 HydraMatic was the substitution of a small hydraulic coupling for the multi-plate clutch, combined with a one-way sprag clutch in place of the reaction band.

Paul Gillan's treatment of the 1956 Star Chief deluxe convertible shows dream-car influence in several areas (side chrome, rear fenders, grille and bumpers). An enlarged V-8 engine provided more power and speed.

Production-model Star Chief for 1956 showed evolutionary design changes only, presenting an image of assured continuity. This was not what the new general manager wanted at all!

In the old system a gear set was locked in direct drive by using a multi-plate clutch to activate the brake band. In the new system, the same action was obtained by filling the fluid coupling whose rotation picked up a sprag clutch and locked the gear set in direct drive. This was a much smoother action than the mechanical-friction method used before.

"Pontiac is proud to be the first to introduce a big and vital General Motors first—Pontiac's new Strato-Flight HydraMatic transmission," Robert M. Critchfield told the press. "In over two million test miles this revolutionary transmission system demonstrated smooth, effortless shifting. This new Strato-Flight HydraMatic transmission combined with Pontiac's more powerful V-8 engine will give Pontiac owners a new experience in positive efficient performance. There is no interruption in transmitting power to the rear wheels and gear action is barely noticeable. This positive action insures unhampered acceleration for quick, safe maneuvering."

Styling changes were intended to add emphasis to the car's power and speed capacity. Bodies were facelifted, and longer rear fenders added an extra 2.4 inches to the overall length. A lineup of fifteen different body styles included six Catalina hardtops, three two-doors and three four-doors. This marked the introduction of the four-door hardtop at Pontiac, one year after this innovation had gone into production at Buick.

The adaptation of this body to Pontiac was engineered by the same man who had been responsible for the division's first two-door hardtop, Herman Kaiser. He was born in Dayton, Ohio, in 1905 and attended the University of Michigan, University of Detroit, American School, and La Salle University. Arriving at Pontiac in 1928, he went to work as a chassis designer. He worked on Pontiac frames, suspension, steering and brakes until car production was halted in 1942. The following year he was transferred to Fisher Body Division to serve as a project engineer on the Allison engine. Coming back to Pontiac in 1945, he was named chief body draftsman, and got promoted to body engineer in 1955.

During 1956 Pontiac Motor Division came in for big organizational changes. In May, Critchfield was made head of GM's process development staff—a position he was to hold until his retirement in December 1959. He lived in Birmingham, Michigan, until he died on December 4, 1973.

Looking back over the Critchfield years at Pontiac, there is no doubt that the division made progress while he was running it. But Ed Windeler is one who takes a cynical view of Critchfield's contribution to Pontiac's welfare: "Critchfield was one of the most successful general managers we ever had, but very little of it was his own doing. The time was right for people to buy cars, and the V-8 engine, which he didn't have anything to do with, was there to spur them on."

About half a year after Critchfield's successor took office, George Delaney applied for early retirement, at the age of sixty-one. He was not ready for some of the changes that he could see coming, and opted to leave Pontiac. He started his own engineering business and operated for a number of years as director of the Pioneer Engineering and Manufacturing Company. Assessments of Delaney and his work at Pontiac are not unanimous. A former Pontiac engineer admitted he was disappointed in the division's product evolution under Delaney: "We had our new V-8, but when we were at the proving grounds, the Cadillacs would go whipping by us." In complete fairness, the same man rushed to state: "Delaney was a good man to work for. He was smart and he was objective."

Others have blamed Delaney for not being a man of innovation. But Ed Windeler disagrees. "You could say he was not innovative but, for instance, he was the guy who got us the automatic transmission. Anibal would not allow automatics in our cars, but just as soon as Delaney became chief engineer, we began to install HydraMatics." And Russell Gee adds: "Delaney was a good organizer and a highly respected engineer. He didn't receive any credit for the high-performance equipment that came along later, but actually, he was involved. Some of the groundwork was laid by Delaney."

Inevitably his dress and manner marked him, to some subordinates, as a man of the past: "There goes George Delaney," they would say, "with his high white collar and his high black shoes." We can only conclude that he was a man who held to his own standards and did not slavishly follow fashion. Perhaps the truest appreciation of George Delaney was his obituary in *Automotive Engineering* (formerly the *SAE Journal*): "He was a man's man and an engineer's engineer. True wisdom, integrity and clear thinking were his hallmarks.

"George Delaney was not a verbose man. He had a great capacity for listening and sorting out the facts . . . arriving at judicious solutions

The 1956 Custom Catalina hardtop in the Star Chief series carried a price tag of $2,401 (or $172 more than the Chieftain 870 Catalina with the same body but lower trim and finish level).

to sticky problems. When he spoke, men listened because he had something meaningful and significant to say. His good friends will not only remember George for his intelligence, but for his joy of living as well. He enjoyed good fellowship, a good cigar, a funny story, and an occasional game of golf."

After leaving Pontiac, Delaney remained active in the Society of Automotive Engineers, serving as its treasurer for a number of years. He died on July 5, 1974, survived by his wife Barbara.

The year 1956 marks the end of an era in the annals of Pontiac Motor Division. On the horizon, a new dawn was breaking. The story of how the day went is told in the next chapter.

CHAPTER 6

Bunkie

DESPITE THE NOTABLE advances made in product engineering at Pontiac, the division's sales took a beating in 1956. With deliveries of 358,668 cars, Pontiac had slid more than 158,000 cars behind Buick and over 75,000 cars behind Oldsmobile. General Motors actually strengthened its position in a market that failed to sustain the boom of the previous year, but it was mainly due to Chevrolet's success. Pontiac's market share dropped to 6.02 percent.

On the first day of June 1956, Critchfield's successor moved into the general manager's office at Pontiac. His name was Semon Emil ('Bunkie') Knudsen, and he was to reshape Pontiac's fortunes in spectacular fashion. But he got there too late to have much influence on the 1957 models and Pontiac's sales that year.

How Pontiac sales went in 1957 must be seen in relation to the sales performance of its sister divisions and the market as a whole to be fully appreciated. By the end of 1956 General Motors had achieved its primary objective of taking half the market, with a penetration of 50.7 percent. Chevrolet alone accounted for more than half of GM sales. The market remained constant from 1956 to 1957, with total car registrations each year of just under six million units. But something was changing in the buyer preferences that again upset the established order. General Motors was running into quality problems. Factories were working above capacity, and cars were coming off the assembly

lines with parts missing, faulty parts, and all sorts of shoddy workmanship. A lot of people switched from GM cars to Ford and Chrysler.

In 1957 General Motors' market share dropped below forty-five percent. Only Chevrolet and Cadillac managed to more or less hold their own, while Pontiac, Oldsmobile and Buick were badly hurt. Buick was ousted from its third place, ending up fourth, ahead of Oldsmobile (fifth) and Pontiac (sixth). Pontiac dealers had sold only 319,719 cars, which earned the division no more than a 5.34 percent share of the market.

What was happening? Chrysler's steal of three extra percentage points was a passing phenomenon. So was Ford's slim rise of about two points. But the really significant factor in the 1957 market was that imported cars more than doubled their penetration, from 1.65 to 3.45 percent of the market. The actual numbers were still small, but there was a message in the public's sudden acceptance of foreign cars that was to elude Pontiac's leaders as well as the top men at General Motors, Ford and Chrysler for years. It was a protest, and that much was recognized. But what it was a protest against was not clearly understood in Detroit at the time.

Those who understood best were no doubt Ed Cole at Chevrolet and Bunkie Knudsen at Pontiac. Both instituted compact car programs

Bunkie got to the top at Pontiac by his own drive, not because his dad had once been president of General Motors. He turned Pontiac around and made it number three in the industry.

A research technician who became an Oldsmobile engineer—that was Pete Estes before he came to Pontiac. Later, he ran Chevrolet, and is now president of General Motors.

Cleaner lines appeared on this 1957
Pontiac prototype. Paul Gillan was
chief designer of the Pontiac studio
from 1953 to 1957 and directed the
shaping of the Chrysler-inspired tailfins and Mercury-inspired grilles.

to have the products ready when the demand reached the kind of
volume that would make it worthwhile for the GM car divisions to
mass-produce them. But that was not Bunkie Knudsen's top priority.
He had carefully analyzed the situation and lucidly concluded that
Pontiac's key problem was image. Changing Pontiac's image became
his first order of the day, and he set about doing it with dauntless
determination.

The image of a car is a composite of symbols, and Bunkie realized
he first had to destroy the old symbols before he could imprint a new
image on the Pontiac car. He began by killing the Silver Streak, the
wide belt of chrome trim running down the middle of the car from
stem to stern, that had adorned every Pontiac since 1935. It was
identified with the stolid and sedate Pontiacs of yesteryear and had no
place on the kind of Pontiacs Bunkie wanted to build. Later on, he
decided that the Indian-head hood ornament was a symbol of the
same past, and it was phased out in 1957.

Next, Bunkie looked askance at the engineering staff Delaney had
assembled, and moved to put new and younger talent in key positions.

He wanted new men in production, in sales, everywhere. It was to be
a complete rejuvenation of Pontiac's decision-making personnel, and
he did it by raiding the other GM divisions for men that had been
moving up fast and were ready to take command.

Bunkie himself was that kind of a man. He was born in Buffalo,
New York, on October 2, 1912, the son of William S. Knudsen, who
was then running the John R. Keim Mills that were later taken over
by Ford. The senior Knudsen had a lot to do with Ford's spreading out
into overseas assembly, but left in 1922 to go to work at Chevrolet. He
ran Pontiac as general manager for a period in 1932, and then served
as executive vice president of General Motors from 1934 to 1937 and
president from 1937 to 1940.

Bunkie got his nickname as a small boy, on a hunting trip with
his father, sharing the same bunk, which led his dad to call him his
bunkmate or bunkie.

Bunkie graduated from the Massachusetts Institute of Technology
with an engineering degree in 1936 and worked for two other
companies before he joined General Motors in 1939 as a tool engineer
at Pontiac. During his first spell with Pontiac, Bunkie worked as an
inspector, and then became involved in processing parts and setting
up assembly lines. During the war he was assistant chief inspector of
gun operations. About 1947 Bunkie became general master mechanic
at Pontiac.

He spent ten years at Pontiac before he was made director of
GM's Process Development section in Detroit in 1950. He stayed there
for three years. Then Bunkie went to Allison in Indianapolis in 1953 as
manufacturing manager. Later that year, Edward B. Newill at Allison
promoted him to manager of aircraft engine operations until he was
transferred to the Detroit Diesel Engine Division as general manager
in 1955.

At forty-four, Knudsen was GM's youngest car-division manager
in 1956. Jack Wolfram at Oldsmobile was fifty-seven years of age;
Edward T. Ragsdale at Buick, then fifty-nine, was even older. At the
end of that year Don Ahrens at Cadillac retired at sixty-five and was
replaced by forty-nine-year-old James M. Roche (a future GM
chairman). Even Ed Cole at Chevrolet was forty-seven, three years
older than Bunkie.

Bunkie had always been closer to Pontiac than to the other car
divisions, since that's where he got his start in business, and he did
not come to Pontiac without a plan. He knew he had to change the
product, and that had to begin instantly, with things that could be
changed without delay. Lead time for a completely new car was about

five years at the time, and planning truly new models needed both corporate approval and interdivisional cooperation.

A Pontiac staff engineer at the time, Bob Knickerbocker, reflects on Bunkie: "Knudsen had the general background and, most of all, the executive ability to utilize the resources—both human and material—and it's my opinion that Bunkie did not make numerous technical decisions. But he made damn sure that he had good people to make those decisions and to provide the data for him. And he had the confidence to approve the changes which he felt were right. I see Knudsen as being the prime executive, and I see the engineering innovations coming from Pete Estes."

Estes—he was the man Bunkie had stolen away from Oldsmobile to replace Delaney as chief engineer of Pontiac. And the two formed a brilliant team. Today 'Pete' is president of General Motors. His real name is Elliott M. Estes, and he was born at Mendon, Michigan, on January 7, 1916. He grew up in Constantine, Michigan, and was an auto enthusiast as far back as he can remember. As a boy of about twelve he made his first car by rigging up a one-cylinder engine on a coaster wagon.

Estes joined GM in 1934 as an eighteen-year-old cooperative student at the GM Institute, where the tool crib supervisor gave him his nickname Pete. His first job was to make sand-casting molds and guide pins for making Chevrolet parts. After graduation from the GM Institute, he went to the University of Cincinnati for two years and left in 1940 with a degree in mechanical engineering. Then, back to GM.

Once again assigned to the Research Laboratories, Estes worked under the legendary Charles F. Kettering, the inventive genius who had perfected the electric self-starter back in 1911, invented the modern ignition distributor in 1925 and developed the two-stroke diesel from 1927 to 1935. At first, Estes worked on diesel engine injectors. Then he was involved with a two-stroke radial aircraft engine that Kettering wanted to test in a car.

In 1946 Estes was transferred to Oldsmobile after Kettering, Darl F. Caris and the other combustion experts had completed their studies of the high-compression V-8. At Oldsmobile he worked in various engineering assignments, and was promoted to assistant chief engineer (under Harold W. Metzel) in 1954.

To take over from Crawford in sales, Bunkie hired Frank V. Bridge, a veteran and an enthusiast, away from Buick, where he had set sales records year after year with monotonous regularity. He hailed from Plankington, South Dakota, where he was born in 1904. He got into

the automobile business by becoming a retail salesman for a Buick dealer at Rapid City, South Dakota, in 1926.

"Frank Bridge inherited a disgruntled group of dealers who were accusing the division that Pontiac had never been able to put two good years back to back," recounted Jim Wangers, who was then account executive with Pontiac's advertising agency, MacManus, John and Adams. "Frank was an old-line fire-breathing, heavy-drinking, dealer-loving salesman, and he didn't get involved with product or marketing—he just went out by himself to rebuild that dealer body. And he did a magnificent job."

The image that Bunkie sought for Pontiac can be summed up in one word: performance. In this he had the full support of GM President Harlow Curtice, a former Buick man of flamboyant taste, who was eager to see Pontiac transform itself from Caspar Milquetoast to Tarzan. Both Bunkie Knudsen and Pete Estes were smart enough to know that looking like Tarzan was not enough; the car also had to pack Tarzan's muscle. At the same time, they were keenly aware of the importance of styling.

And they understood the need for fast action. Steve Malone, who later became chief engineer of Pontiac, recalls: "I guess you've heard the story about Bunkie going down in the prototype garage with a screwdriver and taking off the chrome moldings for the Silver Streak. Well, it's not true. He just gave the order to kill the Silver Streak and it was done, practically overnight. It had a dramatic effect on people at Pontiac, for Knudsen took away twenty-one years of tradition with that order."

Russell F. Gee, once assistant chief engineer for power train and chassis, corroborates Malone's account, adding that you could not simply remove the Silver Streak, for there were recesses in the sheet metal, and it needed a new mold. These molds were physically hand-formed, and the body engineers had to make a new one without streaks. "It was a dramatic change in a near-frozen design," says Russ Gee. "The decision came very, very late in the development of the vehicle. It was no big engineering change, but it had a dramatic effect. It was part of a new attitude." Pontiac did search for some other type of decoration that could serve to identify its cars. "Yes," relates Russ Gee, "of course, we put a spear on the side of the car, to serve as a streak or a mark, wide out at the back, and put the stars in there."

Bunkie also realized that Pontiac could not acquire a performance image by merely making the performance available and leaving it

The 1957 Super Chief Safari was built on a 122-inch wheelbase and had an overall length of 208.8 inches, with body sides featuring two-tone paint with Starlite coloring. The Super Chief was a new series instigated to fill the gap between the Chieftain and Star Chief.

for the customers to discover it. He knew it had to be demonstrated. For that purpose, Bunkie decided to go racing.

Pontiac had been getting its feet wet in stock car racing before his arrival, for Critchfield had sponsored the preparation of two Pontiacs by Indy veteran mechanic Louie Meyer for the Daytona Speed Week in February 1956. "It was one of our first organized factory efforts," ex-Pontiac engineer Bill Collins recollects, "and the cars ran pretty well, but didn't finish." Ed Windeler adds: "Though we were not successful then, that enabled us to get the data we needed. It laid the groundwork."

It is not our purpose in this book to chronicle Pontiac's involvement in all the forms of racing its cars were used in, from stock car events to drag strip competitions or the use of Pontiac engines installed in special vehicles for straight-line speed runs. A supplement listing Pontiac's NASCAR victories is included in the appendices. In addition, we do want to mention some highlights of this period, so as to show what Pontiac's racing flavor was built on, because it came to have a bearing on the character of the cars and the way people regarded the Pontiac car.

The 1956 Pontiac was a pretty hot car as it came off the assembly line, and with new factory-installed power options such as a 285-hp version with high compression ratio and a four-barrel carburetor, it became a veritable projectile.

Colorful Ab Jenkins, then a youthful seventy-three, drove a stock 1956 two-door sedan Pontiac with this engine on the Bonneville Salt Flats on June 26, 1956, posting a new twenty-four-hour speed record with an average of 118.337 mph for twenty-four hours. A retired contractor and former mayor of Salt Lake City, David Abbott Jenkins had won fame in the 1930's for his single-handed stints of long distance speed-record driving at the wheel of his aircraft-engine-powered Mormon Meteor, running in a great circle on the dry salt bed known as Bonneville. With the same Pontiac, Jenkins ran one hundred miles at an average speed of 126.02 mph, breaking a number of international class records.

With Bunkie at the helm, Pontiac began to demonstrate its performance on a multi-front basis. Jim Wangers gives credit to Knudsen for disregarding the 'gentlemen's agreement' inspired by Ford and subscribed to by all Automobile Manufacturers' Association members to keep their companies out of organized racing. "Knudsen broke right out of it, using Catalinas as race cars," said Wangers. His dedication was boundless. "Bunkie didn't want to get left behind. He even spent his own money in certain areas," Wangers continued. "He subsidized Smokey Yunick out of his own pocket."

Henry 'Smokey' Yunick had seen service as a bomber pilot in World War II and back in civilian life opened a garage in Daytona Beach; later he became a franchised GMC dealer. On the back of his overalls were embroidered his name and the slogan 'The best damn garage in town.' He was an expert mechanic with a talent for performance tuning and began to prepare racing cars for local events, gradually branching out into open-wheel single-seaters for Indianapolis and other USAC (United States Auto Club) events. By 1958 he was an essential link in Pontiac's stock car racing activities. Another Pontiac team had been running since 1957, with cars prepared by Ray Nichols of Highland, Indiana, one of the pioneers of midwestern stock car racing.

Impressive as it was that Bunkie could get Pontiac cars to the race tracks so quickly, the attempt would have failed if the cars had lacked the speed and stamina to win. For this, great credit is due to the engineering staff, which had been working on high-performance equipment as part of the development program for the V-8 engine, dating back to about 1953. Ed Windeler confirms: "Much of the high-performance hardware that went into production under Knudsen had actually been developed prior to his arrival, but he was the catalyst that moved the whole thing ahead." Bunkie's theory was that the huge audience of racing fans would soon spread the word if Pontiac could beat the established leaders and that winning races would translate directly into growing showroom traffic and sales.

The racing program was not just a promotion to create a performance image for the Pontiac car, but also a valuable tool for improving the product. New performance equipment issued from the experimental department at an astonishing rate, and Estes saw to it that valid innovations from racing were transferred to the production engines. "When Estes came in," recalls Russell F. Gee, "he almost overnight increased all our compression ratios and put more performance in, using faster-opening throttles and other tricks."

Russ Gee was running a fleet of test cars at the Arizona proving grounds when Estes left Oldsmobile and came to Pontiac. Naturally, he did not expect to see his chief engineer until he made a routine visit back to Pontiac. Great was his surprise when he came face to face with his new chief only a day or two after his appointment, right there on the test tracks outside of Phoenix. Estes and Windeler had flown down, just the two of them. "The idea was for Estes to get a precise idea of the Pontiac product, to see for himself how it handled and what it performed like," Russ Gee explains.

Right after that, the basic Pontiac car began to evolve in a performance-oriented direction, and new marketing strategies were tested.

For the 1957 models, displacement of the V-8 engine was increased to 347 cubic inches by lengthening the stroke. Several interesting modifications were made in the induction system on this power unit. Intake valves were vented to the atmosphere to prevent the formation of a vacuum in the port areas, which could cause oil to be sucked into the combustion chambers through the clearance between the valve stem and guide. The intake manifold for engines outfitted with two-barrel carburetors included two 0.47-inch holes in the carburetor flange to prevent icing in the throats. These holes were eliminated for 1958, when gasoline containing de-icer additives (alcohol) eliminated the need for carburetor heating. A high-performance

Styling for the 1957 Custom Catalina sedan (not a hardtop) followed the same Star Flight theme that marked the silhouette of the whole line that year. New paints were lucite lacquer with metallic pigment in 19 two-tone combinations.

camshaft was offered in 1957, combined with special hydraulic valve lifters.

In addition to the standard two-barrel and optional four-barrel carburetors, the 1957 Pontiac was available with a setup advertised as Tri-Power. It consisted of a special manifold with three two-barrel carburetors mounted in line. With cylinder heads giving a 10.25:1 compression ratio, Tri-Power engines delivered from 294 to 321 SAE gross hp. One Tri-Power Pontiac, privately sponsored by none other than S. E. Knudsen, ran in the 1957 Daytona Speed Week and set a new lap record at an average speed of 131.747 mph.

The 1957-model Chieftain with four-barrel carburetor, three-speed synchromesh transmission and a 3.42:1 axle ratio had a top speed of about 115 mph. How much power this car actually had was shown in a

First production model to carry the Bonneville label was this 1957 convertible with fuel injection and 389-cubic-inch V-8 engine. Side decor shows traces of Oldsmobile styling.

story told by Tom McCahill, reporting his experiences in *Mechanix Illustrated*: ". . . one night I discovered just what a sleeper this car is. I was stopped for a traffic light on U.S. 1 when a messy-faced young kid sidled up to the Pontiac driving one of those weird vehicles known to the Pilgrim fathers as a 'rod.' Mind you, until now I had paid the Pontiac less attention than P. Samuel Whiteman might give to a ferryboat fiddle player. The light snapped green and the kid in the rod shoved his foot through to the front axle.

"The Pontiac momentarily stood still while the wheels spun and then—zoonk! I whipped past and away from the kid so fast that if his radiator cap hadn't been screwed on tight, my vacuum would have sucked the water out of his cooling system. I had driven the Pontiac around Daytona for many miles and never had a suspicion that this

car, with an engine that idled as smooth as hair tonic over a bald head and was as well behaved in traffic as a New York City police horse, contained under its hood one of the most hairy-chested, fire-eating, explosive screamers I'd ever driven. Here was a bomb with finesse."

That sort of talk helped transform Pontiac's wan, ashen image into flaming Technicolor. "Bunkie was the architect of the whole scheme," according to Jim Wangers. But all agree that he could not have done it without Pete Estes.

Bob Knickerbocker confides: "Pete motivated the people who worked at Pontiac and knew how to lead them toward successful efforts. He set an example that was damn hard to follow. The Knudsen/Estes team was the perfect combination."

Estes had long been interested in fuel injection, and had some experience with fuel-injected engines from his days at the GM Research Laboratories. Fuel injection had proved its value as a means of raising power output in aircraft engines for a number of years, and had recently come into use in racing cars. The first in America was seen on a four-cylinder Offenhauser in 1949. This was the Hilborn-Travers fuel injection system (later known as Stuart Hilborn). It was a primitive design, with a single throttle body at each port, feeding fuel continuously under pressure to spray nozzles inside the port areas. Hilborn's injection system adequately met full-throttle conditions with alcohol fuel, but lacked the overriding controls necessary to give the required flexibility for passenger cars. The power gains, however, were so spectacular that they prompted the American auto industry to take a new look at fuel injection.

At General Motors it was Rochester Products Division that led the development of fuel injection, in collaboration with Chevrolet, Pontiac and Oldsmobile, using the Hilborn-Travers principles as a starting point. Oldsmobile rejected fuel injection at an early date in the program, but Pontiac and Chevrolet went ahead. Though it was developed with racing as the primary goal, the system proved acceptable for street use in skilled hands, and Knudsen decided to use it on a new model with its own name plate and distinctive styling. It was given the name Bonneville.

The Bonneville was Pontiac's first attempt to create a car for a small but glamorous market segment, a direct competitor for the letter-series Chrysler 300's and the DeSoto Golden Adventurer. Bunkie Knudsen got authorization to release the Bonneville strictly as a limited-production model. It was made in only one body style: convertible. Standard equipment included Strato-Flight HydraMatic, power steering and power brakes. The chassis was practically unchanged from the standard Super Chief, but the V-8 engine was bored out to 370-cubic-inch displacement.

The fuel injection setup on the Pontiac V-8 was neater than the hurriedly-put-together Chevrolet Corvette package. Pontiac had taken the time to make a one-piece manifold heater with air pipes built up from steel stampings, while the Chevy had a cast-iron manifold heater and separate pressed-steel pipes. Also, Pontiac made its air pipes longer, probably to get better ram effect at high rpm from the pressure waves that increase in strength with the length of the pipe. Chevrolet had short, direct air pipes. While Chevrolet engines carried the fuel-flow meter high up and opposite the air-flow meter, the Pontiac engine had the fuel meter cradled low down under the plenum chamber.

At first, it was accepted that Pontiac would not publish a horsepower figure for the fuel-injected 1957 Bonneville. It implied some of the mystique of the Rolls-Royce, though Pontiac unabashedly stated that the engine delivered in excess of 300 hp so that nobody would mistake their reticence for false modesty. The implication was that there was so much power it really could not be talked about openly. In actual fact, the 347-cubic-inch V-8 with the triple two-barrel setup was more potent.

The fuel-injected 1957 Bonneville took eighteen seconds to cover the quarter-mile, while the Tri-Power Pontiac could do it in 16.8 seconds. In road trim, the 1957 Bonneville had a top speed in excess of 130 mph, however, and would go from standstill to 60 mph in 8.1 seconds. A tuned stock model was timed at 144 mph on the Bonneville Salt Flats. Eventually, Pontiac released the power and torque figures for the fuel-injected engine, claiming 310 SAE gross hp at 4800 rpm and 400 pounds-feet of torque at 3400 rpm.

Though the fuel injection on the Bonneville did not give the expected performance, it most certainly provided a bonus in terms of fuel economy. In the 1957 Mobilgas Economy Run, the Bonneville recorded a precious 20.4 mpg over the road, and a *Motor Trend* test crew completed a one-hundred-mile run at an average speed of 50 mph with a fuel mileage of 16.8 mpg under California traffic conditions.

Like the other models in the 1957 Pontiac lineup, the Bonneville chassis was not developed for sharp curves or S-bends. It was at its best going down the straight, or taking wide turns under full throttle. The brakes were sorely inadequate; the steering was devoid of road feel and very light at parking speeds, with a disconcerting tendency to get even lighter at cruising speed, with a parallel loss of precision. The springs were soft, with long wheel travel and insufficient shock damping, so that Bonneville riders had no better chance to avoid seasickness than passengers in the Chieftain, Super Chief, Star Chief or Catalina, which made up the model range that year. The Bonneville weighed 4,285 pounds and cost about $4,400. Only 630 fuel-injected 1957-model Bonnevilles were built.

For 1958 Bonneville became a series, including a two-door hardtop (sport coupe) and convertible. They were sold with carburetted engines as standard, and fuel injection became an option, priced at about $650. Base prices for the Bonneville dropped to $3,179 for the hardtop and $3,277 for the convertible. For 1958, fuel injection was available on all cars equipped with an automatic transmission, but the high price kept it from becoming a popular option. Only 400 fuel-injected Bonnevilles were produced in 1958, and Pontiac dropped fuel injection entirely for 1959.

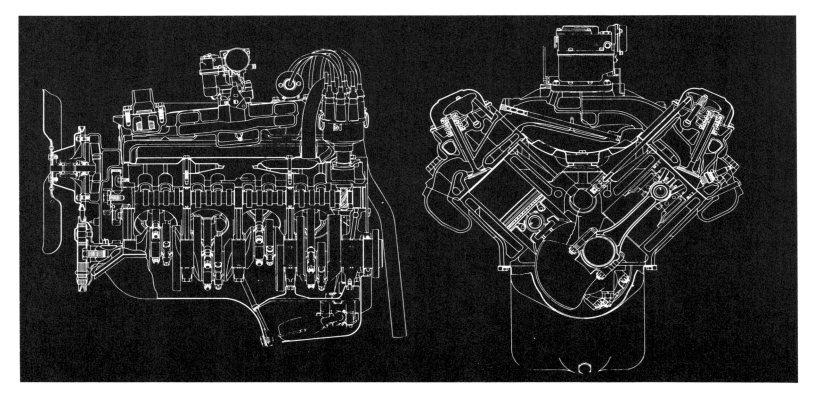

Drawings for the 1958 V-8 engine show the distributor and oil pump drive, rugged five-bearing crankshaft, and induction and exhaust systems.

The Bonneville's bored-out 370-cubic-inch cylinder block was made standard across the board for 1958, and the Strato-Streak label that had been used on all Pontiac V-8's since 1955 was replaced by the name Tempest.

With the use of wider-diameter pistons on the V-8's, Pontiac went to press-fitted wrist pins. New camshaft timing was adopted, with different camshafts for engines destined for automatic and synchromesh transmission cars. Exhaust port size was increased by seventeen percent and a new exhaust manifold had enlarged runners with lower gas flow restriction. New rocker covers had a wider flange

and gasket for better protection against oil leakage. The second compression ring was redesigned for better wear characteristics, and new oil-control rings were fitted for better oil control under high-vacuum conditions.

Pontiac's 1958 engines used intake manifolds with an exhaust crossover to provide heat for vaporizing the fuel. The exhaust passage ran transversely across the manifold, directly below the risers and headers. At the end of the exhaust passage was a connection for the automatic choke heat tube, to open the choke valve as soon as possible during warmup.

The hottest engine options were the 395 A-PK and 395 A-PM (the number 395 representing pounds-feet of torque). The PK version used a single four-barrel carburetor, high-compression cylinder heads and a low-resistance manifold. The PM version had a special flat manifold with short and wide passages, three two-barrel carburetors and high-compression heads. These engines were combined with the Super-HydraMatic transmission, or a three-speed version of a beefed-up Warner gearbox developed for police car duty.

The Safe-T-Track limited-slip differential was made optional for the first time on 1958-model Pontiacs. Pushbuttons were used for heater and air-conditioning controls—an idea that was soon abandoned. A new transistor radio that could be removed and used as a portable was optional.

The Chieftain line for 1958 was expanded from six to seven models by adding a convertible. The two-door and four-door sedans and the two-door and four-door hardtops were carried over. The two-door station wagon was discontinued, so that both the six-passenger and nine-passenger versions had four doors, plus the usual tailgate. The Super Chief line was cut back from four models in 1957 to three in 1958. The station wagon was dropped, leaving a four-door sedan and a hardtop, plus a two-door hardtop. The Star Chief line was trimmed from six to four models. The continuing ones were the four-door sedan and hardtop, two-door hardtop and four-door station wagon. The casualties were the two-door station wagon and convertible.

The total number of models was kept at sixteen despite the addition of a new series. From a manufacturing viewpoint, the lineup was simplified, as the number of different bodies had been reduced from seven to six (by elimination of the two-door station wagon).

In an attempt at restyling without making any large sheet metal changes, Pontiac had fully redecorated front and rear ends and revised side ornamentation. In front view, a wide, low grille was set below a straight chrome bar that curved down towards the ends and lined up with the part of the bumper that curved around the fender. The bumper had two pods, one in each corner of the grille, containing parking lamps that featured a four-pointed compass 'star.' The grille itself had a discreet pattern of small squares. The side view was dominated by a spear—a more elaborate version of the spear used on the 1957 models—pointed at the front and having wings at the rear end. It stretched from the front fender to the taillights.

This restyling for the 1958 Pontiacs was not successful, in the sense that the cars lacked Pontiac identification. The Silver Streak was gone, and no new theme had emerged to replace it. The spear on the sides could be confused with Oldsmobile's rocket theme (not only as used on the 1955–58 Oldsmobiles, but as a representation of what people would expect a new Oldsmobile to look like). Moreover, Buick's sweepspear that year had a huge appendage on the rear

Super Chief Catalina sedan for 1958 was a true four-door hardtop, with no B-post above the beltline. It had a price tag of $2,696 ($153 more than the similarly named but differently bodied car of the year before).

fender, with the inevitable result that the public found the 1958 Pontiac hard to tell apart from Oldsmobiles and Buicks.

But the 1958 Pontiacs bristled with engineering innovations, some of them of far-reaching importance. The chassis had a new simple cruciform frame with five cross-members. The propeller shaft ran through the center of the frame which was expanded to form a narrow tunnel. A totally new coil-spring rear suspension system replaced the leaf springs of the Hotchkiss drive setup used through 1957.

Pontiac's literature described its 1958-model suspension system as Quadra-Poise. The front and rear control arms were set at angles to minimize brake dive, acceleration squat, and sidesway. And as a truly radical innovation, Ever-Level air suspension for all four wheels was made available on the 1958 Pontiacs. Air bellows were installed in the place of the coil springs, with pressure controlled by a central 'brain' to keep the car at constant level. The pressure was provided by an engine-driven pump.

One man who was intimately involved with the 1958 chassis was Stephen P. Malone, who had joined Pontiac in October 1956 as chassis development engineer. Asked if he remembered what his first project was, he burst out: "Yeah, very well! We were working on the 1958 car with the new cruciform frame. It was a new frame concept—different from all previous Pontiac frames. It had some good stiffness characteristics. We wanted a frame with better all-around stiffness, and the cruciform *seemed* to have it. We were also working on a new rear

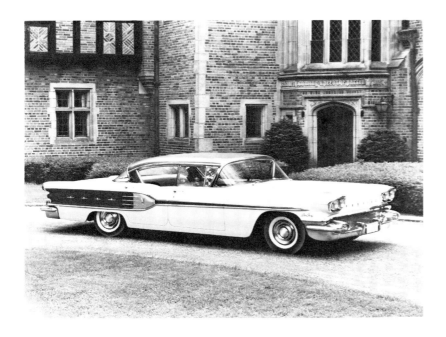

Four-door Catalina hardtop in 1958 Star Chief series was mainly Paul Gillan's design. It remains typical of GM, but lacks Pontiac identification. Grille hints at Buick; sides at Oldsmobile.

A list price of $2,750 was considered high for the 1958 Pontiac Chieftain convertible and it was not a success in the market, despite such options as fuel injection, air ride suspension and HydraMatic transmission.

suspension, that was a forerunner of the four-link design we went to later.

"We wanted to get away from the leaf-spring inter-leaf friction so we went to coil springs—and of course with coil spring suspension we needed some links to stabilize the springs under the car. The 1958 design used two rear links to the axle and a big triangular member that served as an upper control arm. We called it a dishpan because it was all one stamping. The old frame would not accept that suspension, so that's why we developed the cruciform frame."

The air springs were not a Pontiac development, but came from Cadillac. And Cadillac got into it as a knee-jerk reaction to a new French car with oleo-pneumatic suspension controlled by a central

hydraulic system, the Citroën DS-19, which made its debut at the Paris Auto Show in October 1955. Technically, the DS-19 was a bombshell. Seismic shock was felt intensely in Detroit, and especially at General Motors, which was in the process of building its new technical center at Warren, Michigan, and promoting its research and engineering activity under the slogan 'The Spirit of the Inquiring Mind.' Suddenly came a car from Paris which showed that French minds had not only inquired, but found answers that were at once radical, logical and complete.

More or less as a direct consequence, Cadillac wanted something like that, immediately if not sooner. An air spring system was under investigation at the GM Engineering Staff where Von D. Polhemus and Lawrence J. Kehoe, Jr., had not only proved the unsuitability of a scaled-down version of the bus system (used by GMC since 1939) for passenger car installation but also proposed a basic air spring system designed specifically for cars. However, cost considerations dictated an adaptation of the bus system. Development work was accelerated to get it ready for production, and Cadillac engineers Fred H. Cowin and Lester Milliken were given the task of adapting the system for installation on the 1957 Eldorado Brougham. The spring units consisted of an air dome with a diaphragm. The piston was connected to the lower control arm, and acted against the diaphragm. For 1958 the system was adapted to other Cadillacs, and was made available to the other GM car divisions. Pontiac offered it in 1958 for one model-year only.

The adaptation was made by an engineer named Hulki Aldikacti, who then worked in the chassis group but was later transferred to the engine drawing office. Also in the chassis group at the time was Steve Malone, whose background was with Delco. Born in Dayton, Ohio, in 1916, he graduated from Ohio State University in 1940 with a degree in electrical engineering. His first job was with Delco Products in Dayton, where he stayed until called up for military service. He was a pilot in the U.S. Army Air Corps from 1942 to 1945. Then he went back to Delco and worked as a staff engineer until 1956. Malone wanted to get out of accessories and into car engineering and applied to Pontiac, where he was hired in 1956 as a chassis development engineer.

We asked Steve Malone what was wrong with the air springs, and he answered: "First of all we had to have a complete system that would not leak—we needed valves that would not use up more air than could be delivered by the compressor. Valve design had to have high durability. We had to have an air source—and that was an engine-driven compressor which presented some problems we had not been exposed to before, such as high temperatures in hot climates. The lube oil in that compressor could get so hot it turned to carbon and clogged up the valves. The valves were plagued with a multitude of problems.

"Perhaps not enough test and development time. We were committed to 1958. I don't really know why we were committed to 1958 but we had that as our target date and we were developing our cars to that date. Air springs were an option. The idea was very good. It gave the same ride height regardless of load and a variable-rate spring characteristic that would carry the car empty or with a full load with the same spring travel and the same kind of ride motion. It had a lot of merit to it, yeah. We worked like the dickens to develop that air spring but when we went into production there were several things we didn't know about it. We were sort of safety oriented. At the same time we were customer-satisfaction oriented. In the northern parts of the country we did not have too much of a problem with clogged valves, but we were plagued with leaks. The system had over thirty leak points."

At the end of the 1958 model year, Bunkie had been at Pontiac for two years and two months. In that time he had pushed through to the mass-production stage a line of brand-new cars that gave Pontiac not only a new image but a new identity. They were the first of the 'wide-track' Pontiacs, and their story is told in the next chapter.

CHAPTER 7

Wide-Track Drive

At THE DAYTONA Speed Week in February 1958, Pontiac took the six first positions in its category (Class Seven), with speeds over the flying mile of up to 137.693 mph as an average of two runs in opposite directions.

Bunkie had reached his goal of making Pontiac a leader in performance. But the sales picture that year was glum. Pontiac car registrations during the 1958 calendar year reached only 229,740 units, which dropped its market share to 4.94 percent—the division's lowest since 1934. Were these the kind of results the corporation could expect from Bunkie in the years ahead? Of course not. The reasons for the setback were largely external and beyond Pontiac's—and the industry's —control.

During 1958 the American economy suffered a recession, and the demand for new cars shriveled up. The low-priced cars, favorites of the fleet buyers, such as the car rental companies, government agencies, utilities, etc., came through with minor wounds, but the next-step-up cars, of which Pontiac was the most important as well as the most typical, were badly scarred.

Only 4.65 million new cars were sold in the United States during 1958, and 377,819 of them were imported. The imports' share of the market had skyrocketed to over eight percent, and was to pass the magic ten-percent number the following year. The success of small

European cars—Volkswagen, Renault and Fiat, to name a few of the leading makes—in America was to cause an abrupt interruption in the hitherto complacent product planning at General Motors, and Pontiac was already well into the development phase of a compact car of radical concept.

Its production date was still a long way away and, for the moment, Knudsen had put all of Pontiac's eggs in a different basket. A basket labeled wide-track. "Wide-Track Pontiac" was the message that billboards, magazine and newspaper advertisements, radio and television spots blasted at the American public when the 1959 models went on sale in October 1958. It was no empty slogan, for the new Pontiac had a five-inch-wider track, compared with the 1958 chassis. And the new models had an exciting all-new look, lower and wider, with simple but very bold lines. Joe Schemansky, who had replaced Paul Gillan as chief designer of the Pontiac studio in December 1957, had succeeded, in the remarkably short time available, in capturing a dynamic spirit that reflected the relentless drive of Pontiac's management, as well as originating design elements that were to become important Pontiac identification marks in the future.

Strangely enough, the first 1959-model prototypes did not have the widened stance, Jim Wangers tells the story of how it came about: "Knudsen went into the styling studio and looked at one of the styling

Catalina Vista was perhaps the most spectacular model in the 1959 Pontiac line-up. It had a split grille, V-formation tailfins, and panoramic windshield in common with the other series, but was unique as a four-door hardtop with a wraparound backlight.

Bonneville for 1958 shared the principal features of the Catalina with more emphasis on customized trim and decor items. It was also seven inches longer overall, at 220.7 inches.

bucks. Of course, the car did look kind of funny, with that pretty wide body on it and a relatively narrow track. His comment was 'it looks like a football player wearing ballet slippers.' Thus a styling necessity turned out to bring a significant consumer benefit."

Jack Humbert corroborates: "The 1959 body, as it came out of the styling studio, it was lower and it was wider than any previous Pontiac, and in order to make it look right, we moved the track out to sixty-four inches. So it was a combination of having to put the wheels farther apart in order to give the car the right proportions."

In exact numbers, the front track went from 58.74 to 63.72 inches and the rear track from 59.43 to sixty-four inches. "It was the widest track in the industry—by a little bit," was how Steve Malone put it. "The advertising theme was Wide-Track—and you know how that

picked up momentum." According to Jim Wangers, the term Wide-Track was coined by Milt Colson, then a copywriter at MacManus, John and Adams, and now a vice president of the agency.

Phrases such as Wide-Track Ride and Wide-Track Drive were used in early ad proposals. "Knudsen thought it was corny," Jim Wangers laughs. "The agency came back with what they called Sports Stance, supported by a whole series of athletic analogies. But it was Wide-Track that won the day."

Did it really help get better handling or was that just an advertising claim? "It was a combination of things. The wide track did help. Other factors were the link-type rear suspension and the cruciform frame," Malone explained. The frame was basically the same as on the 1958 models, with some structural reinforcements to carry the larger and heavier body. "By that time we had learned all the tricks of the trade about cruciform frames. So the 1959 model was a *big* car and, why, it was a *good* car," Malone slammed his fist on the desk.

Bunkie had set out in 1956 to remove from the Pontiac car everything that related to the Indian chief. On the 1959 models, all that remained was the high-beam headlight indicator, which had the shape of a red Indian head in profile. The reason it was kept was that Pontiac had to use it somewhere to protect its exclusive rights to its former trademarks. Even the model names were changed for 1959 to downplay the Indian connection. Catalina became a separate series, replacing the Chieftain. Only the Star Chief still carried on the tradition.

The 1959 styling represented a return to simple, clean lines with a fleeter look unburdened by excess chrome. Rooflines were thinner and flatter, with a huge increase in glass area. Several distinct roofs were offered, each having a different glass layout. On all, the panoramic windshield was pulled back at the corners, so that the A-post actually tilted forwards. The car's frontal aspect was dominated by the split grille. "Joe Schemansky originated the split grille," said Jack Humbert, "it was he who did the first sketches of it." And that, more than anything, is a styling feature identified with Pontiac to this day.

Dual headlights were mounted side by side, with part of the headlight casing sculpture carried over into the front fender. The bumper was a plain, straight chrome bar surmounting an air intake, with a secondary bar recessed below it, tied together at the corners. Fender cutouts were elongated, recalling the Strato-Star styling, and the rear fenders had a conical flare that symbolically recalled the spear of the 1957–58 models. The beltline was absolutely horizontal from the decorative moldings on the front fender tips to the start of the rear fender crest, which split into a V-motif line and ended in two fins on a base circle above the taillights.

The 1959 lineup included three station wagons with hardtop styling: one customized Bonneville Safari and two Catalina Safaris at lower prices. All Safaris were built on a 122-inch wheelbase.

"Pontiac has broken all bonds of traditional styling and engineering in 1959 with the most progressive change in our division's fifty-one-year history," claimed Knudsen in announcing the new Pontiac line for 1959.

The engineering improvements were wide-ranging, from electrical equipment to engines, suspension, steering and brakes. Electric windshield wipers replaced the vacuum wipers that had lasted through the 1958 model year. A new speedometer with audio-visual warning for exceeding a preset maximum speed was optional. A new crankshaft with longer throws increased the stroke from 3.56 to 3.75 inches, raising displacement to 389 cubic inches. The block was reinforced by casting extra iron into the bearing bulkhead areas, and by increasing main bearing diameter to a full three inches.

The difference in power output between the lowest and the highest horsepower engine was greater than the maximum output of the side-valve six in its final version. The six had risen to 118 hp at the end. Now the range of output from the basic V-8 spanned 130 hp. At the top end was the triple two-barrel Tempest 420A, rated at 345 hp, at 4800 rpm, putting out 425 pounds-feet of torque at 3200 rpm. At the low end, Pontiac had a 215 hp economy engine, the Tempest 420E, available on all cars equipped with automatic transmission. It had a milder camshaft giving less valve overlap, a two-barrel carburetor and a low 8.6:1 compression ratio to enable it to run on regular gasoline.

Engine design engineer Robert J. Dika, who was a specialist in manifold design and air flow, made sure that all 1959 Pontiac V-8's had intake manifolds with all passages equal in length and similar in shape. His designs also gave adequate provision for mechanical mixing of fuel and air and for preheating of the mixture. It had smooth inner walls and no enlargement of the cross-sectional area, assuring high gas-flow velocities consistent with proper cylinder filling.

The triple two-barrel setup was offered from 1957 through 1966. The system evolved over the years, from a start with three small Rochester instruments in 1957 and 1958 to three giant 2 GC Rochesters at the end. From 1959 through 1965 it used one 2 GC carburetor at each end and a small-throat Rochester in the middle, with the central unit being in full-time operation and the outer ones acting as secondaries.

Catalina Safari for 1959 had a roll-down tailgate window and an optional rear-facing third seat. All Safari wagons that year had four-door bodies, shared the same 122-inch wheelbase and 389 cubic-inch V-8 engine.

Chassis modifications, too, were quite significant. Changes in the front suspension system for 1959 included new lower control arms with rubber bushings, greater tilt-back on the upper control arm pivot axis to increase anti-dive effect, larger-diameter front coil springs with lower ride rates, and recalibrated shock absorber settings to go with the softer springs.

The 1959 Pontiacs had a new Saginaw power steering system with a rotary valve and a fail-safe provision that would enable a driver to continue to steer in case of booster failure. The power steering system needed less initial steering wheel movement to bring the power assist into play, and the transition was smoother than on the 1958 cars.

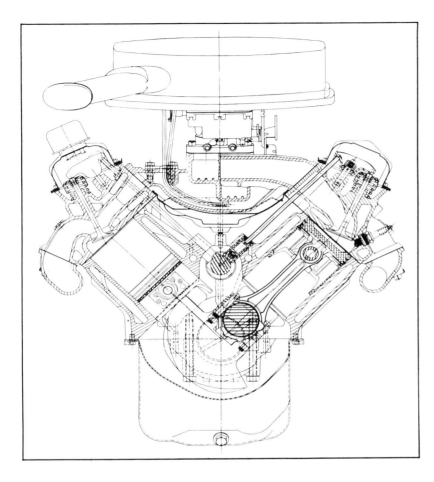

Longest lived and best remembered of all Pontiac V-8's was the 389, standardized for the 1959 models. Combustion chambers are wedge-shaped, and the crankcase is split on the center line.

Front brake drums were thirty-nine percent heavier, to provide a higher-capacity heat sink and reduce the tendency to fade. Brake drum width was increased, and a cooling flange was added around the backing plate. Cooling was improved by additional air space between the drum surface and the wheel rim. On the rear wheels, the drum was widened and moved one inch inboard. Castings were thicker, giving heavier drums. The new brake power booster was smaller and lighter, and featured better interchangeability with the master cylinder used in nonassisted brake systems.

From the customer's point of view, how was the new Pontiac? Jim Whipple reported in *Car Life* (December 1958) on the 1959 Catalina: "Seats are sixty-six inches wide and headroom is good both front and rear. Seating positions remain fairly comfortable because the new floor has been depressed into footwells or pans that drop down below the body sill and frame level to retain the normal relationship of hips, feet and knees.

"The two-door hardtops are the sleekest-looking cars of the whole line, measuring just fifty-four inches from rooftop to pavement. Their front seats are roomy and comfortable as well as being easy for even a six-foot three-incher like myself to slide in and out of. But the back seats of these sport coupes and the convertible are best reserved for dogs and/or agile children, because they are very low, difficult to get in and out of, and are covered by a sweeping sheet of glass that limits headroom but provides unlimited sunlight."

As for its driving qualities, it was an interesting compromise between a stock car racer and a family sedan. "Due to the soft springing, the Pontiac can be made to heel over considerably when slammed into a curve at higher than reasonable speeds," Jim Whipple reported in *Car Life*. "However, shock absorber control is good, and there's no trace of plunging or wallowing. The low center of gravity and wide track gave me a feeling of complete security and control, even at high speed on a winding, crowned dirt road." Summing up, Jim Whipple concluded: "The '59 Pontiac is a big roomy car, with a superb ride, excellent handling, and a soundly engineered chassis, transmission and powerplant. As a solid over-the-road traveler, it's really hard to beat."

Whipple must have come pretty close to a cross-section of public opinion, for Pontiac sold over 382,000 cars in 1959, and its market share was boosted to 6.33 percent. Suddenly Pontiac was ahead of both Oldsmobile and Buick, running fourth behind Chevrolet, Ford and Plymouth, and still in front of George Romney's Rambler, which was beginning to make inroads in the market.

On the racing front, Pontiac's NASCAR effort continued with unabated zeal. Successes were scored from Darlington to Pike's Peak. But NASCAR audiences are concentrated in the Southeast, and Knudsen wanted to reach car enthusiasts all over, particularly on the West Coast, and most of all southern California, which was developing into a trend-setting area in many ways—politics, social attitudes and consumer purchasing. He decided to go into drag-strip racing and got together with Mickey Thompson.

Mickey Thompson was a hot-rodder, then thirty-one years old, from Alhambra, California, who had bought his first jalopy at the age of eleven and spent his time rebuilding it until he was old enough to drive. From building dragsters and tuning engines he soon branched out into manufacturing and selling a line of speed equipment.

Bunkie asked his engineers to develop engines optimized for drag-strip performance, and simultaneously gave Mickey Thompson the same assignment, so he could make comparisons and confront each side with the results obtained by the others. This instilled a competitive spirit at all levels of Pontiac engineering. Mickey Thompson was also given special Pontiac engines and financial aid for his proposed speed-record projects. He built two Pontiac-powered vehicles in 1959, the Attempt and the Challenger.

The Attempt was a narrow-track slingshot dragster with a streamlined cigar-type body. It was unusual in having faired-in rear wheels (though its front wheels stood out in the open). It could be fitted with any one of several interchangeable Pontiac V-8 engines. Thompson built a 303-cubic-inch V-8 engine for Class C, a 412-cubic-inch engine for Class B, and a 435-cubic-inch engine for Class A. All versions had Stuart Hilborn fuel injection, GMC 6-71 blowers and ran on Mobil's nitrated blend of racing fuel.

Regardless of which engine was fitted, the Attempt ran without a gearbox and had a final drive ratio of 2.70:1. Running under USAC (United States Auto Club) observation at March Air Force Base in 1960, it broke several International Class A and B records and set an unlimited record for the standing-start kilometer at 149.23 mph.

The Challenger was an entirely different proposition, intended for nothing less than the world land speed record. Mickey Thompson led the construction project, with Fritz Voigt in charge of the Pontiac engines, George Hill as body designer, Don Borth as body maker and Cecil Shremp as chassis engineer.

In this vehicle, four Pontiac 440-cubic-inch V-8 engines were installed side by side in tandem fashion, the two front engines turned around so as to drive the front wheels while the other two engines drove the rear wheels. A double overdrive system took the power

Mickey Thompson sits at the wheel of the Challenger chassis in 1959. Body parts are visible in the background. Power train layout can be divined from visible elements (see text for details).

flow from each engine and put it through a Cyclone quick-change transfer case, then into a Mickey Thompson overdrive unit, and via short shafts to the wheels.

Four three-speed La Salle gearboxes were hooked up to a common linkage, so that all shifts were made simultaneously by one single gear lever. Similarly, one pedal worked four clutches. There was no suspension system on the Challenger. The axles were rigidly attached

Bunkie grins as he takes the wheel of the seven-millionth Pontiac, a 1960-model Bonneville built in October 1959. It was powered by a 389-cubic-inch V-8 with a four-barrel carburetor.

The 1960 Catalina Vista shows Humbert's restyling touches on what was basically a Schemansky design. His departure from the split grille was only temporary. Catalina's wheelbase remained at 122 inches.

to the chassis. At the wheel of this machine, Mickey Thompson reached 406.6 mph in September 1960 on the Bonneville Salt Flats. But the car suffered a transmission failure and could not make the return leg, so its achievement was not accepted as a new record.

Back at the factory, Pontiac's product planning was once again aimed at new production and sales records. The division built its seven-millionth car in 1959. It was a 1960 Bonneville Vista assembled at Pontiac on October 15, 1959.

A new series designated Ventura was added for the 1960 model year. It was essentially an upgraded Catalina. This increased the number of different Pontiac models to sixteen, in four series: Catalina, Ventura, Star Chief and Bonneville. In appearance, the 1960 models were merely facelifted from the previous year. The most notable difference was a return to an indistinctive one-piece grille, as if nobody at the division had understood the importance of the split grille in connection with the new wide-track theme.

"The split grille, as you know, was dropped in 1960," Jack Humbert explains, "but we recognized it was such a strong mark that we took it again for 1961. And we're still hanging on to it in a sense—using it on some models. It was a unique front." As for his part in it, Humbert explains: "I went into the Pontiac studio in the fall of 1958. The 1959 models were done then. And the 1960 Pontiac was *nearly* finished. The only thing we did was a little cleanup on it."

All Catalina and Ventura bodies, as well as the Bonneville Safari, were built on a 122-inch wheelbase. The Star Chief and other Bonneville models had a 124-inch wheelbase. Counting body modifications, the 1960 Pontiacs had forty-seven new engineering features.

The 389-cubic-inch V-8 continued as the standard power plant in all models, with a multitude of variations in compression ratios, carburetion setups, exhaust systems and camshafts. All incorporated the new Equa-Flow cooling system, which consisted of a new water

The 1960 Pontiac Bonneville in full-scale cutaway shows new cruciform frame, new rear suspension and brake systems. Four-door Vista hardtop had enormous glass area, and a vast trunk.

pump with a divided chamber to give equal coolant distribution to both banks.

A redesigned HydraMatic transmission was smaller and lighter, and permitted a lowering of the floor tunnel. The hump in the front floorboards was one inch lower than before and two inches narrower. The weight of the revised HydraMatic was reduced by eleven pounds to 229 pounds. It was slimmed down by reducing projections in valve-body and shift-control linkage. But the internal parts were unchanged.

The 1960-model chassis had a revised rear suspension system. It included a V-form torque-reaction and locating arm whose pointed end was anchored to a bracket on top of the rear end of the differential housing. The splayed forward ends were anchored to the nearest frame cross-member. All pivot points used large rubber bushings for improved insulation to give a smoother, quieter ride.

Brackets on the underside of the axle housings, as close to the wheel hubs as practical, provided mounting points for the radius arms, which were long and ran straight ahead to the frame cross-member. Vertical coil springs were positioned immediately ahead of the axle,

with their upper abutments inside the frame side-members near the peak of the arch above the axle. Telescopic shock absorbers were mounted outside the frame, slightly splayed (wider apart at the bottom). The torque reaction arm had its rear anchorage point raised one inch, which raised the rear roll center and increased the roll resistance.

Shock absorbers were equipped with nylon-sleeved pistons and used a variable-viscosity fluid for more uniform rebound control at varying temperatures. On cars with synchromesh transmission, a new clutch linkage with improved leverage was fitted. The clutch pedal was brought three quarters of an inch closer to the floor, and so was the brake pedal, to match.

Power steering units were improved for better ease of service. A redesigned upper thrust bearing enabled oil to pass through the bearing case assembly, and reversed fittings in the pump made for easier access to the filter screen and valve assembly. For the first time,

Ventura sport coupe was introduced in 1960 as a mid-range model, priced just above the Catalina. Bonneville convertible was the highest-priced model. It has sculptured side styling extending along both fenders into the door area, presenting a subtle wing appearance.

Magi-Cruise was available as an option. It was not a true constant speed control device, for all it did was to maintain a fixed throttle opening, so that the car slowed down uphill and speeded up downhill —much as with the hand-throttle controls that were common in the 1920's.

For the racing-minded clientele, Pontiac offered the Daytona package in 1960. "That was the first super-duty chassis package made for sale as an option," Jim Wangers stated.

The 1960 stock car racing season was off to a disappointing start, but the Pontiacs soon fulfilled their promise. A 1960 Pontiac prepared by Smokey Yunick led the 1960 Daytona 500 miles race, averaging nearly 160 mph, for practically the whole distance, but lost it all in spinning out, nine laps before the finish.

All NASCAR Pontiacs now had four-speed gearboxes, after the successful running of a factory car equipped with the Warner T-10 transmission in the 1959 Daytona Speed Week events.

Jim Wangers won instant fame as the winner of the NHRA (National Hot Rod Association) championship races at Detroit Dragway on Labor Day in 1960. He was running a Pontiac-powered machine prepared by Ace Wilson's Royal Pontiac dealership in Royal Oak. His car, which looked like a perfectly stock Catalina except for tires and other legal modifications, reached the 100 mph mark inside the quarter-mile and won the title of top stock eliminator.

Engine design engineer Malcolm McKellar had been working for some time on a Super Duty engine for NASCAR racing. With a new crankshaft and a bigger bore, it had 421-cubic-inch displacement and was offered for the 1961 Catalina coupe in 405 hp tune, though super-tuned versions reached 500 hp on the test bench. Pontiac's production engines for 1961 were advertised as Trophy V-8's, since the Tempest name became identified with the division's new compact car (see next chapter).

The 1961 A-body models retained the wide-track idea, but were shorter, lighter and with a new styling theme. Built up on a new perimeter frame, they had modifications in front and rear suspension systems as dictated by the frame. The new A-car was four inches shorter, 2.5 inches narrower, and even lower—up to 0.9 inches. It made great sense. The car became lighter and livelier, handled better, and gasoline mileage improved. But it had its drawbacks in the market place.

Bunkie Knudsen was quoted in *Fortune* (June 1963) as saying: "I pulled back the Pontiac's wheelbase three inches and sweated out 1961 with the same wheelbase as Chevrolet, 119 inches. When you give

Styling mockup for the 1961 Pontiac shows spacecraft inspiration for the side sculpturing, partly derived from the side decor on the 1958 Pontiacs, and partly inspired by Buick and Oldsmobile designs.

6,800 Chevrolet dealers a talking point like that to use against you, believe me, you sweat blood."

Steve Malone explains the redesign: "In 1961 we went to an all-new car that was down-sized from the previous model. That was a corporate decision affecting all divisions. The body was entirely new and we went to a torque-box perimeter frame. Suspension, front and rear, were basically the same as in previous years. It was a narrower car, a little lighter car, with a little better seating comfort."

Pontiac had been working on the new perimeter frame in an experimental way since 1957. Some of the engineers had always been skeptical of the cruciform frame, which had been forced on the division by corporation-wide standardization programs. In a complete reversal, the sister divisions found they were now being led by Pontiac in frame design and development.

Two distinct roof designs were offered for the 1961 Bonneville, a rakish hardtop sports coupe with C-posts that tapered to a very narrow base, the backlight wrapping around to almost meet the side glass; and a more formal coupe called the Vista, where the C-post took the form of a sail panel.

Production-model 1961 Catalina has discreet side sculpturing compared with the prototype. It retains the roof-line eave over the backlight and the same overall proportions.

Star Chief wheelbase was shortened by one inch to 123 inches for the 1961 model and overall length was cut by 3.7 inches to 217 inches. Width was reduced by 2.5 inches and track by 1.5 inches, but wide-track advertising theme was continued.

Though Pontiac sales fell short of Bunkie's targets in 1961, the results were creditable. The division now had a very strong sales team. Frank Bridge had been relieved of a lot of day-to-day chores by the cheerful E. R. 'Pat' Pettengill, who became assistant sales manager of Pontiac in September 1958. He was born in Port Huron, Michigan, in 1905, and joined GM as a cashier in 1925. Together, Bridge and Pettengill managed to move the cars in 1961 as they had done with the thrilling 1959 models. Other key roles in the sales department were played by Ross Thompson in the New York zone office and Tom King in the Chicago zone office.

On the sales front, Pontiac missed the 400,000 deliveries mark by a narrow margin, its dealers having sold 399,646 cars during 1960. The car market had risen from six to 6.5 million units, however, and Pontiac's market share was trimmed to 6.08 percent; the division fell back to fifth place in the sales ranking as the Rambler moved up to fourth spot.

In view of the fact that the car market declined to 5.85 million cars in 1961, Pontiac can be considered to have gone forward, with sales of 372,871 cars. In fact, its market share increased to 6.37 percent, narrowly beating the Rambler. Pontiac captured third place in the sales race in 1961, for the first time in the division's history. And it would not have been possible without a junior line of low-priced compact cars—the Tempest. In fact the arrival of the domestic compacts was the major reason that imported cars saw their penetration cut back to 6.47 percent in 1961. General Motors advanced to take 46.5 percent of the total car market, and Chevrolet strengthened its lead to take twenty-seven percent.

Pontiac was locked into the short wheelbase through the 1962 model year, which was not marked by any important product changes. But the divisional leadership changed hands right after they had gone into production. In November 1961, Estes moved up to the post of general manager at Pontiac. Bunkie had left the office when the corporation tapped him to succeed Ed Cole as general manager of Chevrolet.

The first-generation wide-track Pontiacs, starting with the wonderful 1959 models, had been produced under Knudsen's direction. One could say they were Knudsen cars, but it would probably be truer to say they were Estes cars. Pete Estes and his chief engineer, John Z. DeLorean, were to produce new generations of wide-track Pontiacs for nearly a decade.

But Bunkie was the one who had caused a new awakening at Pontiac, and all was not smooth during his period as general manager. There were some who felt he was shaking things up too much; that he made changes for the sake of change instead of leaving well enough alone. Yet, with the wisdom of hindsight, most of the men who were there now feel that he was right. Steve Malone's description of Bunkie's *modus operandi* sheds some light on how he could get

Jack Humbert created the body shape and styling for the 1961 Bonneville convertible. Semi-recessed grille has waterfall effect, and bumper bars are split to create extra air intake.

such speedy results: "Knudsen, he was the kind of guy who would just get an idea, his own or from some place else, and he would delegate it. He would say 'Hey, why don't we do this!' or 'Let's go and do that!' without getting mixed up in too much of the details himself. He was a good administrator and he was a real car buff. He *knew* cars."

One of the many who held Bunkie in tremendous esteem was Jack Humbert: "Knudsen wanted to build the best Pontiac in the world. He certainly got some good people under him, and they were doing everything they could to be first with the best in engineering, to have the best-engineered car."

CHAPTER 8

The Rope-Shaft Tempest

GENERAL MOTORS' COMPACT CAR program was instituted to offer the American public an alternative to the small imports that were steadily rising in popularity throughout the 1950's. The idea was not to compete head-on with the imports, but to create a new class of domestic vehicles that were cheaper to buy and cheaper to run, while giving almost full-size convenience and practicality in a smaller and lighter package. The concept was far from new. It's just that the big three—GM, Ford and Chrysler—had stayed away from it, while American Motors built its success on the compact Rambler. Before that, there had been the Aero Willys, Henry J (Kaiser) and Hudson Jet. Studebaker's Lark was to follow.

Actually, at one time all of the big three were planning compact cars (though they were not yet called that). It was towards the end of World War II, when the industry leaders imagined they would need new and smaller cars in the postwar market. Chevrolet developed its Cadet prototypes to a high state of readiness before being abandoned in 1947, and Ford's similar project ended up being built in France as the Vedette.

In those days, Pontiac had shown no interest in smaller cars. In response to dealer demand for a smaller car when the Volkswagen was carving out an important market share, Pontiac agreed to import the Vauxhall, made in England by a General Motors subsidiary. It may have helped build traffic in the Pontiac showrooms from 1956 through 1960, but the Vauxhall had a spotty quality record, and both the dealers and the division were glad to get rid of it when Pontiac introduced its own compact car, the Tempest.

Though the Tempest grew out of a corporate project known as the X-100, it was really created in Pontiac's experimental department. Naturally, it had to share certain components with other GM compacts, such as the Fisher Y-body that was also used for the Oldsmobile F-85 and Buick Special. The Y-body originated with the Chevrolet Corvair, which was built on a 108-inch wheelbase and was powered by a rear-mounted air-cooled horizontally-opposed six-cylinder engine. This body was not acceptable to the other divisions, who wanted a longer wheelbase—at least four inches more. This led Fisher to make a longer version of the Y-body for Buick, Oldsmobile and Pontiac. The B-O-P group also shied away from the rear-engine configuration. All three divisions specified a front engine and rear-wheel drive. Oldsmobile and Buick prepared to use conventional rear axles, but not Pontiac.

The man whose inspiration and audacity gave Pontiac this unique compact car was a young engineer from Packard whom Knudsen had

Production-model 1961 Tempest was built on a 112-inch wheelbase and had 15-inch wheels. Standard engine was cast-iron slant-four, with an aluminum V-8 optional.

brought in to serve as director of advanced engineering in 1956. He was named John Z. (for Zachary) DeLorean and he was to leave a trail of engineering innovations on the Pontiac product over a long period.

DeLorean was working on the compact car project almost from his first day at Pontiac. Everything in the technical makeup of the Tempest came about more or less as a direct consequence of his decision to try to make a full six-seater within the dimensional constraints of the Y-body. Providing rear seats and foot space for the front-center passenger were the main problems. They could only be solved by making a flat floor, without the usual hump (transmission tunnel).

Raising the floor level would make for a flat bottom, but unfortunately that would not permit a seat-height and knee-angle relationship that would be acceptable to people of normal build. Raising the seats was impossible, as the need for headroom would then push the roofline up—and no such major changes could be made in

the body shell. Clearly, the propeller shaft had to be routed below the floor—which was already as low as ground clearance considerations would allow. Consequently, that eliminated the use of a conventional rear axle, which bounces on bumps and steals useful space not only directly above the axle but all along the propeller shaft, whose rear end has to move up and down with spring deflections in the rear axle suspension.

The final drive unit had to be divorced from the axle shafts and mounted in the body shell, so that the propeller shaft maintained a constant position relative to the floor pan. In other words, independent rear suspension was required, a feature usually associated with high-priced European sports and luxury cars. So far, so good. But a straight propeller shaft from the transmission output shaft to the

Initial clay model for the Tempest came pretty close to final design. Front end shows strong family relationship with the Catalina, but the side treatment comes closer to Buick lines.

final drive input shaft would not go below floor level. It would intrude into the passenger area, necessitating a floor tunnel, smaller than on the Olds F-85 and Buick Special, but still a hump that would threaten the practicality of the seating plan.

Two things were done to do away with the need for such a tunnel. First, the transmission was removed from its usual location, adjacent to the engine flywheel, and moved back to the final drive unit, forming what is now called a transaxle. That opened up more room on the front seat floorboards without causing any space problems in the rear floor section. Secondly, the engine was tilted up at the nose, so that the drive line ran at an angle pointing down towards the rear end. The transaxle shaft was given a similar tilt in the opposite direction, pointing down towards the front. Now all that was left to do was to hook up some sort of propeller shaft that could run with such angularity in its rotational plane.

An Austin of England patent from 1946 showed how it could be done by a multipiece shaft incorporating three universal joints. But DeLorean had another idea—a flexible propeller shaft that would twist as it turned, without needing any universal joints at all.

William T. Collins worked as a transmission development engineer on the Tempest, and recalls: "When I came back to Pontiac, in 1958, they had been working for a short time on that drive shaft. The drive shaft was, at that time, not enclosed in a torque tube. While the special relationship of the transaxle and the engine were important to keep the bending moments constant in the shaft, which can really be thought of as a torsion bar, they were mounted individually, and it was a real bear to get them lined up." An idea of the angles involved is given by the fact that the shaft's lowest points were three inches below its ends.

Collins continues: "Before the Tempest became the Tempest, we had three or four cars that were built up with that drive line. Then we thought of adding the torque tube. That gave us a tube that we would precisely machine and hold the angles in the special relationship between the engine and the transaxle. Theoretically, the thing was beautiful. The bend in the shaft was not put in it by pushing in at the side, but by applying a moment at both ends. It ended up with constant bending stress throughout the full length of the shaft." Steve Malone, who came into the Tempest project when Knudsen decided to produce it, reminisces: "You know what the funny part of the story is. It's that the most innovative part of the car never gave us any trouble. It was the old standard parts that brought all the trouble."

Bill Collins's explanation sounds plausible: "Because we realized it was critical, that 'rope-shaft' probably received more attention in manufacturing and quality than any other part of the car." Tests had shown that the 5/8-inch-diameter shaft was capable of running more than fifty million flexing cycles at three times the bending stress levels encountered in the Tempest, with up to twice the maximum engine torque.

"The problems we did have with it in my area of concern were due to torsional rattles," Collins continued, "because the drive line was so small in diameter and therefore soft torsionally, it was excited at much lower frequencies than a bigger, stiffer propeller shaft would have been."

As for production cost, Ed Windeler said: "It was more expensive than a normal shaft including two universal joints would have been. The rope-shaft had to be ground along its entire length, and that made it very costly." Leave it to Steve Malone to sum up: "That rope-shaft, I guess, when all's said and done, that was a real, good engineering exercise. But I don't think the specific design sold very many more cars for us." In any event, it did not get low enough to make a completely flat floor. There was a widened, shallow tunnel both front and rear,

Automatic drive transaxle was located at the rear end of the torque tube enclosing the flexible propeller shaft. This 'rope-shaft' was the most controversial feature of the car, and never gave any trouble.

shaped with due consideration to form a platform for the center passenger's feet.

Having committed himself to independent rear suspension for his experimental compact car, DeLorean began to look for existing parts that could be adapted. He did not have to look far, for the rear-engine Corvair had not only the transaxle he needed, but a swing-axle rear suspension system. George Roberts worked on the Tempest suspension design, and recalls: "We more or less took that rear end straight from the Corvair. That saved us the time and expense of developing our own, and we could not have made it at Chevy's cost anyway."

The wheels were mounted on pendulum-type open drive shafts that were jointed at the inboard end only. The driving thrust was taken by diagonal radius arms, and the load was carried by inclined coil springs. The springs were tilted inboard at the top end to conform to the camber changes in the wheel during jounce deflection. In rebound,

the wheel went into a strong positive camber attitude, which tended to cause oversteer, and the Pontiac engineers tried to counteract it by setting the radius-arm axis so as to give increasing toe-in during both rebound and compression of the coil spring. With the swing-axle pivot point at wheel-hub height, the rear suspension had a very high roll center of 14.5 inches above ground level. This provided good roll stiffness at the rear end, but the front suspension had its roll center at ground level, which resulted in a nose-down roll axis with less than ideal roll stiffness distribution.

A paper on the production-model Tempest, written by DeLorean and delivered by George Roberts to an audience of the Society of Automotive Engineers in Detroit in January 1961, claimed: "Another

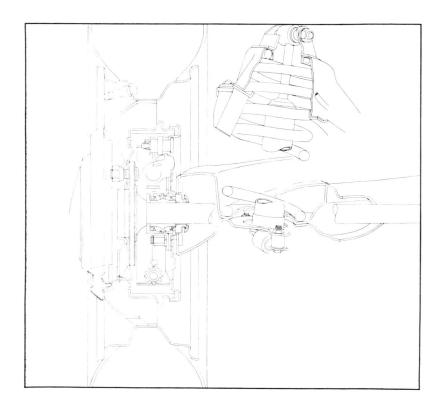

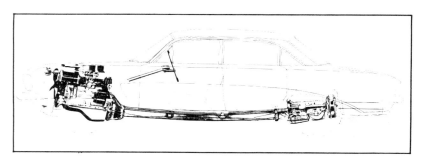

The Tempest swing axle independent rear suspension was taken from the Corvair and brought on the same handling and instability problems. After two years, universal joints at the wheel hubs were added to avoid extreme camber changes.

How nearly flat the floor was in the Tempest is apparent from this side elevation, showing the mechanical elements in relation to the passenger compartment and overall layout.

axle is far less subject to the wheel hop and shake experienced by cars with solid axles.''

Some transaxle changes had to be made from the original Corvair design because of the drive line on the Tempest, and this added to the cost. With TempesTorque, the drive from the engine was taken straight through the mechanical part of the transmission and differential to the air-cooled torque converter mounted at the rear. Output from the three-element hydraulic torque converter was taken via a pinion shaft—concentric with the hollow input shaft and running inside it— to a simple Ravigneaux-type planetary gear set. A two-wrap brake band with high self-actuation was used for locking the front sun gear, so that the power flow was routed to engage low range (a 1.82:1 reduction). The Low-to-Drive upshift was made by releasing the brake band and engaging an overrunning clutch on the input. "The problem was that quill shaft, as we called it, a one-inch hollow shaft about two feet long,'' recalls Ed Windeler. "We said afterwards we never should have done it, because of the expense.''

Cars with synchromesh transmission had the clutch in its conventional position, facing the engine flywheel. The gearbox was mounted immediately ahead of the pinion and ring gear, and was of the same type that was standard on the full-size cars. But all the parts were smaller and lighter, so that the unit weighed twenty-two pounds less despite identical shaft spacing, pitch helix angle, and gear face width. The output shaft was splined to the pinion shaft.

A floor-mounted shift lever was chosen to simplify and shorten the linkage, and to reinforce the sports car flavor the engineers tried to put into the Tempest. The final drive unit was of the hypoid type, with a ring gear of 8.75-inch diameter. Before transaxle prototypes had

advantage of the rear transmission is the improved weight distribution, particularly in terms of radius of gyration to wheelbase. The increase of radius of gyration resulting from moving the transmission to the rear lowers the pitch frequency of the car to such an extent that a 'big-car' ride is possible over a wide variety of load conditions. Also, the swing-

been built, the ring-gear and pinion were road-tested over 35,000 miles in another experimental Pontiac.

The Tempest's front suspension had been used on a number of Pontiacs built in the advanced engineering section, and consisted of stamped-steel A-arms with coil springs, all attached to a box-section cross-member. There were no kingpins, as the steering knuckles were held in ball joints. The upper control arm pivot axis was tilted backwards to provide some antidive effect during braking. All internal and interlinkage wheel forces and shock loads were concentrated into this cross-member, with a view to reducing noise and vibration in the car. The tops of the coil springs were seated against rubber shims. The lower control arm was a two-piece cantilever assembly with a compression strut to reduce the effect of the horizontal forces acting on the wheel when it hits a bump.

General Motors had a long history in unit-construction bodies, starting with Opel and Vauxhall in 1937, but the first American-built unitized body structure for a GM car was that of the Corvair. This Y-body structure was adopted for the Tempest. Instead of a conventional frame, the body shell contained longitudinal hat-section reinforcements, united front and rear by transverse torsional transfer members. Front wheel housings were welded to the cowl and front rails, while the fenders were separate sheet metal stampings that simply bolted on to the underbody structure.

Jack Humbert directed the styling of the Tempest, which shared the split-grille theme of the big Pontiacs. Dual side-by-side headlights were inset in the grille at the outer ends. A simple, straight bumper bar surmounted the modesty panel (the front-end sheet metal that extends below bumper level) with supplementary air intakes and a central license plate bracket. There was no chrome on the body sides of the base-line sedan other than window frames. Accent lines were made entirely by sheet-metal sculpturing which seemed inspired by the dramatically new look of the 1959 Buicks. The beltline extended into a finlike crest above the front and rear fenders, with a sharp crease giving a concave section in the upper part of the door panels. Chrome wind splits were optional decor for the front fender recess aft of the wheel opening.

Wheel openings were slightly flared in front, a bit more in the rear fender. The front fender skirt had a simulated air extractor with a recess that led to an accent line, which ran on a slight rearward slope through the doors and joined up with the lip around the rear wheel opening. The windshield was a one-piece curved glass design, and A-posts were conventional, leaning back at about sixty degrees from the top of the cowl. Front doors had vent windows, and fixed rear

quarter-panel windows were built into the area just ahead of the thin C-post pillar.

The Tempest was designed to go down the same assembly line as the big series, partly to control manufacturing costs, and partly to provide greater flexibility in the product mix than would be possible if the Tempest had needed a separate assembly line. Two body styles were offered at the outset, a four-door sedan and a station wagon. The wagons had a top-hinged tailgate, counterbalanced by torsion bars to ease the muscular effort of lifting it. A two-door coupe was added late in the 1961 model year.

Although the Corvair was a six, and Oldsmobile and Buick were planning to use V-8 engines in their X-100 compacts, DeLorean wanted a four-cylinder power unit for the Tempest. Because most of the money budgeted for the engineering of the Tempest was soaked up by the suspension and drive line development, the engine had to be strictly a low-cost item. There were no funds available for anything remotely experimental, and advances that would have been normal at the time (such as the overhead camshaft, for instance) were out of the question.

The engineers set out five clear-cut aims for the Tempest engine. First, it must give vehicle performance better than any competitive six-cylinder car at equal cubic-feet per ton-mile displacement. What does that mean? Cubic-feet per ton-mile is a measurement that relates engine size and gearing to vehicle weight, and is a good criterion for comparing cars. Specifically, it measures the air volume consumed and discharged by the engine per ton of vehicle weight for each mile driven in top gear. This objective forced Pontiac to search for above-average specific power output (measured in terms of horsepower per cubic inch) which meant high compression and high volumetric efficiency.

Secondly, it must be simple in design, economical in operation and have modest maintenance needs. Thirdly, to compete in the compact car market it must have minimum tooling costs and minimum unit cost. It was decided that maximum interchangeability of parts with the existing production-type 389-cubic-inch V-8 would be an advantage for both production cost and parts availability. This solution also offered maximum integration with existing manufacturing plant facilities, which was the fifth objective.

It was DeLorean's idea to make an in-line, overhead-valve four-cylinder engine by sawing a Pontiac V-8 in two. He felt that development time on the Tempest engine could be significantly shortened by doing the slant-four that way; the valve gear and

Slant-four engine was designed as half a V-8 but ended up being nearly as heavy as the power plant for the Catalina. Optional aluminum V-8 was much lighter. Cross section of Tempest slant-four engine, right, reveals reasons for its weight problem: It's not half a V-8 but more nearly two-thirds, with a needlessly hefty bottom end and odd-shaped block, crankcase and manifolds.

combustion chamber, porting and cylinder head cooling systems were already well proved.

To prove the feasibility of the slant-four, Malcolm 'Mac' McKellar just cobbled up a V-8 in which the four left-bank pistons had large holes in them and the left-bank valve gear was disconnected. It was installed in a standard Pontiac on a whim—not to prove a point, but to satisfy their curiosity. Great was their surprise when the car reached 92 mph and gave reasonable fuel economy.

This led to a series of experimental engines which were actually V-8's with sawed-off left banks, but using four-cylinder crankshafts and camshafts. These were installed in various cars and dynamometer tested. Gradually the engine group was amassing positive proof that the slant-four was an excellent solution—free-breathing and economical at the same time. This led to a full-scale development program towards a production engine.

The four-cylinder design, as it emerged, had certain parts that were definitely its own. That included the cylinder block, which was a separate casting. But because of the way it had come into existence, it could be machined on the V-8 line. The crankshaft was different, and a new intake manifold had to be designed.

The forty-five-degree tilt on the block was retained for the vehicle installation, which left plenty of room on the left for the induction system, accessories and starter motor. The head was a crossflow design, using the standard exhaust manifold from the V-8 on the lower side. The four demanded a smaller carburetor, with air cleaner and silencer to match. It was equipped with a smaller fuel pump, smaller water pump impeller and water outlet fitting, a smaller cooling fan and different pushrod cover. A cheaper ignition coil was used, but the distributor, generator and starter motor were simply modified parts from the V-8. The Tempest camshaft was a slight variation on the V-8 version, and connecting rod bearings, though having different part numbers, were almost the same.

The list of parts that were absolutely identical with those of the V-8 still remained quite long. The four ended up using the same cylinder head, valves and valve springs, rocker arms, rocker arm studs and balls, valve lifters and pushrods. Also identical were the pistons, piston rings, wrist pins, connecting rods, main bearing shells and main bearing caps. Timing chain and timing chain cover were the same, and the oil pump and oil pan were unchanged. The water pump body, crankshaft pulley and harmonic balancer were adopted from the V-8 without alteration, and the water pump and fan drive pulley were the same. The heat stove for the choke was the same, and the crankcase ventilator inlet was unchanged. The standard V-8 dipstick was used, with the same spark plugs. Out of forty-four major parts or assemblies, twenty-eight remained identical, five had minor differences, and only eleven were totally new.

How did it work out in the car? "It was a cheapie way to get a four-cylinder engine, but we had the dickens of a time trying to develop it," said Russ Gee, adding: "Because it was so rough, and the direction of the unbalanced forces was kind of oddball, we had to mount it in real soft rubber to let it move around under the hood so that the vibrations wouldn't be carried into the car.

"That thing was mounted so loosely, it shook the cars. We had to put stabilizing blocks on the engine so it wouldn't run around and bust something up. We used very soft large-diameter engine mounts. They were so juicy we had to stabilize them some way, so we put metal containers above each of them, to keep it from going completely out of control. The design included buffer stops."

Gee went on: "We actually used the chassis to compensate for drawbacks that were inherent in the engine. We really had a problem there, in the shaking forces." The engine itself had only two mounts, one on each side. But Russ Gee explained that it was really a four motor-mount system, because of the transaxle supports and the rigid

torque tube around the propeller shaft, two in their normal positions and two some distance away.

Ed Windeler's thoughts are closely parallel: "Everybody had always had three or four engine mounts, but there were only two on this engine, one on each side. And the torque tube was solid, you know, and that's what held it in place. It couldn't move fore and aft. But it rocked. It required special motor mounts, mainly because it was a large-diameter piston engine—the cylinders had a four-inch bore—and it was the biggest four-cylinder engine of its day. We had to have rebound stops so that it wouldn't go too far."

McKellar had not been unaware of the engine's balance problems, but he thought that by balancing the crankshaft to half an inch-ounce in assembly, with the crank rotating, in addition to using a harmonic balancer and four integrally cast counterweights, crankshaft deflections had been adequately diminished.

Some other problems with the engine were unforeseen and did not show up until it was too late. We got this from Ed Windeler: "There was one thing that was really a problem and that was the timing chain. We had a link-belt type of chain, like everybody uses, but because we had the camshaft in the same position as on the V-8, the same distance from the crankshaft, we couldn't do anything else but use that fine-pitch timing chain, and the torsional vibrations in the four-cylinder engine just tore that thing apart. Unfortunately this problem didn't show up until after we got in production.

"To fix it we had to make a very elaborate chain tightener, a spring-loaded automatic tensioner. We would have gone to a roller chain but the dimensions were such that you couldn't get a roller chain in there. So we were stuck with the V-8 chain and it just wouldn't work without that elaborate chain tightener."

How did the engine perform? *Motor Trend* tested a 1961 Tempest with the high-compression four-cylinder unit and automatic transmission and Chuck Nerpel reported: "Acceleration under full throttle is smooth and rapid, going from 0 to 60 mph in eleven seconds. Part-throttle or traffic-type lugging is equally smooth with an automatic downshift of the two-speed transmission at about 25 mph with part throttle and about 45 mph with full throttle, which gives excellent in-traffic or highway passing acceleration. Here again, engine, transmission and drive-line smoothness is disarming, giving no indication that the speedometer is nudging 85 mph very quickly after a stomp on the throttle."

As for the car's fuel economy, Nerpel's report switched to a manual-drive car with the same engine: "Pulling out in first gear, accelerating to 30 mph, shifting to second and running at full throttle to 50 mph before going into high—where we cruised at a steady 65 mph—produced 24 mpg. Slower through-the-gears starts and 35-mph cruise increased the mileage to 29 mpg. The stick shift, for ordinary driving is no great advantage over the two-speed automatic, except that it produced slightly better gas mileage."

The standard transmission for the Tempest was a three-speed synchromesh gearbox. There was no four-speed option at first. A two-speed automatic transmission was optional. Pontiac's TempesTorque was derived from the Powerglide unit used in the Corvair. Many of the components were identical, but the TempesTorque had a different high-gear clutch that permitted split-torque action (as in the HydraMatic 61-05 used for the Buick and Oldsmobile compacts). The cars equipped with automatic transmission had engines with hotter camshafts, giving twenty extra horsepower and bringing peak power rpm to 4400 (from 3800).

Three versions of the slant-four engine were offered: a regular-fuel job with a single-barrel carburetor and 8.6:1 compression ratio, and two premium-fuel mills running on a 10.25:1 compression ratio and breathing through a one-barrel carburetor in one case and a four-barrel carburetor in the other. In addition, the Tempest was available with a small V-8 engine built by Buick. It was an all-aluminum unit that proved considerably lighter than Pontiac's cast-iron four. The chassis was developed with the four-cylinder engine, and as Russ Gee recalls it, "the V-8 was too light for proper weight distribution—it changed from 60/40 to 40/60, and that was very bad for a car with swing axles."

That was an exaggeration, but the point was well made. The complete slant-four weighed 507 pounds, while the light alloy Buick V-8 weighed no more than 325 pounds. That was enough of a difference to change the static curb weight distribution from 52.3 percent on the front wheels and 47.7 percent on the rear wheels with the Pontiac four to 49.7 percent front and 50.3 percent rear with the Buick V-8 in the four-door sedan. With a five-passenger load, the swap from four to eight cylinders meant going from a 49.4/50.6 percent weight distribution to a 47.2/52.8 percent situation.

The 1961 Tempest was built on a 112-inch wheelbase, with a track of 56.8 inches front and rear. That was enough for Pontiac to advertise it, too, with the Wide-Track slogan. While Buick and Oldsmobile chose thirteen-inch wheels for their compacts, Pontiac was compelled to use wheels two sizes bigger because of the excessive camber changes in the rear suspension.

The fifteen-inch wheels, shod with 6.00–15 tires, carried nine-inch brake drums front and rear, with a lining width of 1.75 inches. Power

brakes were not offered. On paper, that seemed fine. But as Steve Malone observes: "There wasn't anything unusual about the brakes, but we ran into trouble." Field reports came in with complaints about excessive lining wear and a tendency to fade. Nominally geared at 24:1, the steering was very slow, at 5½ turns lock to lock, and gave a turning circle diameter of thirty-eight feet. This was perhaps done to prevent eager drivers from cranking in too much input, and ending up with handling situations that they could not control. For the car was decidedly capricious in its road behavior.

In December 1961, a group of auto press people was invited to Daytona Beach for a preview of the new Mercedes-Benz 300 SE. And the Mercedes-Benz company's chief car development engineer, Rudolf Uhlenhaut, personally gave us demonstration runs with a variety of Mercedes-Benz cars. There was one American car there, for comparison purposes. It was a Tempest. Mercedes-Benz has all-independent suspension, with a swing axle arrangement at the rear. Though far different from the Tempest chassis in execution, the basic principles were the same. The point was to prove that the Germans had done it right while the Americans had done it wrong.

Uhlenhaut set up a grid on the speedway, marked by rubber cones, and at one point the right lane was blocked, so that he had to swerve into the left lane. A couple of hundred feet later, a lane change to the right followed. He made several runs at about 70 mph with the Mercedes-Benz, each time following exactly the same path. He only made one run with the Pontiac. On the first attempt, at the same speed, the tail end swung wide, and despite rapid countersteering, the car spun around and overturned in a shower of sparks. Uhlenhaut, helmeted and harnessed, emerged unhurt. Had he done it on purpose? He never said.

But no one who was there can forget the Tempest's slewing around and rolling over. We could not endorse the handling qualities of that car. Using the Corvair's rear suspension, it could not escape some of the same oversteering phenomena (which played a large part in Ralph Nader's book *Unsafe at Any Speed*, published in 1965).

In a cornering situation, the Tempest body would lean over under lateral weight transfer to the outside. Theoretically this would put the outside rear wheel spring under compression, and put the wheel into a negative-camber angle. But that was only theory. Due to a combination of forward weight bias and a high rear roll center, the outside rear wheel went into a positive camber attitude, and sort of jacked up the tail end of the car until neither rear tire had much tread contact with the pavement. Then the car would go into a skid, which was difficult to correct because of the slow-geared steering.

As for the Tempest's ride comfort, Karl Ludvigsen wrote in the 1962 *Car and Driver Yearbook*: "The ride is very soft and comfortable; you are unable to sense the individual irregularities, yet there is no unreasonable pitching through dips. This is achieved through front springs only sixty percent as stiff as usual, at a wheel rate of seventy-five pounds per inch. Add to this the nose-heaviness and the mere 5½ inches of ground clearance at the front, and you have a car which bottoms out a bit easily. We made a terrible clang entering an underground garage at 15 mph and subsequently found that rough roads traversed at speed would also make the front suspension bottom out."

But it wasn't its lack of road manners that killed the swing-axle rope-shaft Tempest. It was Detroit's ever-present nemesis: cost. According to Ed Windeler, "There was a sizeable dollar difference in the cost of making the Tempest, compared with the Olds F-85 or Buick Special." And Bob Knickerbocker concurs, "Unfortunately it was terribly costly. All that hardware was charged to a single division, and volume wasn't that great. Pontiac couldn't afford to continue it."

That should have been predictable, you might say. But it surely wasn't that obvious, and there were many reasons why the Tempest turned out the way it did. "Pontiac dealers were not interested in marketing a Corvair with a Pontiac name plate on it," remarked Knickerbocker, "That certainly had something to do with it." And Ed Windeler states, "We were trying to get a sports-car image, to improve our sales appeal." The Tempest was competing not only against other American compacts but also against all sorts of imported cars. The Tempest was priced to compete head-on with the Valiant V-200, and closer to the Rambler Deluxe Six than the Super Six. It was positioned above the top-of-the-line Corvair, and safely below the F-85 and Special.

One of the cost-cutting methods backfired. Automatic transmissions had no Park position—and emergency brakes were unreliable. Some people resorted to carrying bricks to keep their Tempests from running downhill when parked on a slope.

There is no doubt the car was too experimental in its character to have gone into production so quickly. Perhaps it had the makings of a great car. It was truly different, at a time when cars were coming to resemble each other more and more. And DeLorean gets more praise for making the attempt than he gets blamed for the car's shortcomings.

When the Tempest was launched on November 3, 1960, DeLorean held the opinion that the vehicle had been adequately tested. Component test vehicles had accumulated over three million miles, and the four-cylinder engine the equivalent of 2,600,000 miles. In

Four-door 1961 Tempest station wagon has independent four-wheel suspension, four-cylinder engine and rear transmission.

addition to the usual test procedure that all new models were put through, which included a 25,000-miles durability run, a 5,000-miles hill schedule, and 5,000 miles on Belgian blocks, the Tempest had to submit to other tests, "some of them almost fiendishly conceived," in DeLorean's words—such as 20,000 miles at 100 mph, and 100,000 miles of general durability operation on single cars.

In the judgment of Russell F. Gee, "John DeLorean was an outstanding engineer. He was always there to guide us in areas we had problems. He was *involved*. And everybody who worked on the Tempest was enthusiastic about it." Bob Knickerbocker says: "There were many people who worked twelve-hour shifts, seven days a week, on that project." There is no record of that happening over the Catalina or the Bonneville, or any other Pontiac. The Tempest wasn't just a car—it was a Pontiac demonstration.

"Before the era of regulation, what set Pontiac apart was an ability that the people there had of coming together in a cooperative way and creating an imaginative new product such as the original Tempest in a relatively short time frame," Bob Knickerbocker states. "In doing that, you certainly turn on the engineers, of course, for the only real satisfaction they get, you know, is creating something."

Aged only thirty-one when he came to Pontiac, DeLorean was a 1948 graduate of the Lawrence Institute of Technology. He was born in Detroit and grew up in Michigan and southern California. His first job was at Chrysler and he attended the Chrysler Institute. Later he went to the Detroit College of Law and collected a master's degree in business administration from the University of Michigan. He was brought in by Knudsen to serve as director of advanced engineering in 1956, and in 1959 Estes named him assistant chief engineer; in 1961 he succeeded Estes as chief engineer of Pontiac.

"He was the kind of a guy," said Bob Knickerbocker about John DeLorean, "who would come in on a Saturday when you were working on a design and had kicked the stuffing out of it and still couldn't overcome the problems. Then he'd spend fifteen minutes at the drawing board and give you a whole raft of ideas and usually one of them worked."

What happened with the Tempest? No changes of importance were made for 1962, but Pontiac dropped the optional aluminum V-8 for the Tempest at the end of the 1962 model year. Ed Windeler comments acidly: "Not many were sold, because at that time it wasn't a real good engine." About ninety-eight percent of Tempests built up to that date had been equipped with four-cylinder engines. Tempest sales for the first 2½ years were eighty percent conquest, i.e., 'plus' business. The Tempest brought to Pontiac customers that the division's other products could not reach.

For 1962 a convertible and a two-door coupe were added. This sports coupe in the 1962 Tempest series was the first production-model Pontiac to carry the LeMans name. The name had previously been used for a 1961 show car based on the Tempest coupe, outfitted with a supercharged slant-four, wire wheels and bucket seats. Pontiac ads even explained the pronunciation—"Luh Mahnz"—which may have been intended to help its salesmen around the country more than any clients who knew of Le Mans as the site of Europe's most famous endurance race but were not familiar with how it is pronounced in French. In any case, Pontiac got it wrong or wilfully Americanized it, for in French the name ends in a nasal 'ng,' the 's' being mute. LeMans became a separate series in the Tempest line for 1963.

At the same time, Pontiac switched from swing axles and trailing arms to double-jointed shafts and semi-trailing arms in the rear suspension. That meant adding universal joints at the outboard end of the drive shafts, so that the camber angle on the wheels was no longer dictated by the body height relative to the ground.

Pontiac discontinued use of the aluminum V-8, which was a very expensive item indeed. Instead, Pontiac produced a new, smaller version of its cast-iron V-8. Introduced for the 1963 Tempest, the 326-cubic-inch V-8 was structurally similar to the 389 but had a smaller bore, 3.72 inches compared with 4.06 inches. It was about thirty pounds lighter, because of a less hefty crankshaft and thinner casting walls.

The four-cylinder engine was improved, too, with a new cylinder head. The combustion chamber cavities had a different shape intended to give shorter flame front travel and increased quench area. The generator was replaced by a Delcotron alternator, which produced current right down to idle speed, had sealed-for-life bearings, and reduced weight.

The automatic transmission had been revised and two new versions were adopted, one for the four-cylinder engine and one for the V-8. The difference between them was mainly the size of the torque converter, and the number of clutch plates. The torque split feature was eliminated, so that one hundred percent of output now flowed through the hydraulic converter. Two different control systems were used, too, one for the standard column-mounted selector lever, and one for the new console-shift that was offered exclusively on the LeMans. Both included a Park position, and shift points were vacuum-controlled, eliminating the throttle-valve cable between engine and transmission that was used earlier.

The Tempest body was stretched by five inches for 1963—mostly in the form of rear overhang. The deck lid was three inches longer, and some extra luggage capacity was gained. The new body was two inches wider, and the track was widened to 57.3 inches in front and a full fifty-eight inches in the rear, an increase of 0.5 and 1.2 inches, respectively. The 1962 model had not had a split grille, but a dropped center section flanked by a grille-and-headlight combination that was a cleaned-up version of the 1961 design. Now, the split grille came back, with a simple horizontal pattern, with the usual side-by-side dual headlights.

The side sculpturing was toned down, and the shape became essentially slab-sided. Three chrome wind-splits remained to suggest the air extractor in the front fender skirt, and chrome strips were added above the wheel openings and at doorsill level. Something new, and the start of something big, appeared in the rear fender. There was a slight kickup from the beltline, and a widening around the wheel, giving a hint of the Coke-bottle shape that was then making its mark on the full-size Pontiacs.

Let's not leave the compact Tempest without making it clear that with the revised rear suspension, all its vices in the handling and controllability area had been eliminated. Nothing could make the four-banger a pleasant car to drive, but equipped with the new V-8 the Tempest was an understatement of refined power and performance.

Despite all the improvements in the 1963 Tempest, it was passed in sales by both the Plymouth Valiant and the Dodge Dart, and was

closely threatened by the Olds F-85 and the Rambler American, ending up eighth among compacts, two steps down from its usual position. In its first year—1961—the Tempest ran sixth among the compacts, behind the Ford Falcon, Corvair, Mercury Comet, Rambler American and Plymouth Valiant. The Tempest accounted for 29.55 percent of Pontiac sales that year.

In 1962 it also had to contend with competition from the new and lower-priced Chevy II, but the Tempest still stayed sixth though the leaders changed. Now the Tempest followed behind the Falcon, Chevy II, Corvair, Comet and Buick Special, having moved ahead of the American and Valiant, leaving the Dodge Lancer and Oldsmobile even further behind. During 1962 the Tempest accounted for 6.24 percent of the compact car market and 1.99 percent of the total market.

Pontiac built its eight-millionth car on April 12, 1962. It was a Tempest convertible. Tempest sales grew sharply at this time, with a thirty-five-percent increase from 1961 to 1962. In its first year, roughly one Tempest in five had been a station wagon. That share fell to one in ten the following year, with a one-third drop in sales volume.

The 1963 Tempest price range started at $2,188 for the two-door sedan, which was only $132 more than the cheapest Corvair but $203

Restyled Tempest for 1963 was taking shape as a clay model back in July 1961. The side treatment became pure Pontiac, and the front end was cleaned up—this grotesque center divider slimmed down to a thin vertical post.

Production-model 1963 Tempest was a pretty and practical car, but did not sell well. The aluminum V-8 was scrapped in favor of a small cast-iron V-8, and a new rear suspension was adopted.

above the lowest-priced Falcon, about $100 below the Special and $200 less than the F-85. Additional charges for options were $189 for the TempesTorque automatic transmission and $75 for the power steering which had been made available to meet public demand for faster steering response.

Even before the 1963 Tempest went on sale, it was becoming clear to the marketing men at Pontiac that the compact field was overcrowded, and probably that was not where the Tempest belonged. A new and larger car—with utterly conventional engineering—would carry that name from 1964 onwards.

CHAPTER 9

One of the Top Three

SKILLFUL, CLEVER MERCHANDISING was as essential for Pontiac's rise to third place in the industry as the soundness of its engineering. Nor must the part played by styling be underestimated. But above all, it was leadership that mattered, and it was part of Bunkie's success that continuity was assured when he went to Chevrolet in the fall of 1961.

Continuity of management and engineering, which went hand in hand at Pontiac, was assured by repeatedly promoting the chief engineer to general manager when the top post became open. The pattern was set when Estes succeeded Knudsen in 1961. When Estes followed in Bunkie's footsteps to Chevrolet four years later, John Z. DeLorean, chief engineer since 1961, took over the helm at Pontiac. All three of these men were to share the glory of Pontiac's years as one of the top three makes in the industry. Knudsen put Pontiac in third place, Estes consolidated the position, and DeLorean defended it until he, in turn, was transferred to Chevrolet in 1969.

Not all engineers make good managers, but Pontiac trained and promoted men of exceptional ability, and Estes was, if anything, a better manager than an engineer. Steve Malone, now chief engineer of Pontiac, remembers his former boss as "a demanding kind of guy—but he had charisma . . . he just attracted people and he was always

friendly. Congenial. But when you worked for Estes you soon learned that he didn't take an answer that he didn't want to hear. He would keep challenging you: 'Did you look at this? Did you look at that?'

"He has another characteristic. When he wants to get something done, he'll ask a lot of people to do the same thing. In a way, that's a waste of manpower, but we always came up with several different answers to the same problem. He would tell one man: 'Wish you would take care of that.' Then he'd go down the hall and ask somebody else: 'How about looking into this?' And a third: 'We really should get into that!' All directed toward the same objective.

"We used to laugh around here when somebody said he had an assignment. How many other guys got the same assignment? He is probably the most knowledgeable automotive guy that I've ever known that really knew the nuts and bolts—really knew what a car should be like, yet without getting bogged down in the details and try to do it all himself."

Pontiac chief designer Jack Humbert has nothing but praise for Estes: "He was probably more engineering-minded than Knudsen. He was a great guy to work for, who appreciated cars. And he understood what we in the design studio wanted. He was easy to talk to—and he would listen to you."

Pontiac offered four wagons in 1962, culminating with this luxurious Bonneville. The lowest was a compact wagon in the Tempest series, and the remaining two were six- and nine-passenger versions of the Catalina.

General Motors discontinued its Motorama exhibitions in 1961 but each division continued to build advanced-engineering experimental cars as well as pure styling prototypes.

Pontiac continued to display special show cars from time to time. Bob Knickerbocker explained the situation: "The normal mode of our operation is to build preliminary pretest type automobiles on a continuing basis, and these models are used for development work and for demonstration to the management of the division—and management of the corporation—and still are today. These cars actually run and often incorporate new types of materials and components. Show cars, on the other hand, are primarily constructed for viewing and represent, usually, the design staff and the divisional design studio's concept of some future model."

"We used to have a car every year we called the X-400," says Jack Humbert. "The first one, as far as I can recall, was made in 1959. It was a convertible. The V-8 engine had a big GMC blower on it, and we put a special hood on the car. Then every year we'd update that car. We showed one in 1960, and another one in 1962. They were big hot-rods! These show cars allowed us to get a feel for some shapes. The 1963–64 production model design came out of one of the X-400's. It was a regular design exercise. We learned a lot from them."

Jack Humbert came from Canton, Ohio. He was drawing cars from the moment his hand learned to hold a pencil, and he was sixteen

Clay model for the 1962 Pontiac was shown to top corporate officers in July 1960. Split grille theme is carried forward, and dogleg A-posts are returning towards a safer, more robust design.

Torque-box perimeter frame was used for the 1962 Pontiac chassis. The 389-cubic-inch V-8 is mated to a four-speed HydraMatic. Car has all-coil suspension.

when he bought his first car. He worked in gas stations, used-car lots and auto paint shops. He was barely out of high school when he was drafted for military service. Returning home in 1945, he had experience from a combat engineering battalion and the armored field artillery. Without a job lined up, he decided to go back to school and attended the Central Academy of Commercial Art in Cincinnati. One of his teachers suggested he should try to see Harley Earl at GM Styling. He did, and was hired in the fall of 1948.

Humbert made no big changes in the 1962-model Pontiac bodies. But for 1963, the designers and clay modelers in the Pontiac studio came up with a dramatically new look. The frontal aspect was strikingly different, and the side view was fresh, smart and gave the new car a poise it had lacked before.

Headlights were stacked, with the fender line forming a hood over the top-mounted lamp, which widened the grille. The grille elements were slightly recessed, and the center divider was toned down. There was no more panoramic windshield, and the A-post was now set to coincide more or less with the windshield rake. In side view, the front fender line tapered off in the door panels, blending in with the start of a rear fender sculpture, which spanned the full height of the

sheet metal, from doorsill to beltline. Here, at last, was something that helped set the Pontiac apart from the other GM cars built on the Fisher B-body.

How did this new look come into being? "There's nothing I can tell you we used as a theme," says Jack Humbert. "We just did a lot of work and took the best parts for the final design. We just tried to do the best job we could and come up with something fresh. Finally, for 1963 we hit on what we called the *Venturi* theme. I don't know if anybody on the street ever called it that. It was known as the Coke-bottle shape. I don't know if it could have become a Pontiac trademark, in a way, for then everybody started using it. We weren't the only ones."

This is significant, for it shows that Pontiac was becoming a trend-setter in styling. At General Motors, Cadillac had always been the accepted style leader, with the other divisions following in its footsteps. Now Pontiac was openly challenging Cadillac's position. And there can be no doubt that styling leadership—not just innovation, but leadership in the sense that one's designs get copied by others—has a great influence on the public's readiness to buy the product that has it, no less than styling which projects a brand-name identity.

"Our philosophy has always been to—not revolutionize—but to show a little heritage," Humbert explains. "You want some continuity through all the model changes. You must have some mark there that gives the divisional identity." People were taking notice of Pontiac, and sales soared.

The national auto market expanded from 5.85 million cars (including imports) in 1961 to 6.9 million the following year. General Motors boosted its market share from 46.5 percent to 51.9 percent, with 1962 calendar year sales of 3.6 million cars. Pontiac accounted for 528,654 of them. From 1961 to 1962 Pontiac raised its share of the domestic new-car market from 6.37 to 7.62 percent. Pontiac was solidly in third place for the second consecutive year. A Pontiac Bonneville produced on March 14, 1962, was the seventy-five millionth General Motors car produced since the corporation had come into being in 1908.

Mechanically, the 1962 Pontiac was essentially the same as the 1961 model. But that year Pontiac demonstrated its forward-looking mentality by being first in the industry to offer a factory-installed full-transistor ignition system as an extra-cost option. By 1964, Pontiac's lead in the use of transistorized ignition had been followed by the Chevrolet Corvette, Ford Thunderbird, and Mercury.

Appearance changes for 1962 were relatively minor. The A-body had a straight, horizontal beltline with just a hint of fattening at the rear fender, repeated by an accent line bending down in an easy arc just ahead of the wheel opening. The spear on the body sides was slimmed down to continue the headlight profile right back to the taillights, switching from convex to concave in the front door panel. A very clean split grille was used, with the dividing sheet metal rising to start a crease straight down the middle of the hood. Dual headlights were mounted side by side, as before.

The emphasis on performance was pushed relentlessly. Pontiac cars had finished 1-2-3 in the 1961 Daytona 500, setting a new record for the race, with a winning average of 149.601 mph. Back at the factory, Mac McKellar was turning out new and hotter cams faster than if his middle name were Isky. The fairly mild McKellar No. 6 had the standard lift, but intake duration was extended to 283 degrees and the exhaust duration to 293 degrees. The standard camshaft for the 389-cubic-inch V-8 had a 0.40-inch lift with an intake opening duration of 273 degrees and exhaust opening duration of 283 degrees.

The McKellar No. 7 cam was hotter and made the engine more temperamental, with its 0.414-inch lift and opening durations of 301 degrees for the intake valves and 313 degrees for the exhaust valves.

The HO optional camshaft also had a lift of 0.414 inches, but shorter opening durations (288 degrees for intake valves and 302 degrees for the exhausts). It was a good road-racing camshaft, giving great top-end power and putting out peak torque somewhere around 4000 rpm, but

hopeless for street use and not really suited for the drag strip.

McKellar No. 10 was made for solid lifters and intended for drag-strip use. Valve lift was raised to a full 0.52 inches. It gave valve opening durations of 308 degrees for the intakes and 320 degrees for the exhausts. Its cam profiles were later modified for use in combination with hydraulic lifters.

Anything that worked on the Pontiac V-8 was naturally adaptable to the slant-four. The Tempest was going to have a racing career, too. Mickey Thompson installed a GMC blower on the four-cylinder Tempest in the spring of 1961. This boosted its output to about 250 hp at 5600 rpm. A Tempest coupe powered by this setup could go from standstill to 60 mph in seven seconds flat and cover the standing-start quarter-mile in 15.5 seconds. It had a top speed in excess of 125 mph. On the Bonneville Salt Flats in 1962, it was timed at a flying-mile two-way average of 120.8 mph.

A 1961 Pontiac Catalina with its 389-cubic-inch V-8 prepared by Mickey Thompson had a high-lift high-overlap camshaft, lightweight valve lifters and pushrods, and larger-diameter valves. It was bored out an extra 0.06 inches and forged aluminum pistons with a loose fit were used. This engine delivered about 390 hp. *Car Life* magazine tested the car and reported acceleration from zero to sixty miles per hour in 4.6 seconds. It covered the standing-start quarter-mile in 13.7 seconds with a terminal speed of 108 mph.

In another experiment, Mickey Thompson turbocharged a 389-cubic-inch V-8 installed in an innocent-looking 1960 Catalina. It was as quiet and docile as a standard machine on light throttle, but had a real punch when the throttle was opened, and Mickey Thompson used to amuse himself by blowing off unsuspecting hot-rodders on the streets around Los Angeles.

Mickey Thompson then proceeded to saw up a few 421-cubic-inch engine blocks to create two-, three- and four-cylinder engines. He devised new crankshafts to provide proper phasing, but kept the same production-type Pontiac valve gear on all. With a GMC 4-71 blower, he was getting about 110 hp per cylinder. These engines were to be used in a new streamliner called Assault, built to attack international class records in the lesser-displacement groups (Classes D, E and F). The four-cylinder Class D engine (180-cubic-inch displacement) delivered nearly 500 hp on nitromethane fuel, and the Assault was timed over the standing-start quarter-mile at 9.94 seconds at March Air Force Base. Tests for maximum speed gave readings up to 151.59 mph.

Running at the Bonneville Salt Flats a few days later, the same car established a whole new set of Class D records. It covered the flying kilometer at 153.64 mph and ran 1,000 kilometers at an average of

Split grille with sunken air scoops is flanked by dual vertical headlamps on 1963 Star Chief four-door hardtop Vista.

Grand Prix X-400 show car appeared in April 1963. It was the third show car to carry the X-400 designation. Supercharged 421-cubic-inch V-8 breathed through four side-draft carburetors.

A drag-racing engine of this type also appeared in 1962. It was bored out to an actual 428-cubic-inch displacement and fitted with a high-overlap camshaft and solid valve lifters. Oversize valves were closed by dual coil springs, and Mickey Thompson-forged aluminum pistons (with forged steel connecting rods) gave a compression ratio of 11:1. Two Carter four-barrel carburetors were mounted on an aluminum manifold. A heavy-duty oil pump kept the flow going under normal pressure from idle speed to peak rpm. Pontiac claimed 405 hp for this mill, but that figure probably errs on the side of modesty. Users said it delivered 445 to 450 hp.

Then Pontiac took a stock Catalina sedan to Indianapolis Speedway in the winter of 1962 for an attempt at the 500 miles and twenty-four-hour stock car records. It broke Ford's record, set in 1956, for 500 miles by 1.37 mph by clocking an impressive 113.25 mph for the 500 miles; and it pulverized the twenty-four-hour record, set by Chrysler in 1953, with an average speed of 107.7 mph—no less than 17.81 mph faster than the old record.

Things got out of the experimental department and into field use with remarkable alacrity in those days. In the spring of 1962 Pontiac made available to its racing customers a new, improved 421, officially listed as delivering 432 hp. In addition to all the special parts of the basic Super Duty engine, this one also had a forged-steel crankshaft and a high-pressure oil pump. Roger Huntington reported in *Motor Trend* on a test of the 1962 Catalina with the Super Duty 421 engine, quoting a standing-start quarter-mile in 13.9 seconds with a terminal speed of 107 mph under conditions of far-from-ideal traction.

A Pontiac win in the Firecracker 250 miles race at Daytona on July 4, 1962, was attributed more to the better aerodynamics of the Pontiac two-door sedan bodies than to out-and-out power superiority over Ford (whose Holman & Moody-prepared engines were perhaps the highest-powered in NASCAR racing at the time, but whose two-door bodies had a squared-off roofline with a high drag coefficient).

Mickey Thompson rebuilt a Super Duty 421 in 1962 for competition in what the National Hot Rod Association called its Factory Experimental Class. Using a standard Catalina body over a dragster chassis, this Pontiac-powered monster covered the standing-start quarter-mile in 12.22 seconds at a terminal speed of 117.27 mph.

Thompson also prepared a 1962 Catalina with the Super Duty engine for a new crack at some international class records. It ran the flying kilometer at 150.66 mph and the flying mile at 150.552 mph at March Air Force Base.

Pontiac's engineering department was literally overflowing with experimental high-performance parts. As the various items became less

137.78 mph. It set a record for the one-hour run at 142.09 mph and averaged 143.12 mph over three hours. Still, the NASCAR circuit continued to form the backbone of Pontiac's racing program.

The Pontiac that won the Daytona 500 in 1962 was prepared by Smokey Yunick. Its Super Duty 421-cubic-inch V-8 ran with a single four-barrel carburetor and delivered about 440 hp. It set a qualifying speed of 158.744 mph and averaged 152.529 mph in the race.

and less experimental in view of their race-proved endurance, it was suggested that they could be sold as special production options. The management was considering a catalog of speed equipment, with distribution through the full Pontiac dealer organization.

But Frank Bridge ("who was probably wiser than all of us," Jim Wangers recalls) said that was unacceptable. It would cause all sorts of confusion among dealers and customers alike. It could give rise to endless service and warranty problems. He said that one single dealer should be selected to handle such parts, one whose qualifications were not to be questioned and whose ideas of promotion tallied with those of the factory. Out of this conference came a decision to let Royal Pontiac in Royal Oak, Michigan, handle all the high-performance stuff. Ace Wilson was its boss, and he had proved his ability.

Royal Pontiac had a broad base. The company prepared cars for its own stable, and ran a mail-order and over-the-counter business of special high-performance Pontiac parts. It even built complete, modified stock cars (for street and track use) for sale to the public as well as to actual racing competitors. The Royal Bobcat appeared in 1962 and was basically a Catalina coupe with the 421 Super Duty engine in its 348-hp version, heavy-duty chassis, and specific exterior identification.

An even wilder arrangement was the Royal 348 Super Chief, in which the 421-cubic-inch V-8 carried carburetors with larger jets and the heat risers were blocked off. About 370 hp was claimed for it. And that's a believable figure, for the Royal Bobcat with the four-speed T-10 Warner transmission was capable of reaching 60 mph from standstill in 6.5 seconds.

The Royal Tempest Tiger also dates from 1962. It was a Tempest coupe outfitted with a 185-hp version of the slant-four. In straight-line acceleration, it could make the zero-to-sixty run in under ten seconds.

"The reason Royal Pontiac's cars were so good," recalls Jim Wangers, "is that the stuff came from us." When Wangers says "us," he means Pontiac Motor Division. Though technically employed by the advertising agency, he actually worked for Pontiac on a full-time basis, even to the extent of sitting on a product-planning committee. The equipment was developed and tested by the factory, and when judged valid for a specific purpose, released to Royal Pontiac.

Racing-image names were added to the lineup of production models. A new car, labeled Grand Prix, was introduced for 1962. Its story is told in chapter thirteen on A-body variations. Royal Pontiac was not slow in getting its own version.

The Royal Grand Prix also came on the scene in 1962. It was powered by a Paxton-supercharged 389-cubic-inch V-8 delivering about 400 hp at 5600 rpm. The Paxton supercharger was a centrifugal blower of relatively low pressure, delivering 5.5 to 6 psi boost. Royal Pontiac's usual chassis modifications and cosmetic touches were part of the package.

A new X-400 was shown in the winter of 1962. Based on a production-model Grand Prix, it was powered by a Mickey Thompson-tuned 421-cubic-inch V-8 using four side-draft carburetors and a GMC Roots-type blower. This car proved capable of covering the standing-start quarter-mile in 14.92 seconds with a terminal speed of 97.82 mph with a four-speed manual transmission.

Pontiac's Super Duty 421 for NASCAR events in 1963 was equipped with a single four-barrel (due to new regulations, intended to cut power and reduce speeds) but had pistons and cylinder heads giving a 12:1 compression ratio. It delivered 390 to 400 hp. Another version was intended for the drag strips. It had the same compression ratio but breathed through dual four-barrel carburetors and delivered 405 hp.

Pontiac was all set for another season of victories on all fronts. Suddenly the division withdrew all factory support, by corporate edict, and Fords finished 1-2-3 in the Daytona 500 miles race in February 1963. Pontiac channeled its initiative and energy into more conventional forms of sales promotion, marketing and dealer incentives. And with good results.

The 1963 Catalina was listed at $2,795 for the four-door sedan, which was only twenty-three dollars more than the suggested retail price of a V-8 powered Chevrolet Impala! For upward comparison, the lowest-priced full-size Oldsmobile was the Dynamic 88 at $2,995 and in the Buick stable the senior-series price leader was the LeSabre at $3,104. The 1963 Bonneville four-door hardtop had a list price of $3,423, but in those days you had to pay extra for automatic transmission ($231), power steering ($108) and power brakes ($43). The Star Chief (only model designation still carrying an Indian flavor) filled the middle of the range.

With these cars, Pontiac's sales soared above 600,000 cars for the first time ever. The overall car market expanded from 6.9 to 7.5 million cars and General Motors maintained its position of taking half the market, with a margin of between one and two percent. Pontiac's market share increased to eight percent, beating its former best-ever of 7.67 percent in 1941. Its third-spot position seemed increasingly secure.

CHAPTER 10

From Estes to DeLorean

ALTHOUGH PETE ESTES had been general manager since 1961, the 1963 Pontiacs were basically engineered under his direction. Steve Malone, who was one of his closest assistants, expressed tremendous admiration for his understanding of cars: "Estes is one of the few men who can ride blindfolded in a car and tell you almost exactly what's in it, in terms of power unit, drive train and suspension. He feels whether it's acceptable, whether its ride is right, whether it's shaky or whether it's solid. He's got a sixth sense about that stuff. I've never known another guy like that. He really knows his business."

Estes had reorganized the engineering department in 1959. Mark Garlick was executive engineer, H. R. Field was chassis engineer and John P. Charles was assistant chief engineer in charge of testing and reporting. On the engine side, Ed Windeler was design supervisor, and Clayton B. Leach and Mac McKellar were design engineers. DeLorean was still in charge of advanced engineering at that time, and after he became chief engineer, he proceeded to change the organizational setup again. He explained his theory of engineering management in an article that was published in *Automotive Industries*, November 15, 1963: "We believe in a small, hard-hitting force of top-calibre people. We try to maintain a balance of experienced elder statesmen and younger high-powered line people. A great deal of our engineering management effort is devoted to training our engineers through job rotation, actual classwork, and progressive responsibility techniques.

Out of 159 engineering personnel, 97 changed jobs in the last two years. We're very proud of our engineers, both in terms of accomplishment and their capacity for work. We have 200 fewer people and 50 percent less floor space than any competitor with a comparable product line. However, our size has not limited our creativity."

A modicum of the creativity DeLorean was referring to showed up in the 1964 Pontiacs. The 1964 models were fundamentally carried over from 1963, with a facelift and a far greater number of options. The front end was made even bolder, with the headlight bezels integrated with the bumper. On the sides, the lower body sculpturing was coming in for greater attention.

With the 1964 models, Pontiac launched the Bonneville Brougham and the Catalina 2+2 as special options. On the senior series, the four-speed HydraMatic with hydraulic coupling was replaced by a new type of transmission that borrowed much from Buick's pioneer work on the Dynaflow, consisting of a torque converter with three-speed planetary gearing. HydraMatic executive Sherrod Skinner was named as the man whose support for the fluid coupling kept the torque converter out of HydraMatics for so long.

Pontiac built its nine-millionth car, a 1964 Catalina station wagon, on December 9, 1963. How did the sales go? Pontiac widened its lead over Oldsmobile and Buick in 1964 with total registrations of 687,902

Bonneville convertible for 1964 came on the same 123-inch wheelbase as the Bonneville sedan, with an overall length of 220 inches. Coke-bottle shape is emerging visibly in door-to-rear-fender transition.

cars, boosting its market share to 8.5 percent and reaffirming its claim to the third spot. The total car market had gone to eight million units, and GM held forty-nine percent of it. Import penetration grew again to six percent.

With Catalina sales of 215,000 cars in 1964, Pontiac had a first-class runner that outsold the Chevrolet Biscayne and could approach the Bel Air for sheer numbers, while leading the best-selling series of Buick and Oldsmobile by comfortable margins. The big Mercury was outdistanced, and the big Dodge was completely outclassed.

Now an intermediate, the Tempest's sales performance suddenly put it third in its class behind the Fairlane and Chevelle, and its popularity was high enough to beat all compacts except the Falcon! Tempest sales picked up tremendously in 1964, with deliveries of over 240,000 cars (including 15,000 station wagons), raising its share of Pontiac's total to thirty-five percent. The 1964 Tempest was a brilliant case of Pontiac being ready with the right car at the right time. With the growing prosperity of American consumers came a new emphasis on upward mobility in the car market.

General Motors reacted swiftly to Ford's intermediate-size Fairlane, introduced as a 1962 model to fill the gap between the compact Falcon and the full-size Galaxie, and began preparing a whole family of intermediates on a 115-inch wheelbase. But there was a big difference in marketing strategies between Ford and General Motors.

While Ford kept the Falcon in production for a decade, General Motors replaced all its compacts (with the exception of the low-volume Corvair) with intermediates that inherited their model names from the compacts.

As had been the case with the X-100, the 1964-model intermediates were not divisional projects but came out of a corporation-wide program. In contrast with the unit-construction compacts, the new intermediates were to have separate frame construction, and Fisher was to produce an all-new A-body to be shared by Buick, Oldsmobile, Pontiac—and Chevrolet.

Jack Humbert's styling for the Tempest was patterned on the Catalina theme, with a split grille carrying the same basic motif as the front-end design of the senior series. Side-by-side dual headlights were mounted at the outer edges of the grille, as in the 1961–62 full-size cars.

While the compact Tempest had used plain glass for the side windows, the new A-body had curved side glass, which enabled the designers to form a smoother transition from doors and side panels to the roof sections. In side view, the first intermediate Tempest was quite neutral, to the extent of almost lacking an overall theme. Front

Styling mockup for the 1964 B-body car shows alternative front ends with different grille and headlight treatment for visual evaluation. Right-hand side won, but underwent further modification.

Catalina two-door hardtop for 1964 was built on a 120-inch wheelbase and the body sides were developing more pronounced sculpturing. Catalina power options ranged from 230 to 270 hp. Lowest-priced Catalina was listed at $2,735.

overhang was very short, and rear overhang quite long. The body had a straight beltline, and a horizontal accent line stretching from the front wheel opening to the taillights, about twelve inches up from the doorsill molding. Wheel openings were slightly pear-shaped, providing a little extra air aft of the wheels, between the tires and the sheet metal.

The 1964 lineup included the plain Tempest, Tempest Custom and Tempest LeMans. The hardtop was available only as a LeMans. Five body styles were offered: four-door sedan, two-door coupe, two-door hardtop, convertible and station wagon. Tempest prices went up with the growth in car size, starting at $2,259 for the two-door six.

Yes, Pontiac had discontinued the slant-four and brought out a six. The slant-four as it existed in 1963 delivered insufficient power for the new and bigger car coming for 1964. It could perhaps have been enlarged enough to cope with the greater weight of the new Tempest, but its other drawbacks were what killed it. Above all, it was roughness and vibration that made it so unsuitable for the intermediate Tempest.

The intermediates were designed with separate frame construction and open propeller shafts, eliminating the torque tube of the rope-shaft Tempest. In such an arrangement, the slant-four would have made impossible demands on the engine-mounting system. In addition, it was unreasonably heavy in relation to its displacement. As Russ Gee tells it: "After the rope-shaft Tempest went out, the engine could not be used for anything."

Mac McKellar began design work on a new six as soon as GM's top management made the decision to increase the size of the Tempest along with Buick's Special/Skylark and the Oldsmobile F-85 and Cutlass. But there wasn't enough time! He designed a lovely, very modern six with an overhead camshaft and a high performance potential, but it needed extra time for testing and development as well as new and special tooling. Consequently, during two model years (1964 and 1965) the division's second-string models used another six, which was assembled by Pontiac, but mainly from Chevrolet parts. Pontiac did some machining and produced some parts, but it was really a Chevrolet engine, with overhead valves using that division's pushrod and rocker arm system.

It was heavy (635 pounds!) and sturdy. Breathing through a single-barrel carburetor, with conservative valve timing, it was developed for high torque at very low speed, and modest maximum rpm, so that it was always running understressed and with a promise of very long life indeed. But Russ Gee described it as "a bad, ratty, cream-vanilla engine with no sex appeal." As a performance option for the Tempest, Pontiac continued its 326-cubic-inch V-8. Buyers paid $108 extra for the V-8. Most Tempest buyers chose V-8 engines. Less than one in four Tempests came equipped with the baseline six in 1964.

The standard transmission for both sixes and V-8 Tempests was a three-speed column shift with non-synchromesh first gear. A four-speed all-synchromesh floorshift transmission was optional with the V-8. For buyers who wanted automatic drive, Pontiac had a new two-speed HydraMatic available with the V-8 power unit. It was a simplified and lighter transmission than the HydraMatic used in the senior series, with air-cooling instead of water-cooling, and mechanical

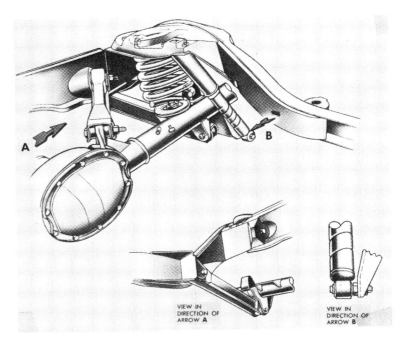

down-gearing in one instead of two steps. Six-cylinder cars with automatic drive used the HydraMatic 61-05 that had been developed for the compacts.

Ed Windeler held responsibility for the whole power train, from engines and transmissions to axles and wheels. Suspension systems, steering and brakes were engineered by a group headed by Mark Garlick, a Pontiac old-timer with young ideas.

He was born in Kansas City, Missouri, in 1905, and educated at schools in Dallas, Kansas City and St. Louis. While attending the University of Michigan he worked summers at the GM proving grounds at Milford. He graduated in 1928 and joined Oakland Motor Car Company as a service representative. In 1931 he was transferred to the technical data section of the Pontiac engineering staff, and advanced to development engineer in 1937. He was named project engineer in 1942. Garlick was promoted to experimental engineer in 1950 and assistant chief engineer in 1954. On March 1, 1958, he became executive engineer for experimental, production, and field engineering. DeLorean placed him in charge of chassis engineering.

He was not given too much freedom. For cost reasons, Pontiac could not scale up the independent rear suspension from the 1963 Tempest, but instead had to use a rigid rear axle with a coil-spring suspension system that was derived from the Catalina/Bonneville. The front suspension was a Chevrolet design, with A-arms and coil springs, based on the Impala's. A young engineer named James Lagergren

With the switch from compact to intermediate size for 1964, the Tempest went from unit body construction to a perimeter frame without cross-bracing. It had low torsional rigidity; in fact, the body shell was what contributed structural stiffness to the car.

Four-link rear suspension for the 1964 Tempest used coil springs tilted forward at the top, and splayed shock absorbers anchored as close as possible to the wheels.

played a big role in the development of the 1964 Tempest. His job was to adapt the new A-body to Pontiac's frame, and vice versa.

While the full-size Pontiacs were built on frames made in Milwaukee by A. O. Smith, Estes and DeLorean decided that Pontiac should produce its own frames for the Tempest. If the intention was to raise the division's profitability by manufacturing a higher proportion of basic components, it backfired. Bob Knickerbocker recalls: "We built the best damn frame in the world—and we lost our shirt doing it."

The 1965 Catalina was said by some critics to be a whole styling generation ahead of its competition. It was indeed a remarkable car by virtue of its exterior appearance, though its engineering was in no way backward. John DeLorean, right, became general manager of Pontiac in 1965 after nine years with the division, including four as chief engineer. He left Pontiac in 1969 to take over the top post at Chevrolet.

Parallel with the development of the 1964 Tempest, Pontiac engineers had undertaken a major effort to prepare totally new senior-series 1965 models. This was part of a closely coordinated corporation-wide scheme. Much of the planning and development work was carried out jointly with the other divisions, each one specializing in one or two areas and sharing the results in order to cut development costs. There was little interdivisional engineering coordination until 1962. Relations became closer when work began on the new B- and C-body cars for 1965.

In 1964 General Motors split up certain engineering functions among the car divisions to avoid duplication of effort. Pontiac was placed in charge of rear suspension design, and was also given responsibility for carburetion jointly with Rochester Products Division. Air conditioning, too, fell to Pontiac, with an assist from Harrison and Frigidaire. Chevrolet was given responsibility for front suspension, Buick for brakes, Cadillac for driver visibility and Oldsmobile for steering.

"Harry Barr—or the guy before him—down at the Tech Center doled that stuff out, and a lot of it didn't make sense," said a former Pontiac engineer, now in retirement. For the time being, each division retained full control over its engine design, development and manufacturing.

A new cylinder head had been developed for the production-type 421-cubic-inch V–8 (no longer Super Duty) that became optional in 1964. This head was made standard for all Pontiac V–8's the following year. Its key features were larger valves, with a 1.92-inch intake valve head diameter and 1.66-inch exhaust valve head diameter. Ports were enlarged to take full advantage of the increased valve area, and the intake manifold was opened up to permit a corresponding increase in the air-flow mass.

The 1965-model full-size Pontiacs had new frames and bodies, new front and rear suspension, new steering gear and linkage. And the power train had come in for considerable refinement.

Some designs had originated at other divisions and had to be adapted to the Pontiac. Other components and systems were pure Pontiac developments. With so much new at the same time, it is very easy for things to go wrong. Nevertheless, the 1965 Pontiac engineering was cohesive, and the product impressed one as representing the end result of long breeding, with its separate entities well matched to each other and creating a balanced whole.

This is seen as largely due to the experience and skill of another Pontiac old-timer, John P. Charles, who had held the title of executive assistant chief engineer since November 1961. Charles had been on Pontiac's engineering staff since January 1928. He had two years' experience from working as a project engineer on the GM proving grounds at Milford, Michigan, where he went after graduating from Purdue University. A born Hoosier from Mount Auburn, Indiana, he

First mockup for the 1965 Pontiac dates from July 1961. A year later the Venturi or Coke-bottle profile took firm shape. The doorsill treatment is particularly interesting.

Two-door coupe on 1965 Bonneville chassis had a spectacular profile, with its long 124-inch wheelbase and 221.7-inch overall length. Standard engine was a 389-cubic-inch V-8 rated at 333 hp at 5000 rpm. Turbo-HydraMatic was an extra-cost option at $231.

Clay model for the 1965 Bonneville is contrasted with the final product. Pointed nose was later used for Grand Prix. Stacked headlights, dating from 1963, went out in 1967.

was then twenty-five years old. After a wide variety of engineering assignments, he was named assistant chief engineer to Delaney in 1951.

In every way, the 1965 models were bristling with the kind of creativity John DeLorean had been talking about. The new B-body concept had been laid down as early as October 1961, and GM's divisional styling studios went to work with the same unalterable basis, each intent on achieving its own look. In the Pontiac studio, Jack Humbert and his assistants made sketches and clay models showing various new ideas. Some of the most promising themes and shapes were selected for three full-scale clay models made early in 1962. These served to fix actual dimensions and to produce surface drawings for all models—sedan, coupe, convertible and station wagon. The final design process was the fiberglass model, finished inside and out in complete detail and hard to tell apart from a finished automobile.

Now began the work of coordinating the new body with engineering, as every detail in the design from bumpers to windshields to carpeting, item by item, had to meet the calculated price and fit into the production apparatus. Steve Malone was mainly responsible

for directing this work in his capacity as assistant chief engineer for body and styling. The collaboration with Fisher Body Division was handled by Joe Whitesall, now chief engineer of GM-Holden's in Australia, who also directed the Pontiac body engineering design work carried out by R. D. Chrisman, chief body draftsman; H. E. Kadau, styling engineer; and A. N. Gray, body development engineer. The

The 1965 Tempest was built on a 115-inch wheelbase and had a typical Pontiac look despite only very symbolic signs of the Coke-bottle shape, such as the convergence of the dual beltline into one aft of the B-post.

liaison with the power train and chassis engineering groups was handled by James Lagergren.

One day in August 1963, the 1965 models were shown to the GM board of directors for the final approval. Only at that moment could tooling orders go out. "We are constantly at work on means to reduce our tooling lead times," said John DeLorean in an *Automotive Industries* article. "Obviously, the longer we can defer a styling decision, the better feel we have of the marketability of the current products, both ours and our competitors'."

The 1965 Pontiacs were just spectacular. They looked fantastic, and they looked right. In side view, the 1965 Pontiac had a decidedly aggressive profile. The front fenders ran straight forward, and gave the impression of leaning forward of the bumpers, so that the car looked poised for takeoff. The gutter line, which had emerged as a strong styling element as early as 1962, became the dominant accent line along the side view.

A sizeable but smooth kickup in the beltline at the start of the rear fender conveyed the idea of power, acceleration and speed. Vertical louvers in the front fender, just aft of the wheel opening, evoked the racing image that Pontiac sought to preserve despite having withdrawn from the sport two years earlier. The front end showed how a drastic change could be made in an evolutionary pattern over the course of a few years.

The 1965 Bonneville had a split grille with painted sheet metal separating the two grille elements which were strictly horizontal. The grille frames included a central horizontal divider. The bumper face had a flat top and did not intrude at all on the grille. The overall impression was one of extremely clean lines. Stacked headlamps in overlapping circular bezels formed the fender heads and ended the grille on both sides. The hood had a slight bulge, tapering from a wide base at the cowl to a small bulb above the grille. A V-shaped emblem was attached to the painted sheet metal in the center, and the letters BONNEVILLE appeared on the left forward edge of the hood. Stainless steel plates covered the Bonneville's lower body panels, which were tilted inward at the bottom, giving a kind of 'gutter' effect.

A former GM styling man, Robert Cumberford, discussed the exterior design of the Catalina in the 1965 *Car and Driver Yearbook* and found it "one full styling wave ahead" of the competition: "The extruded look is gone, replaced by some very graceful shaping of sheet metal forms. All the elements are as before, and the derivation of the '65 from the '64 Pontiac is clear to the dullest eye. But what a difference! There are some gimmicks and tricks, of course—there are on all GM cars that reach production—but some of the trickery is very clever and is going to sell a great many Pontiacs. A good example is the severe outward flare toward the bottom of the body. When you look at the car, you think the body has stopped where the flare turns back under. Result: a car that looks six inches lower than its competitors."

At the same time, the Tempest styling was becoming more assertive. In side view, the 1965 Tempest was much crisper than its predecessor. Front overhang was increased, and the rocker panel and door sheet metal were acutely pulled under to meet a narrower doorsill line, emphasizing the lowness of the body. A new front with stacked headlights and a squared-off split grille of very aggressive aspect made the car look wider and heavier. Also, the hardtop coupe, previously sold only with the LeMans label, was extended to the basic Tempest line for 1965.

These were the cars that John DeLorean had to sell when he became general manager. Pete Estes had launched them before leaving to become boss of Chevrolet.

In 1965 GM regained a full fifty percent of the car market, and Pontiac increased its share to 8.93 percent. Its lead over Buick and Oldsmobile grew to about a quarter of a million cars. The Tempest overtook the Ford Fairlane and was second in the intermediate field, close behind the Chevelle. Chevelle sales were around 350,000; Tempest about 315,000; and Fairlane 227,000. The compacts were on

the wane, for now the Tempest outsold even the Falcon. The planners at Pontiac congratulated each other for having spotted a trend and exploiting it.

Bottlenecks in the production apparatus were becoming obvious. In 1965 three new building projects were completed. They included an addition to the foundry and a new finishing room, plus a spare parts warehouse. Altogether they added about a million and a half square feet to Pontiac's home production facilities.

DeLorean built a new engine plant in 1966 and increased production capacity in the Pontiac home plant. But when more cars are built, quality problems usually follow. To forestall this danger, DeLorean had started his Zero Defects program in 1965, in order to build quality-consciousness among the workers more than for exterior publicity, and made some changes in the manufacturing setup. The responsibility for formulating and implementing the Zero Defects program fell to H.A.C. Anderson. Born in Newport, Rhode Island, in 1913, he had joined Pontiac in 1949 in the sales department and since 1960 he was Pontiac's director of reliability.

Pontiac Motor Division was responsible for the quality of all the cars built at its own plants in Pontiac, while the corporation acted as a competitor with Pontiacs assembled under GM's auspices, in 1965, at Fremont and South Gate, California; Arlington, Texas; Atlanta; Kansas City, Kansas; Linden, New Jersey; and Baltimore.

There was a continuous comparison being made on a warranty-cost basis between the cars assembled by the corporation and those actually built by Pontiac. The actual figures are closely guarded secrets, but it was said in the industry that Pontiac-assembled cars dropped behind in quality in the years 1962–64 and began to pull even in 1967. A good deal of the credit for this recovery must go to F. James McDonald, who had replaced Buel E. Starr as works manager when

Starr retired. Starr had served as works manager since 1961 after a long career at Pontiac that started when he joined Oakland in 1927. But recovery must also be credited to John F. Blamy, who had been named general manufacturing manager of Pontiac in August 1964. Blamy had left Whitman, Massachusetts, where he was born in 1912, to attend the GM Institute in Detroit, and joined Pontiac in 1934 in the standards department. He was promoted to director of manufacturing in 1967, and D. Robert Bell was then named general manufacturing manager of Pontiac. Born in Lafayette, Indiana, in 1916, Bell had joined Chevrolet at the Detroit gear and axle plant in 1938, and transferred to Pontiac later.

A high proportion of the intermediate Tempests were assembled at the Pontiac home phant, and the rest in the B-O-P Assembly Division's facilities around the nation. Beginning with the 1964 Chevelle, Chevrolet cars were added to the B-O-P program and in 1965 the division was renamed GM Assembly Division. Two years later it took over the first of Chevrolet's regional assembly plants, a large facility at Framingham, Massachusetts. This served Pontiac in providing a New England production center.

On the sales front, Thomas L. King succeeded E. R. Pettengill as general sales manager of Pontiac in 1966. (Frank Bridge had retired in 1964.) Born in Kingstree, South Carolina, in 1910, King had graduated from Wofford College and joined Pontiac in 1946 as a district manager.

Richard Y. Case of Uniroyal developed the camshaft drive-belt for Pontiac. It is made of rubber but reinforced with fiberglass to prevent stretching. Sprockets are cogged to match the belt.

With drive-belt cover removed, the cogged belt is visible. Sectioned camshaft cover bares cams and bearings. Carburetor is cut away to show primary and secondary throats in four-barrel edition. Stylized camshaft cover and drive-belt cover were common for both versions of the overhead-camshaft engine. The four-barrel-carburetor version also had a chrome-plated low-profile air clean-e.. The seven-bearing crankshaft was Chevrolet, otherwise the engine was pure Pontiac.

In the late summer of 1965 Pontiac switched from making the Chevy-based six to its own more advanced six-cylinder engine. It became standard in the 1966 intermediates. "Our overhead-camshaft engine was developed as a—not exotic—but successful European type without the romance of a twin-cam," said Russell F. Gee. "The original design came out of an advanced design group which at the time was headed by John DeLorean," explained Mac McKellar, "and then it was put into my area for development, and I redesigned it for production."

McKellar is a round-faced, crew-cut, soft-spoken individual of medium height. He is almost self-effacing in his modesty and reluctance to take credit for his engineering accomplishments. But at the same time he has the quiet assurance of one who is cocksure of what he's talking about, and he never hesitates in answering a technical question.

He made a careful analysis of Pontiac's objectives and the means of attaining them, and concluded that an overhead camshaft was essential to success. The reason was that elimination of the pushrods and rocker arms, obtained by moving the camshaft to the top of the cylinder head, would give higher horsepower at higher rpm without loss in

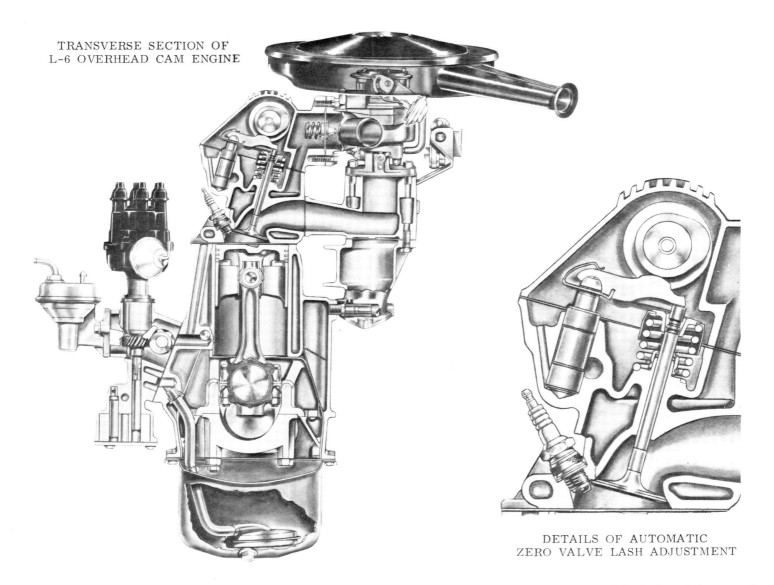

TRANSVERSE SECTION OF
L-6 OVERHEAD CAM ENGINE

DETAILS OF AUTOMATIC
ZERO VALVE LASH ADJUSTMENT

Cross section of Pontiac's overhead-camshaft six shows tall, narrow structure
and neat arrangement of accessory drive and mounting. Detail at right gives
close-up view of valve gear and wedge-type combustion chamber.

Tempest lineup for 1966 included this four-door station wagon, using the sedan's 115-inch wheelbase, with a single, fixed side glass pane aft of the doors. Tailgate was one-piece 'platform' type. A 326-cubic-inch V-8 was optional, overhead-cam six standard.

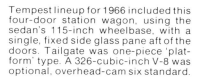

Full-size clay model for the 1967 Catalina shows uncertainty about the side sculpturing and hesitation in the backlight treatment. Production model was much sharper in all respects.

low- or medium-speed torque, and without loss of smooth idle characteristics.

The play, flexing and lost motion associated with pushrod and rocker arm types of valve gear, plus the inertia loads of the moving parts in the system, imposed limits on camshaft design and engine performance, which the overhead camshaft would get around.

Design goals included a quiet, positive, reliable camshaft drive, and a valve train to include automatic, hydraulic zero-lash adjusters. Out of these stipulations came the cogged belt drive and the finger-type cam follower arrangement.

In contrast with the crossflow head of the V-8 engines, the six was designed with intake and exhaust ports on the same side. All valves

were arranged in a side-by-side pattern, inclined fifteen degrees from vertical, away from the spark plugs, giving a very compact combustion space.

Compared with the Chevelle engine, the overhead-cam Pontiac valve gear was forty-five percent lighter, while the effective inertia at the valve was reduced by twenty-seven percent. Maximum valve lift was increased from 0.333 inch to 0.4 inch, and the valve event duration was shortened from 126 to 114 camshaft degrees. Valve overlap was reduced from thirty-eight to fourteen degrees.

Contrary to Pontiac's claims, it was not the first U.S.-made overhead-cam six, for Wills Sainte Claire had one in 1926. That was a 273-cubic-inch design with vertical shaft and bevel gear drive to the camshaft (a typical World War I aircraft engine design feature) and splayed valves above hemispherical combustion chambers, each row of valves having a set of rocker arms whose inner ends bore against the cams on the centrally located camshaft.

Pontiac was first in the U.S. with a belt-driven camshaft, but not first in the world, for the sixty-cubic-inch four-cylinder engine of the

Ventura was an optional hardtop in the Catalina series for 1967. Grille was combined with bumper, and windshield wipers were concealed under the hood lip.

A 400-cubic-inch V-8 became standard in the Catalina for 1967. It was derived from the famous 389 and was destined for a 12-year production life.

German-made Glas 1004-S coupe used one in 1963. What Pontiac *was* first with was the combination of hydraulic zero-lash adjusters with an overhead camshaft.

These adjusters were located in the side of the camshaft cover. Their internal design was very similar to the hydraulic valve lifter of Pontiac's V-8 engine. Its plunger served as a mounting base for the finger follower, which was secured by a spring steel clip. The follower had a milled groove for the valve stem tip, so that no lateral movement was possible, keeping the follower completely stable without the aid of the camshaft.

Fully machined, contoured wedge-type combustion chambers, patterned on the Pontiac V-8 design, were incorporated in the cylinder head. Pistons were flat-topped except for an indentation to prevent contact with the valve heads.

The cylinder bores were spaced at 4.4 inches, which provided ample room for efficient porting. Intake valve heads had a diameter of 1.92 inches, while exhaust valve heads measured 1.6 inches across. The neoprene camshaft drivebelt had a fiberglass tension member which prevented any stretch and eliminated the need for a tensioner, such as was commonly used with chain drives. It also needed no lubrication, made no noise and showed no wear.

Early experiments centered on high-carbon steel cable reinforcement, which worked well except for corrosion problems. They were cured by going to stainless steel, which in turn ran into fatigue failures before 100,000 miles. In the end, fiberglass proved best in this application.

The nodular-iron crankshaft—the only part in the whole power unit that was not made by Pontiac but came from Chevrolet—ran in seven main bearings of 2.3-inch diameter, with two-inch crankpins. With a 3.25-inch stroke, that provided a very generous overlap of 0.525 inch.

Two versions of the 230-cubic-inch engine were built, one with low compression (8.5:1—for regular fuel) and a single-barrel carburetor. The other had high compression (10.5:1—needing premium fuel) and a four-barrel carburetor. The intake manifold for the one-barrel setup had siamesed ducts, two direct ones to the center pair and twin extensions to the front and rear pairs, while the four-barrel manifold had separate headers to each port.

The base engine had a standard exhaust manifold, while the four-barrel unit had a more efficient dual-outlet exhaust system. The four-barrel engine also had a different camshaft, with increased overlap. It developed peak power at 5200 rpm, 10.6 percent higher speed than the base engine, and its output, 207 SAE gross hp was 25.5 percent higher.

The six was installed in twenty-four percent of 1966 Tempests and 21.5 percent of Tempests made in the 1967 model year. People preferred the V-8, though the four-barrel high-compression six was nearly as good in performance and far more economical. The 1967 Tempest with the optional 207 hp six-cylinder engine would go from standstill to sixty miles per hour in nine seconds flat and cover the standing quarter-mile in 16.5 seconds at a terminal speed of eighty-four miles per hour. On the road, the six-cylinder Tempest would get twenty miles per gallon easily, even when driven briskly.

The engine was enlarged to 250-cubic-inch displacement for 1968. The overhead-camshaft six was used in Pontiac Tempest, Firebird and LeMans through the 1972 model year. Then Pontiac began to install the pushrod-overhead-valve six made by Chevrolet. The overhead-cam six was simply taken out of production. Chevrolet had done the same with its pushrod six, and since Pontiac was using the Chevrolet crankshaft, the change was almost mandatory.

"It was a pretty good engine," says Russ Gee, "but costly to build. It was too expensive to build, because of the small quantity we made. The belt drive never gave any trouble. But the overhead camshaft never helped sales. The timing was wrong. It came too soon." What he meant is that its balance of economy and performance made no difference in the market of the late sixties, but would have made a lot of difference in the fuel-saving-conscious world of 1973/74.

Pontiac had only one car line when DeLorean joined the division—the full-size models. The secondary car line—Tempest—was mainly his own creation. During his reign as general manager a third line was added, the Firebird. He changed the Grand Prix from a giant float with muscle to a magnificent road car. And the Tempest, which had grown to intermediate size in the meantime, sprouted an offshoot that became famous as the GTO.

One cannot get a proper picture of how Pontiac evolved under DeLorean's command unless these cars and the public reaction to them are examined and understood. Consequently, we must interrupt the chronological review of the division's fateful way through the sixties and devote our attention to some of its most distinctive products.

Front end of the 1968-model Executive broke with recent trends and started a new series that was never allowed to evolve in a logical pattern but zigzagged wildly from shades of Edsel to Olds and Buick grilles.

CHAPTER 11

GTO:Gran Turismo Omologato

O**F ALL THE CARS** John DeLorean was responsible for, none has been covered in greater glory than the GTO. That car has been described as a Tempest with a Bonneville engine, and that gives one an idea that is at the same time right and wrong. It is right, because the GTO vehicle belonged in the Tempest series, and its engine was basically the same unit that was standard in the contemporary Bonneville. And yet it is wrong, because the GTO was, of course, far more than an engine swap for the Tempest.

It was a carefully developed car, with heavy-duty suspension as standard (and extra-heavy-duty suspension as an option), heavy-duty brakes and fast-ratio power steering. It had its own sports-type steering wheel and special instrumentation including a large tachometer. It had front bucket seats and a four-speed floorshift as standard. Early cars used a Warner T-10 transmission, before Chevrolet built up capacity at its Muncie transmission plant to supply four-speed all-synchromesh gearboxes to all GM divisions that wanted them. Then Pontiac used the 'Muncie' box for the GTO. Pontiac had its own shift linkage as standard, with the Hurst dragstrip-type shifter as an option. The clutch was also a heavy-duty mechanism, dimensioned to withstand the stress of drivers popping the clutch at 5000 rpm and laying rubber for fifty to sixty feet on dry pavement. But it was not just a dragster. The chassis also offered some measure of sports-car handling, so that it was a formidable road car.

The GTO engine even had its differences from the standard Bonneville 389-cubic-inch V-8. The cylinder heads for the Bonneville power plant had a 1.88-inch intake valve head diameter and a 1.60-inch exhaust valve head diameter. But the GTO version of the 389 had the heads from the 421-cubic-inch V-8, which had larger valves, intake valve heads measuring 1.92 inches and exhaust valve heads 1.76 inches across.

The GTO first appeared in 1964. Was it an offshoot of the racing program, or a merchandising gimmick? Again, the answer is neither, though there is some truth to both.

"I had the idea for the car," says Jim Wangers. He had been working at Pontiac's advertising agency, MacManus, John and Adams, since September 1958. He also had a background as a successful drag-strip racer. Jim Wangers started his automotive career in 1952 as a member of the Kaiser-Frazer advertising department. He joined Campbell-Ewald in 1956, to work on the Chevrolet account, but left within a year to take a job with Chrysler Corporation as assistant sales promotion manager of Plymouth. In 1958 he moved again, this time to Pontiac's advertising agency (which later became D'Arcy-MacManus and Masius).

As Wangers sees it, the GTO was the answer to a marketing problem: "We were still in the middle of trying to build image for the Pontiac car line itself and for the maker itself as a builder of pretty

The GTO was introduced as a Tempest LeMans option for 1965, combining the Bonneville engine with the intermediate A-body car. It became the pacesetter for Pontiac's growth in the sixties.

sophisticated, kind of specialized machines that were well worth the extra dollars above the Chevrolet," Wangers recounts.

"And a kind of image that would live somewhere in-between that low-priced Chevrolet and the so-called accepted image that Oldsmobile had—something like the 'gentleman's hot-rod.' That's a difficult niche," Wangers went on. It became even more difficult, for in December 1962, the corporation told Pontiac to get out of racing. "The order came from Jim Roche himself," said Wangers: "This time we mean it. We'll not just play games and watch you go under the table. We know all the tricks you've been pulling. Not only do we want you out, but we want you to sell all your inventory!"

That was the message—not verbatim as it came from the GM chairman, but in the rough-and-tumble vernacular of the racing crowd. That message put Pontiac face to face with two urgent needs: first to stop racing, and second, to preserve its racing image.

Bill Collins, who headed an advanced engineering group at the time, makes no bones about it: "We snuck in with some fairly hot Tempests before the GTO, with the 326 V-8, and then a dozen to sixteen super-duper models that we built in the 1963 model year. That summer (1963) John and Pete were both big on having Saturday rides at the proving grounds. They spent a lot of time trying out next year's cars. I was there, and we had a 1964 LeMans coupe on the hoist.

"It occurred to me that if we moved the wheels back—an inch roughly—that car would qualify for NASCAR racing. So we tried to see how we could do that, but it didn't work out very well. In the back of my mind also was the fact that the base engine was the 326. And

121

Special instrumentation, bucket seats, console-shift automatic transmission (or four-speed floorshift) were GTO hallmarks.

GTO convertible for 1965 was distinguished from the LeMans by a hood scoop, identification letters in the left-side grille element, and special wheels and tires.

externally, the 326 was identical to the 389 which meant we could put a 389 in it."

Collins went on: "So that's really kind of where and how the GTO was born. Then John came in the following Monday and said 'let's call it the GTO.' Then we got into development of a car that to my mind was not a Woodward Avenue dragster; my objective was to try and come up with a car based on what we have in this country and make it handle and have the performance of a good European car."

There is an apparent contradiction here. Wangers is saying he had the idea for the car six months after Collins says it had been brought into existence. They are talking about the same GTO, but in different contexts. For Collins, it was the hardware combination, and for Wangers it was the marketing concept. DeLorean gets credit for the name. No doubt Wangers had a part in that (the two often met privately on weekends).

Looking for an exotic name for Pontiac's newest high-performance car, they picked a label that was intended to convey the idea that here was a car to rival the Ferrari. There was a Ferrari that became known as the GTO, but it was never an official Ferrari model designation. The car was really a 1961-model 250 GT Berlinetta. And why was it called GTO? It was a misunderstanding. Ferrari entered one in a Grand Touring race, and on the entry form put an 'O' further along on the line that stated make and type, to indicate 'Omologato' for homologated (which is racing lingo for registered, recognized, approved) so as to confirm that the car indeed belonged in a GT race. The race organizers who didn't grasp the meaning of the O tacked it onto the GT when they printed the program, and race reports all over the world talked about the new Ferrari GTO. It was a consistent winner in its class and, to racing fans, the letters GTO spelled Ferrari. But the Italian manufacturer never used it on a car, and never copyrighted it. The GTO name was in the public domain until Pontiac snapped it up.

One of the direct predecessors to the GTO in Pontiac's stable was the 1964 LeMans with the HO (for High Output) option. It was one of those 'hot Tempests' Bill Collins had referred to. The HO option included a four-barrel Carter carburetor and ran with a 10.25:1 compression ratio, Pontiac claiming 280 SAE gross hp at 4800 rpm and

355 pounds-feet of torque at 3200 rpm. That corresponds to 0.86 hp per cubic inch, which was very high at a time when no American production engine had yet reached the magical 1:1 ratio between horsepower and cubic inches.

The 1964 *Car and Driver Yearbook* had a report by Jan P. Norbye on the Tempest LeMans V-8 HO. The test car was equipped with the new Chevrolet Muncie four-on-the-floor transmission, but the LeMans linkage was found unsatisfactory. The gear ratios were well enough spaced. First gear took the car just short of 50 mph. It ran to 65 mph in second and to 83 mph in third. Top speed was estimated at 122 mph. Its 3.36:1 final drive ratio had been selected for performance and not fuel economy, which could be as poor as 12 mpg. But the car was a real goer, for the report stated it could accelerate from standstill to 100 mph in nineteen seconds flat, while covering the standing-start quarter-mile in 16.3 seconds with a terminal speed of 92 mph.

Just like the Catalina of the same period, the LeMans was stable, with basic understeer. Ride comfort was considerably improved, with softer springs to accompany the change from fifteen-inch to fourteen-inch wheels. The car was decidedly front-heavy, carrying 56.5 percent of its 3,232-pound curb weight on the front wheels.

The car had some wheelspin problems, and the 7.00-14 Uniroyal Tiger Paws were less than satisfactory on curves. Norbye's report stated "body roll is restricted, and tire squeal sets in well before the roll angle becomes objectionable—a fact which is as much due to the properties of the tires as to the roll resistance of the car." But the report also pointed out that the tires gave a feeling of greater (than with standard equipment) security during braking.

The HO option for the LeMans did more than provide a starting point for the GTO. It showed up the worst inadequacies of the basic chassis, and consequently, pointed the way for the most-needed modifications when a 389-cubic-inch V-8 was put into the car. They were made, and they were made fast.

From the first, the GTO prototypes impressed everyone. The next question was how to build a market for it. And even the first one could not be sold without cheating. The corporation had laid down a rule that said "nothing bigger than 330-cubic-inch displacement in intermediate cars." This applied to all divisions. And here Pontiac sat with a whopping 389-cubic-inch V-8 in the Tempest! Would this marvelous car be condemned to death while still in the prototype stage? One solution would be to use the GTO chassis with a super-tuned 326-cubic-inch V-8. But even that would just not be a GTO.

Both Estes and DeLorean balked at open insurrection. Their very jobs were at stake if they did not heed corporate orders. Then one

day, as Bill Collins recalls it, someone said: "We think we've got a way around it. Let's *not* make it a model." All looked quizzical. "Say it's an option. When the customer goes down the line through the order form, there is this GTO option. What you've got to buy is a LeMans. That way you don't have to clear with the corporation. It's not a catalogued model. Give it a model name and a number—then you've got a problem. But if it's an option, you can get it out and get distribution on it before the corporation finds out about it—and then they'd have a hard time stopping it." Estes took a deep breath and said: "Let's do it."

"As you know, that GTO just went to the moon," Jim Wangers smiled at the memory. But things did not always run smoothly. "Frank Bridge was getting on, and said no way did he want anything to do with it. That led to a split between DeLorean and Bridge. Estes acted as a sort of mediator and finally got Bridge to take 5,000 cars. They sold 31,000 that first year—could have sold 62,000," said Wangers.

"Those cars—our performance cars—they were the ones that were selling the Bonnevilles and the Catalinas and the LeMans. The whole thing was running on the strength of the GTO. A LeMans looked just like it, except it had no hood scoops and it had a 350 in it instead of 400. When a guy saw it in the showroom—two minutes later he was driving it—it was just what he wanted."

GTO's sold for street use were capable of quarter-mile times down to thirteen seconds, and could blow off a stock 327 Corvette. Zero-to-sixty mph acceleration was usually a matter of a mere six seconds. GTO's running on drag strips got down to 10.5 seconds for the quarter-mile. The GTO was the talk of Detroit, and the corporation relented its ban on big engines in intermediate cars. Before long, Oldsmobile had its 4-4-2 and Buick its Skylark GS (Gran Sport). Even Chevy brought out its Chevelle SS 396. But Pontiac's GTO had been the first in the field and it was recognized as the leader.

Jim Wangers summed it up: "GTO was the first really true, hot street-machine. It started in cold weather. It had an automatic choke, and it used hydraulic valve lifters, despite a rev limit as high as five-five. But the reality of that vehicle is far more significant than almost anybody has given it credit for. It was a social statement. It appealed to youth. It was something they could identify with. Car songs got popular at that time, starting with one called 'Lil GTO' by Ronnie and the Beach Boys."

The Tempest LeMans GTO was listed as a separate series in 1966. It was available as a two-door coupe, two-door hardtop and convertible. The coupe had a list price of $2,783 which made it an exceptional buy for an era when the whole industry went on a 'muscle car' kick—most

Restyled LeMans for 1966 provided new excitement for the GTO, now powered by a 400-cubic-inch V-8 metrically identified as a 6.5-Litre. Hurst-Shifter gear-change linkage was adopted.

makers set very high prices in order to milk that market for maximum profit right away, as if they knew it couldn't go on forever.

Pontiac began offering Tri-Power manifolds for the GTO in 1965, and the following year offered a new Ram-Air option for GTO's with Tri-Power engines. The Pontiac Ram-Air device had its beginnings at Royal Pontiac in 1964, when a GTO dragster was fitted with a forward-facing air intake on the right side of the hood, feeding air under the pressure of ram effect (caused by the car's speed) via three flexible hoses to a metal box plenum chamber covering the throats of the triple two-barrel carburetors. It was raced in 1965 and proved successful.

The production type Ram-Air for the '66 GTO was not the same as the racing prototype. Paradoxically, it did not have the benefit of any ram effect, because the hood scoop was so positioned that it could pick up only boundary layer air. However, it did admit cool air, thus assuring higher volumetric efficiency. The air cleaner was combined with a plenum chamber that covered the carburetor air horns and was sealed against the closed hood (and hot under-hood air) by thick gaskets made of foam rubber.

In appearance, the GTO went where the Tempest went, sharing the coupe and convertible body sheet metal and brightwork, with trim changes, special wheels, tires and identification markings. For 1966 the Tempest had a new look, though actual body changes were relatively inexpensive. The front remained basically the same, though the grille was widened towards the ends, giving it something of a bow-tie flavor. The bumper had a flat upper face, underlining the grille, and wrapped around the fender tips.

The Coke-bottle side treatment, inspired by the larger Pontiacs, was now conferred upon the Tempest. The front fender line swept downwards from the cowl, only to rise again as it approached the rear wheel opening. Wheel cutouts remained asymmetrical, coming down to a fairly flat lip above the tire and opening up behind it. For the 1966 models, Pontiac introduced four-door hardtops in the Tempest Custom and LeMans series.

The GTO was definitely playing a role in promoting sales of the Tempest and LeMans. Pontiac's intermediate kept up with the Chevelle in 1966, again leaving the Ford, Chrysler and American Motors rivals far behind. Aided by the overhead-camshaft engine, six-cylinder Tempest sales climbed from 60,000 in 1965 to 95,000 in 1966.

There was practically no styling change in the 1967 Tempest. The front end kept the same lines, and its most obvious mark of distinction was the fitting of a series of vertical bars inside the grille elements. The lower side-panel accent line was pulled down to near doorsill level, and the lower part of the sheet metal curved under as if to link up with the frame, while the beltline was sharpened for 1967 and given a Riviera-like treatment from the cowl back, stressing the wide stance.

Was it sporty? Luxury and convenience options did better than sports equipment. Bucket seat installations ran just over half of output. In 1967, seventy-seven percent of Tempest buyers specified and paid extra for an automatic transmission. About fifteen percent were willing to pay a similar price for four-on-the-floor while the standard three-on-the-tree synchromesh transmission was used on less than ten percent of the cars. Power brakes became optional on the 1967 Tempest, and over thirty percent of customers ordered them. Three out of every four Tempest buyers in 1967 specified power steering.

Tempest/LeMans sales declined from over 350,000 cars in the 1966 calendar year to just short of 280,000 cars in 1967. That's a twenty-percent drop. Still, it remained the second most popular intermediate, well ahead of the Ford Fairlane, surpassed only by the Chevelle. GTO sales, too, fell off after the first two years. What went wrong? Jim Wangers ascribes the decline to the new sales manager: "Tom King didn't understand the car. Tom was absolutely a detriment to the division. They didn't get a good, strong sales guy in there until after DeLorean left—the guy who is now running Cadillac, Ed Kennard."

The 1967 GTO came with a choice of power plants, from the 400- to the 455-cubic-inch V-8 engine. The larger one had completely new cylinder heads with greatly widened ports and enlarged valves. Intake valve head diameter was increased to 2.11 inches, with a corresponding figure of 1.77 inches for the exhausts.

New tunnel-port cylinder heads (so-called because of their rounded cross-section) became available during the 1968 model year, and came with a new intake manifold. Further progress, in the form of an additional ten-percent increase in sectional port area, was made for 1969. It is worthy of attention that the 400- and 455-cubic-inch Pontiac V-8's were not redesigned engines, but enlarged and refined versions of the original design, which speaks volumes for the soundness of the division's first V-8 engine.

A serious research effort on ram induction led to new developments for GTO's (and later, Firebirds). The Ram-Air II option was introduced in 1968 and featured dual air scoops on the hood, which resulted in getting some ram effect. This was replaced in 1969 by the Ram Air III version, which incorporated a two-way flap valve in the

GTO for 1967 continued without major changes. It became the most imitated car in the industry, not only from the other GM divisions, but also Ford, Chrysler and even AMC.

air scoop inlet, controlled from a knob on the dashboard. It gave the driver the possibility of closing the cool air entry and running on warm under-hood air whenever desired.

Despite its impressive power and performance, the GTO was also one of the more reliable of the muscle cars. Yet it had some problems. What were they? "Nothing unique," says Russ Gee, explaining: "When you do put out high-performance engines in the hands of the general public, there are some manufacturing processing and reliability controls that are very important to the success of the product. I'm not sure that we had any more problems than anybody else. But we had some. And we had to get on top of them quickly. They were mainly in the drivetrain, not particularly in the engine. The single biggest thing we saw in the field was probably oil pressure. We were concerned about that. We just continued to increase the oil pressure in those high-performance engines, from 30–40 to 50–60 psi, by changing pumps. The GTO engine was a development project that helped improve all Pontiac engines. It paid off even in our bread-and-butter power units, especially in a metallurgical way, and in the structure. The high oil pressure experiments resulted in a spinoff into mass production."

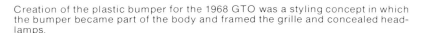
Creation of the plastic bumper for the 1968 GTO was a styling concept in which the bumper became part of the body and framed the grille and concealed headlamps.

Twin air scoops and hood-mounted tachometer were introduced on the 1968-model GTO, setting it apart from all other cars in the LeMans series. Wheelbase was shortened from 115 to 112 inches. Built as a two-door coupe and convertible only; concealed wipers were new that year.

For 1969 Pontiac offered a GTO model known as The Judge (from television's "Here come de judge"). It was made for high performance at a reasonable price, with visual distinction in its rear spoiler. But it failed in the market place.

While participation in organized racing was banned, there was no rule at General Motors to prevent Pontiac from demonstrating the power and speed of the GTO in the Union/Pure Oil Trials. This was a good opportunity, but there was also the temptation to use experimental parts for even better results. In 1967 the two GTO's were

the fastest in their class, by a suspiciously generous margin, and the NASCAR officials began to investigate. They found nonstandard cylinder heads and carburetion setups, and disqualified the GTO's. In the 1968 Union/Pure Oil Trials Pontiac was playing it straight. Results were not outstanding and full credibility was restored.

The 1968 GTO that ran in the Union/Pure Oil Trials accelerated from 25 to 70 mph in 6.85 seconds, which compares with 5.875 seconds for a hemi-head Plymouth GTX and 7.135 seconds for the Chevelle SS-396. Fuel economy of the 1968 GTO as tested in the Union/Pure Oil Trials was 15.9 miles per gallon. That compares with 13.5 for the Plymouth GTX that outdragged it, and 16.7 for the slower Chevelle.

The 1968 GTO was built on a shorter, 112-inch wheelbase, and its appearance was marked by greater distinction from the standard LeMans. DeLorean wanted to make it a style-leader as well as a performance leader. For instance, the 1968 GTO had a plastic front section which enclosed the two narrow sections of the split grille, while also serving as a bumper structure.

"Pontiac began to use plastic bumpers earlier than anybody else," says Jack Humbert. "Plastic bumpers are easy to work with for styling. You just model the shape and then they cast them. But in engineering they probably tore their hair out to make it work."

A hood-mounted tachometer, looking from the front and sides like a reverse air scoop in front of the driver, near the cowl, was first used as a GTO option in 1967, and became standard on the 1968 GTO.

For 1969 Pontiac offered a lower-priced version of the GTO. It was a hot car for straight-line acceleration, but lacked the roadholding and handling precision of the regular GTO. What was good about The Judge was the use of aerodynamic aids such as a front spoiler and a rear wing, although for most customers the effects of these items was less important than being able to display them. Also, the car carried its name (The Judge) in psychedelic lettering several places on the body. The true enthusiasts stayed away from The Judge, and the guys who bought it were usually regarded as flakes and dudes. The Judge was discontinued at the end of the 1970 model year.

A new power climax was reached by the Ram Air IV package, which was made optional for the 1969 GTO—including The Judge. Instead of using hood scoops, cool air was admitted to the air box around the carburetor throats from openings in the grille via two large-diameter flexible tubes. Manual open/close control was not provided, since this was almost a pure competition setup, with a special camshaft, rounded-off intake ports and exhaust manifold heads, and stiffer valve springs good for avoiding valve flutter right up to the engine's 6000-rpm red-line. In fact, some press reports claimed running it up to 6200 or 6250 rpm without trouble.

The Ram Air IV engine had standard-size valves (2.11-inch valve head diameter for intakes and 1.77 on exhausts) but new cylinder heads had round exhaust ports with thirty-six percent greater sectional area. The camshaft was the wildest yet released by Pontiac engineering, with its lift raised from 0.413 to 0.480 inches and overlap stretched from seventy-six to eighty-seven degrees. Intake opening duration was extended from 301 to 308 degrees, and exhaust opening duration from 313 to 320 degrees. This camshaft gave a notable increase in mid-range torque without hurting peak power.

Valve heads were hollowed out on the face, taking between three and six grams out of their weight, and reinforced pushrods, 1/32-inch thicker than standard, were adopted to prevent bending at high rpm.

Forged pistons replaced the former cast aluminum ones, saving about fifty grams per piston while gaining strength.

But Ram-Air IV was soon eclipsed by Ram-Air V, which became available as a 1969½ option for the GTO, GTO Judge and Trans Am Firebird. It featured the new tunnel-port cylinder heads and the McKellar No. 10 solid-lifter camshaft on the 400-cubic-inch block with beefed-up web areas and four-bolt main bearing caps. The pearlitic malleable cast iron crankshaft was replaced by a forged steel crankshaft that had cross-drilled main journals for better oil circulation. Connecting rods were new designs, evolved from the 421 Super Duty model with special bracing in the cap and beam areas. Pistons were forged aluminum, giving an 11.0:1 compression ratio, with cam-ground contours and tin-plated skirts.

Pontiac invented what were called wobble-ground pistons for the GTO engines. Cam-ground pistons were standard in most American V-8's by that time. Pontiac's idea was to use two cams rather than one, making the pistons (in plan view) more oval at the top but near-circular in the skirt area. The pistons come out flared, to avoid scuff when hot and slap when cold. Pontiac also found they did not require steel inserts to control thermal expansion, which kept them lighter.

All 1970 GTO engines had molybdenum-faced piston rings. The top compression ring was a reverse-twist, barrel-faced design with molybdenum filling, and the second one was similar except for being taper-faced. Two chrome-plated rails with slotted stainless steel expanders served as oil control rings.

For the Ram-Air V a single four-barrel Holley with a flow capacity of 800 cubic feet per minute replaced the Rochester Quadrajet used on previous versions.

New tunnel-port cylinder heads had fully machined combustion chambers. Valves were chrome-plated and hollow-stemmed. Valve head diameter was increased to 2.19 inches for the intakes and 1.77 inches for the exhausts. The cam had altered cam profiles but the same lift and duration was used for the Ram-Air IV (i.e., 0.520 lift and 308/320 degrees).

Before he left Pontiac, John DeLorean had helped bring into existence the hottest GTO yet, which went into production as a 1970 model. The 400-cubic-inch V-8 remained standard for the GTO, and the 455-cubic-inch engine was made optional. Some significant modifications were incorporated in the engines.

The Pontiac V-8 had always been a wedge-head design. For the 1970 the Pontiac engineers devised a new variation on the wedge. They called it the spherized wedge. The basic principle in this design was to undercut the chamber shape to unshroud the valve heads. It gave

1970

1970

For 1970 the GTO went to uncovered headlamps, with squared-off chrome bezels inset in the plastic bumper. Modesty panel provided extra air intake and mounting for parking lights.

The Judge was kept in the lineup for 1970, featuring special stripes on the fender accent lines, and continuing the rear-deck aerodynamic spoiler.

good breathing without abnormal combustion, and provided enough residence time and a closely defined temperature belt for the combustion to keep emission levels low.

With a 10.25:1 compression ratio and a single four-barrel carburetor, maximum power in the 455 was 360 hp at 4300 rpm. Torque went to 500 pounds-feet at 2700 rpm. With Ram-Air and 10.5:1 compression, this engine gave off 370 hp at 5500 rpm, while the torque curve was completely sacrificed, so that its peak fell to 445 pounds-feet at 3900 rpm.

The Ram-Air system used on the 1970 GTO had double doors. The hood scoops were manually controlled by the driver. On each side, vacuum-operated doors opened or closed according to manifold pressure. At part-throttle, during warmup, the vacuum-operated doors drew preheated air across the exhaust manifold. At full throttle, after warmup, the underhood air supply was shut off to let the engine run on a flow of fresh air from the hood scoops.

The M4 Rochester QuadraJet carburetor was used on regular 455 GTO's. It was ideally suited to such vast variations in driving, with its small primary throats of 1.375-inch diameter and huge secondaries of 2.25-inch diameter. It also comprised an air valve controlled by gas velocity to assure smoothness during abrupt throttle movements, prevent over-carburetion at low speeds, and give the extra mixture needed on wide-open-throttle acceleration.

Over the years, Pontiac's tests with a variety of experimental cylinders showed that the production-type wedge-head was the right answer for both high performance and low emissions. With a compact combustion space on one side of the cylinder, there is high turbulence, excellent mixing, fast flame front travel, and near-complete combustion. It permitted very high compression ratios without running into pre-ignition problems.

Camshafts were computer-designed for maximum accuracy, flexibility, and to save time in getting them into production. Limited-travel hydraulic lifters were used to prevent over-revving on the 455 with ram-air. They usually had a lash limit of 0.03 to 0.05 of an inch.

The basic GTO with the 400-cubic-inch V-8 had substantial valve overlap of fifty-four degrees. The intake opened at twenty-three degrees before top dead center and closed seventy after bottom dead center, which gave a 270-degree opening duration. The exhaust valve opened at seventy-eight degrees before bottom dead center and

A new hood with air scoops moved up near the front edge was used on the 1971 GTO, combined with a revised grille-and-bumper structure.

A revised spoiler design was used for the 1971-model Judge, going into its last year of production. Special identification and striping were toned down.

closed thirty-one after top dead center, giving an opening duration of 289 degrees.

On the Ram-Air version of the 1970 400-cubic-inch GTO V-8, valve overlap increased to sixty-three degrees. This was done by starting to open the intake valves thirty-one degrees before top dead center and keeping them open until seventy-seven degrees after bottom dead center, while simultaneously kicking the exhaust valves open ninety degrees before bottom dead center and not closing them till thirty-two degrees after top dead center. This camming gave a 288-degree duration for the intake valves and 302 degrees for the exhaust valves.

On the 455-cubic-inch GTO V-8 the timing was the same as for the Ram-Air 400. However, the 455 was also available with the hottest Ram Air V camshaft (380/320). Valves on the Ram-Air 455 were ten percent larger than on the other units to provide the flow characteristics necessary to deliver its full power potential. Valves were made of special steel. The intake valve material was chosen for very high heat resistance on the face, and chrome plating was used on the stems to reduce wear. The necks were aluminized to reduce seat erosion. Exhaust valves were made of very-high-temperature steel, with projection-welded tips to reduce fatigue. Stems were chrome-plated and necks aluminized, too.

Dual-coil springs were used, with two concentric coil springs, wound in the same direction, to promote regular valve rotation. The inner spring had the primary duty of damping main-spring oscillations. A windage tray was installed to keep the crankcase oil from foaming. Power-flex fans were used, to eliminate the power losses incurred in the standard design with its fluid fan clutch.

At this time Pontiac was also experimenting with an overhead-camshaft V-8 engine for the GTO. Since 1967 Pontiac had been in contact with the Australian Repco firm, which built the racing engines for Jack Brabham's Formula One Grand Prix cars, to see how Repco technology could help Pontiac's high-performance engines. In the end, no deal was made, but the talks had helped Pontiac's thinking.

Pontiac's own overhead-cam V-8 was a narrow-angle hemi-head unit, using a duplicate set of rocker arms with zero-lash valve adjusters for each bank. Cylinder block and heads were light alloy die-castings, and the crankshaft was forged chrome-alloy steel. With a bore of 4.257 inches and a stroke of 3.75 inches, total displacement was 427

Most noticeable innovation on the 1972 GTO was the adoption of the honeycomb light-alloy wheel, which was later to adorn other Pontiacs such as the Grand Am and Firebird.

cubic inches. With a 12.1 compression ratio, output was estimated at 640 hp at 7500 rpm.

A Turkish-born engineer named Hulki Aldekacti (who was responsible for the air-spring adaptation on the 1958 Pontiac) headed the experimental engineering group that designed this engine. He took a unique approach to engine design in that he applied styling to all external parts. The cam covers, front cover, oil sump, flywheel housing—all were designed to look good. The ram-air ducting and filter were designed to protrude through the hood, permanently on view, but the idea was to present a stylish view under the hood, too. Aldekacti knew how many boys spent their whole weekends looking at each other's engines. . .

Camshaft drive was by twin cogged belts, adapted from the six, one for each bank. The overhead valves were splayed at an included angle of sixty degrees, with maximum valve head diameters of 2.4 inches for the intake and two inches for the exhaust. In addition to sets of three and four two-barrel carburetors on a common manifold, Aldekacti was also toying with a new type of Rochester fuel-injection system. Repco built several test engines to Pontiac designs, but the project was doomed not to get beyond the experimental stage, and one day in 1971 it was given up. Pontiac needed all its engineering capacity for more urgent tasks.

The 1970 GTO had the Tempest body but its own front-end design, with a plastic bumper conforming in color to the body paints. The grille was a split-oval design with a recessed grillework, the left-side unit carrying three bold-faced letters: GTO.

By this time the GTO had grown to nearly the same weight as the most powerful Catalina of 1963. No wonder it needed more power, for without it, older cars could blow off the newer ones at the street lights. And that was considered unacceptable until 1971, when the corporation forced all divisions to make only low-compression engines so as to run on regular fuel. And from then on, the GTO went downhill.

To insiders, the GTO was identified as a DeLorean car, and the new general manager was blamed for its demise. Most vocal of the GTO's defenders, Wangers disagreed with everything McDonald said or did, and quit within a year of his arrival. "Jim McDonald was no *automobile guy*," Wangers spits the words out. "He had no courage. And he had a lot of leftover ideas about styling. He thought the GTO didn't have enough chrome on it. And he believed you shouldn't ever show the bottom of your front end."

For its last appearance in 1974, the GTO was built on the compact X-body (shared with Ventura). Power was a 350-cubic-inch V-8, with an air cleaner projecting through the hood and a rear-facing air scoop ('shaker' hood).

Bill Collins, the engineer who had worked so hard to make sure that the early GTO steered and handled well, had been given other tasks after the car went into production. We will meet him again in the next chapter, which relates the story of the Firebird. As for Jim Wangers, he left the ad agency in April 1970 and became a partner in a Chevrolet dealership in Milwaukee.

By 1976 the idea of the muscle car was dead, but the 'image' car was beginning to come into closer focus for Wangers. The following year he formed Motortown in Troy, Michigan, to create special 'image' cars for the industry. He did no business with Pontiac, though. Most of Motortown's work was for Ford.

CHAPTER 12

Pontiac Firebird

UNLIKE CHEVROLET, which began production of the Corvette roadster in 1953, Pontiac has never built a pure two-seater sports car. But while DeLorean was chief engineer, two such projects came into existence. One was principally a show car, but the other was a very serious proposal for a production model, which the corporation turned down. Both remain important stepping stones towards the car that became the Firebird.

The first experimental two-seater was displayed at the Los Angeles Auto Show in January 1962. It was called Monte Carlo. This name plate was never to be used on a Pontiac production car, but Chevrolet picked it up for a personal/specialty car introduced as a 1970 model. It was a short-wheelbase Y-body Tempest—a unique, open roadster-type of car designed for Bill Mitchell in the Advanced Studio at GM Styling.

The Monte Carlo was built on a ninety-seven-inch wheelbase, which increased the severity of the arc in the bent drive line and probably excluded the car from being seriously considered as a production model. Heavy-duty suspension was used on all four wheels, along with wide-rim wheels and special tires.

The 195-cubic-inch slant-four engine with an 8.25:1 compression ratio was outfitted with a Roots-type supercharger to give increased power output. Figures on compressor boost and power output were not released. Actually, the supercharged slant-four was not an engineering development project, but a 'quick and dirty' way to put some glamor into the car. A four-speed all-synchromesh transmission (reworked from the Corvair unit) was chosen. This was the time when novelty had gone out of automatic transmissions and the kids were looking for four-on-the-floor as a driving skill and performance symbol.

The interior had blue leather bucket seats with lap belts featuring automatic retractor spools. The special instrument cluster combined four large circular dials, the speedometer being flanked by a tachometer. The three-spoke steering wheel was inspired by Italian racing cars and had a wooden rim.

The car had an overall length of 175 inches, and the body was seventy-two inches wide. The low windshield reduced overall height to forty-four inches. Twin head fairings blended into the rear deck and twin rows of louvers and a Supercharged label were placed on the left side of the hood. Stainless steel cowlings were fitted on the fenders, and the grille was split in typical Pontiac fashion. Black-painted grille bars, deeply recessed, set it apart from the production models.

The Monte Carlo may have done what it was supposed to as a show car, but it was a dead end as far as product planning went. "When I

Production-model Firebird from 1967 is compared with the first GM vehicle to carry the Firebird name, a gas-turbine-driven experimental car built in 1953.

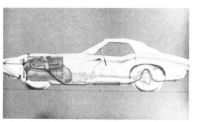

Open roadster named Monte Carlo was shown in February 1962. It had a short-ened 'rope-shaft' Tempest chassis and a supercharged four-cylinder engine. Monte Carlo was finished in white pearlescent lacquer with two blue rally stripes. The low windshield kept overall height to 44 inches. Bucket seats, left, gave extra side support for hard cornering. Tachometer was console-mounted. The car also had retractor-type seat belts.

XP-833 prototype could have be-come the Firebird. It was a light-weight two-passenger car, proposed as coupe and convertible. Side eleva-tion of the XP-833 shows overhead-camshaft six-cylinder engine instal-lation and Corvette-like proportions. Its engineering relied heavily on standard A-body car parts.

was in charge of advance design, in 1964-65, we designed and built two prototype two-passenger sports cars," reveals Bill Collins. "This was not the Banshee. Banshee was a name that DeLorean assigned to a four-passenger car which appeared briefly at the New York Auto Show in 1966 and got yanked out by Roche. The car I'm talking about never really had a name. We proposed it as a production model, and the project number was XP-833.

"It was a 2,200-pound two-passenger sports car and it had our overhead-cam six-cylinder engine in it as the base, which with that weight car would make it a viable performing vehicle as opposed to the old Blue-Flame Corvette," Collins explained. William T. Collins had joined Pontiac after graduating from Lehigh University, and went to work in the test and development section. He left in 1954 to go into military service.

"It was not a fun place to work and that's why I didn't go back there after my time in the service," he confessed. "I worked for Yale and Towne for a year and a half and that was even worse. So I went back to Pontiac in 1958 and found it a totally different place. I worked as a test engineer, following up on advanced design projects," Collins went on, "and served as a transmission development engineer on the 1961-63 Tempest. After that I had the title of advanced design project engineer, and became director of advanced engineering in 1964.

"This project started after Mitchell's prototype Corvair Monza had been shown. We wanted a car like that, but with a front engine. So we took the six and laid it over so it was only fifteen degrees from horizontal to get the hood line low enough."

That kind of engine installation was common on Indy-type single-seater racing cars from 1950 until they all went to midships engines in the mid-sixties. "But Pete said, 'You can't get at the plugs,' and so we had to stand the engine up," explains Collins. The second car was powered by the 326-cubic-inch V-8 engine. Both were built on the same short ninety-inch wheelbase, with front and rear track of fifty-eight inches. Overall length was 167.6 inches, and overall width seventy-one inches. The coupe was forty-five inches high overall.

Most of the chassis components were standard parts from the A-body car. Tempest steering knuckles, ball joints, front and rear brake assemblies, and its Salisbury rear axle were used. Mass-production Chevrolet three- and four-speed gearboxes and the small two-speed HydraMatic were readily available.

Many other components were Tempest production units, such as clutch assembly, brake master cylinder, wheels and tires, heater and heater controls. Most of the body hardware was in production at Ternstedt. The radiator was a Buick crossflow type, and the instruments were basic GMC units with specific faces. The body was based on an integral-construction steel underbody, with fiberglass-reinforced plastic panels outside. Seats were in fixed positions, for minimum cost and maximum safety, so that the pedals had to be mounted on an adjustable bracket, and the steering wheel was carried on the telescoping steering column that was optional on the Corvair.

Why wasn't it put into production? Bill Collins tells the story: "John was nice enough to let me make the presentation to Roche—and Donner—and they said the return on investment just isn't good enough. Now, I think the record will show that within one or two months of turning us down, that's when the Opel GT was approved for probably about the same amount of money."

When the Firebird came along, it was not a sports car, but a sporty car. It was not a two-seater but a two-plus-two, following the pattern set by Ford's Mustang. As soon as the Mustang hit the market in April 1964, Chevrolet started design work on a project of the same type. That became the 1967 Camaro. Donald McPherson was the executive engineer for that car. A wily Canadian, he had a special knack for making use of mass-produced components without giving up any of the virtues that are most precious in a sports car—handy size, light weight, smart looks, decent power, accurate steering with fast response, and predictable road behavior with stable cornering.

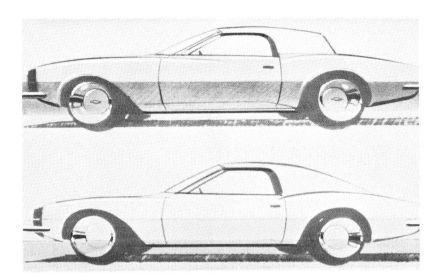

The 1967 Firebird was more Chevrolet than Pontiac, sharing the Camaro's F-body. The concept started at Chevrolet with these sketches.

Corvette-like fender treatment and long sloping hood were toned down by the time drawing-board work ended and clay work for the Camaro/Firebird began.

Since he was also associated with the development of the 1968-model Chevy Nova, he found it easy to make maximum use of its X-body inner structure and front stub-frame for the Camaro's F-body. The rear suspension, with single-leaf springs, was taken straight off the Chevy II, and the front end was the same as the new suspension and steering systems designed for the Nova. Instead of having the front coil springs mounted above the upper control arms, as on the Chevy II, the Camaro and Nova had the springs anchored on the lower control arms.

Drum brakes with 9.5-inch diameter and 2.5-inch lining width were used on all four wheels. Both front and rear units were of the duo-servo type for maximum self-energization, thus eliminating the cost of power brakes. Ventilated front disc brakes were optional, though, right from the start.

The car was built on a 108-inch wheelbase and weighed 2,700 pounds with fuel, water and oil. The rear roll center was located 9.3 inches above ground level, exactly as calculated. But at the front end a design intended to place the roll center 1.3 inches up instead turned out to have its roll center 1.8 inches below ground level. Rather than having an even ten-percent roll understeer both front and rear, the car ended up with 9.5 percent in front and 8.5 percent in back. Static weight distribution percentage, with the base six-cylinder engine, was 51/49.

Known under the code name Panther since mid-1965, this was the car that was offered to Pontiac. DeLorean was eager to have a sporty model in the range, and the idea found favor with the dealers who had watched their Ford-franchised rivals rake in Mustang profits hand over fist. Pontiac decided to call it Firebird. The name comes from Indian mythology—a deity that symbolized action, power, beauty and youth. General Motors had used the name before, first on an experimental gas-turbine-driven car in 1954, and then on two others, Firebird II of 1956 and Firebird III of 1959.

"The first Firebird we just kind of inherited from Chevrolet," said Bill Collins. "The 1967 Firebird body had all Chevrolet sheet metal and all the same exterior hardware except for the grille and the taillamps." GM's F-body cars followed the proportional arrangement that had made the Ford Mustang so popular, with a long hood and short deck. Pontiac styling under Jack Humbert's direction did a lot to set the Firebird apart from all the other 'ponycars' as the press had begun to call the Mustang and its imitators.

Pontiac's advertising agency was unhappy about having a Chevy on its hands, and Jim Wangers complained that the 1967 Camaro was outdated from the start, coming out 2½ years behind the Mustang. "It

was kind of a dud—dumb-looking, with a low price. It presented a poor image for GM relative to Ford. And the car just floundered around. Pontiac had very little time to dress it up, but we tried to make it look like a real Pontiac, with a lot of development behind it. We put wide-oval tires on all, for sheer looks. And we had five models, the baseline car, the Sprint, the V-8, the HO, and the 400. They took off like gangbusters."

Pontiac advertisements characterized the base Firebird with six-cylinder engine as the car for regular-gas lovers "who want to swing easy." The Firebird Sprint was described as "Our European thing. 215-hp OHC-6, floor shift, road rigging." The Firebird 326 V-8 was given the title "Our family sportster. 250 lively horses on regular gas. Yes, 250!" Then came the Firebird HO: "Our 285-hp light heavyweight. Those stripes mean what they say." Of course the stripes said absolutely nothing. Firebird 400 for 1967 was proclaimed to be "The ultimate driving machine." The ads stressed power: "400 cubic inches of chromed V-8 churn out 285 hp with no strain."

In side view the first Firebird borrowed a lot from the two-door LeMans coupe. It was lower and shorter, but made use of the same styling devices. It had front overhang that nearly matched the rear fender skirts for length, a sloping hood, and a rear fender kickup. Halfway between the beltline and the doorsill line was a horizontal accent line, running the whole length from front to rear bumper. A split grille was adopted, with a strong vertical center chrome member integrated with the bumper structure, which served as a frame for the whole grille design. Side-by-side dual headlights were mounted close to the outer ends of the frame, with a discreet horizontal bar in the middle of the grille elements.

Mechanically, Pontiac had managed, in very little time indeed, to create a vital difference from the Camaro. The Firebird made use of Pontiac's own engines, and had the engines set further back in the vehicle for better balance. This gave less understeer. The 1967 Firebird also had traction bars to hold the rear axle in place and prevent spring windup.

Still, the Firebird wasn't ready at the start of the model year, as the Camaro had been. The cars were to be assembled on the same line in the corporate plant at Norwood, Ohio. Pontiac needed about four months more than Chevrolet (which had a long head start) and the Firebird was announced on February 23, 1967.

There were two Firebird models in 1967: the coupe, listed at $2,666, and the convertible, listed at $2,903. Both were positioned about $200 above their Camaro counterparts. Firebird sales were off to a flying start, with 93,262 deliveries during 1967, and running at a

monthly rate better than 8,000 by the end of the year. Still, the Firebird sold less than half of Camaro volume despite their small price difference during 1967 and 1968. Break-even point for the F-body cars was probably around 250,000 units a year, so that with Camaro sales above 200,000 and the Firebird somewhat short of 100,000 GM found it profitable to compete in the sporty-compact market.

Contrary to Pontiac's sales prognosis, nearly four out of every five Firebird buyers in 1967 preferred the V-8 over the six. Two-thirds of Firebird buyers in 1967 ordered the extra-cost power steering, but disc brakes were slow to catch on. Just over 6,000 cars (7½ percent of output) were so equipped. That first year, one-third of all Firebirds made had synchromesh transmission with three-speed or four-speed floorshift. The remaining two-thirds had automatic transmission.

The original Firebird was carried over into 1968 practically without any styling change. There were some engineering improvements in the suspension and ventilation systems. For the HO option, a version of the new 350-cubic-inch V-8 power plant was adopted. And a ram-air option was offered with the 400-cubic-inch V-8 engine.

The 1969 models had a facelift and new outer skin. The frontal appearance introduced a new theme in Pontiac styling: the split grille within a narrow frame leaving the headlamps on the outside. A very bold chrome-plated frame, pointed at the center, contained two horizontal rectangular grille elements with rounded-off corners. This frame also served as a bumper structure. The side-by-side dual headlights were set in circular bezels and surrounded by painted sheet metal. Parking lights and turn signals were combined into one round lamp below each outer headlamp unit.

The first Firebird Trans Am was introduced in the spring of 1969. Pontiac called it the "ultimate performance ponycar of the day." It had a ram-air version of the 400-cubic-inch V-8, rated at 335 hp.

Cirrus show car of 1969 was destined to have long-term influence on the Firebird, though there was no immediate transfer of technology or styling features. The Cirrus had no side doors, passengers entered through a hatch into the cockpit.

Side treatment on the 1969 Firebird had a sharp horizontal crease above each wheel opening, thereby playing down the beltline and the rear fender kickup. A dummy air vent of the waste-gate type was placed in the front fender skirt.

The 1969 Firebird V-8 was about the middle of the field in fuel economy, at 18.5 miles per gallon, compared with a low of 17.9 for the Cougar and a high of 20.1 for the Mustang, as tested in the Union/Pure Oil Trials. In acceleration the Firebird beat all comers, however, with

Firebird for 1970 was notable for having no side glass other than the door windows and a very sleek fastback roofline with a full-width backlight. The '70 Firebird had a new F-body with plastic bumper enclosing entire front end. Innovations included concealed wipers and radio antenna laminated into the windshield.

a 25-70 mph run in 9.65 seconds. The Cougar was next best at 9.84 and the slowest was the Javelin at 12.27.

Pontiac had a brand-new Firebird ready in 1970. It was planned for normal introduction time, in the fall of 1969, but the tooling was late, and production could not start till February 1970. Pontiac continued producing 1969-model Firebirds in small numbers well into the 1970 model year.

Prices were higher for the new model: starting at $2,875, it was still tremendous value in a car. The new Firebird had a very sleek body, conforming to a certain ovality from every angle, and with better streamlining. The convertible disappeared, and the coupe was almost more a fastback than a notchback, though it had a normal trunk lid. No side glass was used other than in the doors, which were very long, running right back to the sail panel.

This Firebird body came into being when Pontiac was also preparing a show car named Cirrus, which was notable for not having side doors at all. Entry to the cockpit was from the rear, between the front bucket seats, as in a jetliner. A hatchback provided the necessary opening. The Cirrus—named after the cirrus clouds of the stratosphere —was not to be taken as a serious experimental car, with its spaceship

styling and space-age instrumentation and interior design. Still, some of its exterior styling elements were to find their way into the Firebird, in modified form, years later. By then the Cirrus was forgotten by most. Built strictly as an attention-getter for the moment, no production studies were ever made for this prototype.

The 1970 Firebird had no grille in the conventional sense but two nostril-like air intakes with deeply recessed wire-mesh to protect the radiator and other parts against flying debris. It was an all-plastic front end, with a painted plastic bumper surrounding the grille inserts; there was no chrome, and no conventional bumper. Single headlamps were mounted separately, away from the grille.

Throughout its first three years, the Firebird/Camaro situation was under constant review at Pontiac. The redesigned model was under preparation, and Jim Wangers said the talk then concentrated on "what's Chevrolet done wrong, and what can we do right?" And Bill Collins tells how engineering and styling got involved with the marketing on the new car:

"We tried to do a couple of things and the guy that really did it at Styling was Bill Porter, the head of our styling studio. He and I sat down and came up with this marketing plan, and we said, well, the sales department, like all sales departments, *must* have one *el cheapo* for some reason. They keep thinking that you sell on price. So we gave 'em one, you know, the standard Firebird. And then we said, let's do two things. Let's do a car that has all the visual luxury a stewardess-

type buyer might want. That was the Esprit—the one with all the chrome on it and a deluxe interior but just the standard engine and nothing exotic in tires or suspension. And then we said: OK—on the other side we'll have a car called the Formula. It will have none of those visual things, but we will concentrate on suspension and tires and that's how the Formula series came out.''

The Formula had a hood with two dummy air scoops, and was available in only one version, Formula 400, which meant the 400-cubic-inch V–8 engine. ''Then with the Trans Am, we said, let's go all out and do the best job we can for a car that really is as close to a legal street

1970 Trans Am stands out for its front air-dam and the rear-facing hood scoop feeding cool ram-air to the carburetor. The engine was the 400-cubic-inch V-8 rated at 345 hp.

Trans Am for 1974 received new front end with dual air scoops below the bumper face. Rear-facing ram-air scoop was retained. Firebird emblem covers the whole hood.

Honeycomb texture was chosen for wheels and grille inserts on the 1972 Firebird Formula 455. Distinctive hood scoops were opened up for customers who specified ram-air, otherwise they were phony.

Pontiac Banshee was a 1974 show car based on the Firebird chassis. Built to test safety concepts as well as styling, it had a soft-face bumper system of body-color urethane over an energy-absorbing foam plastic base. Banshee had fixed side windows fitting flush with the body sheet metal. Louvers around backlight have high-level lighting for traffic safety.

Firebird Esprit for 1974 had new front end with bumper structure sloping back into the hood for reduced air drag. The F-body sheet metal remained unchanged.

Trans Am for 1975 received radial-ply tires and the suspension system was retuned for the tire characteristics. That year one out of every three Firebirds sold was a Trans Am.

machine in a road-racing car as can be, and that's where those spoilers were all developed—not in the wind tunnel like the MacManus ads said. On the road we optimized those spoilers for drag and front and rear lift. The shaker hood really was a trick, to permit, well—without modifying the bodywork—a guy could have a high-rise manifold in there."

The 'shaker' hood was a hood with the sheet metal cut away around the air cleaner, so that the driver could see it shake as the engine rocked and vibrated.

The Trans Am was to be the most serious rival the Corvette had ever had, and its owners and protagonists just as fiercely loyal. It was developed by an enthusiastic young engineer named Herb Adams. "He had a lot of good ideas about what the Trans Am really ought to be," says Bill Collins. "He had done a car called the Firebird Sprint Turismo

back in 1968 which didn't have all the spoilers but had a really hot overhead-cam six-cylinder engine in it."

Actually, Herb Adams had a background in pure racing machinery and was not to stay very long at Pontiac. He was born in Chicago and loved cars. He wanted nothing more than to be an automotive engineer, and he was still a teenager when he built his first sports car, using Ford power. His coming to Pontiac was decided by his entry in the 1957 Fisher Body model competition. His model won him a scholarship, sponsored by Pontiac, and he enrolled in the GM Institute as a student engineer, graduating in 1961.

There was not much glamor in his first assignments at Pontiac. He recalls working on the heating, ventilation and air-conditioning systems for the 1963 Catalina, for instance. But in his spare time, he built race cars in his home, and shook up a lot of midwestern road racing aficionados with his weird creations. One was powered by a Mercury outboard motor, another by a two-cylinder Saab two-stroker, and a third by a pair of 250 cc Suzuki motorcycle engines. The latter

Highest-powered engine for the 1978 Trans Am was the 400-cubic-inch V-8 with a four-barrel carburetor and ram-air. Aerodynamic improvements do not affect the basic F-body sheet metal.

Formula 305 for 1978 shows revised hood scoops and rectangular headlamps inset in the grille inserts. Bumper structure includes front spoiler for improved aerodynamics.

led to a still faster one, using twin 350 cc Suzuki engines, and finally a car powered by a single 500 cc Kawasaki engine. After rounding out his experience with a stint in production engineering and working as a test engineer at the proving grounds, Herb Adams was transferred into the advance design department, and by 1967 he was assigned to the X-4 project.

By 1969 Adams was working on retuning Pontiac's suspension systems for radial-ply tires, and after that he was involved with the GTO Judge. But his pet project was the Trans Am.

He wanted the Trans Am to be capable of winning races, and was in charge of developing a 303-cubic-inch Special Duty V-8. He was part of the design team that drew up the four-cam small-block V-8 that was built for Pontiac by Repco in Australia. He also headed a project for a 366-cubic-inch racing V-8 which he installed in a Firebird and drove himself at Daytona. Finally, he led the team that developed the 455 Super Duty V-8 in 1973. By that time, he was sensing the corporate pressure to make him stop these racing activities, and left Pontiac. He moved to California and set himself up as a builder of sports cars based on Pontiac and Oldsmobile.

A partial restyling of all Firebirds came in 1974, after John Chinella had become head of the Firebird section of the Pontiac studio. The underbody structure was not touched, and in fact all sheet metal remained the same, though the car got a fully redesigned front end,

with a thin bumper line and a sloping grille panel. The grille inserts, first evidence of Cirrus influence, were recessed in rectangular frames and separated by a plastic panel carrying a prominent Firebird emblem. The Formula had twin (dummy) air scoops on the hood, facing forward, while the Trans Am had a true air intake on the hood, with a rear-facing inlet. Single headlamps were retained, but in new bezels that were squared-off at the fender tips.

Equipped with the 400-cubic-inch V–8 and Turbo-HydraMatic drive, the 1975 Trans Am had a top speed of a true 125 mph and could go from standstill to 100 mph in 28.5 seconds. It could cover the standing quarter-mile in 17.2 seconds, with a terminal speed of 82.5 mph.

The Super Duty 455-cubic-inch engine had been made available on the Firebird in 1973, with ram-air and a special camshaft with 308/320 timing, a stronger cylinder block with provision for dry-sump

Type K sports wagon was a Firebird-based show car from 1977. Rear side windows extended into roof panels and opened gullwing-fashion to give access to cargo area.

the most powerful Firebird engine became the 400-cubic-inch V-8 with four-barrel carburetor and dual exhausts.

To explore the public interest in a sports-wagon based on the Firebird, Pontiac made its Trans Am Type K (for Kamm-heck) show car in 1977. Its roofline continued in an easy slope till it was abruptly cut off at the tail, of which the upper one third was glass, the central part a ribbed panel, and the lower part bumper. There was no tailgate, but huge side windows that were hinged in the roof and opened up, gullwing fashion. It was put into auto shows in Europe as well as in America, but the reaction has been pretty cool, and Pontiac has no plans to build a Firebird sports-wagon at the time of this writing.

Rarely has a Pontiac been so long in production without major changes as the current Firebird. Indeed, its popularity is ever-increasing. From a low point in 1972, when the rumor mill in Detroit had it headed for extinction, it bounced back during the fuel crisis. For, despite its sporty style, people were wont to regard anything with a six-cylinder engine as an economy car. Its fantastic sales record is shown here.

lubrication, and a number of other improvements. Steel-belted radial tires became standard on all Firebirds in 1974, and suspension systems were tuned to match the tire characteristics.

Bold new front styling with dual rectangular headlights set the 1977 Firebird apart from its predecessors, and the engine availability list was completely revised. The Buick 231-cubic-inch V-six became standard, and Pontiac's new small V-8 (305-cubic-inch displacement) was added as an option. The 455-cubic-inch V-8 was discontinued, and

Year	Base Firebird	Firebird Esprit	Firebird Formula	Firebird Trans Am	Total Firebird Production
1967	2H 67,032				
	2C 15,528				82,560
1968	2H 90,152				
	2C 16,960				107,112
1969	2H 75,362				
	2C 11,649			697	87,708
1970	37,835		7,708	3,196	48,739
1971	23,021	20,185	7,802	2,116	53,124
1972	12,000	11,415	5,250	1,286	29,951
1973	14,096	17,249	10,166	4,802	46,313
1974	26,372	22,583	14,519	10,255	73,729
1975	22,293	20,826	13,670	27,274	84,063
1976	21,209	22,252	20,613	46,701	110,775
1977	30,642	34,548	21,801	68,745	155,736

2H = Two-door hardtop
2C = Two-door convertible

Trans Am for 1979 retains basic 1970½ body with different grille and bumper structure, front and rear spoilers, and wider fender skirts to accommodate the wider tires. 'Shaker hood' cool-air intake is still in use.

CHAPTER 13

Variations on the A-Body Theme

WITHIN THE CONFINES of divisional authority DeLorean pulled off a real coup. Bridge players would call it a grand slam, and poker players a royal flush. He called it the Grand Prix—not even bothering to invent a new name. Pontiac had been building cars with the Grand Prix label for several years, but the 1969 model was the one that had the zing. And what made it possible was what had happened to the Tempest, the trusty intermediate-size car.

General Motors introduced a novel concept for all its 1968-model intermediates. It consisted of building the two-door models on a four-inch shorter wheelbase than the four-door models. Until now, the intermediates had used the same wheelbase for all models, as was the case with the full-size cars. Previously, two-door models were able to have different rooflines because the rear seat was moved forward relative to the axle, which remained at the same distance from the front wheels. Now, the difference was going to involve many more parts—frames and propeller shafts, underbody and central body panels.

The two-door models adopted a short 112-inch wheelbase to get the benefits of sports-coupe styling, and the four-door models were built on a 116-inch wheelbase to provide adequate interior space for a whole family.

The whole family of A-body cars had wide torque-box perimeter frames and separate body structures. The opportunity that DeLorean saw earlier than anybody else was to take the long-wheelbase chassis and put the short-wheelbase body on it—giving a two-door coupe with a long hood. And that, in essence, is what the 1969 Grand Prix was. Its importance, however, can only be realized after a study of how Pontiac had been fooling around with the Grand Prix name for another type of car for years.

The original Pontiac Grand Prix was an addition to the line in 1961. It was a sports coupe based on the Bonneville, using the same B-body, and sadly lacking in special identification and 'image.' This Grand Prix concept was not unique to Pontiac. Oldsmobile had tried it with the Starfire coupe, Dodge did it with the Custom 880, Rambler with its 990, and, of course, Buick did it with the Wildcat.

It wasn't even a new concept really. The same car had been around for years, with other names and special options. Jim Wangers expressed it his way: "For years the hottest Pontiac you could buy was a Catalina with a so-called Bonneville engine. That was nothing but a goddam 389 with a four-barrel on it. That Bonneville label, because of the name, had a great image."

The Grand Prix had a somewhat different flavor, and the name did Pontiac no harm. Purists protested that Pontiac had never built a Grand Prix car and had no right to use the title, but were made to realize that the term is really meaningless, since at various trade fairs around the world, a Grand Prix (or grand prize, simply) can be awarded to all sorts of products, from cheese and beer to shoes and socks.

Grand Prix started off as a special coupe using a B-body and the Bonneville power train. This 1962 model had front bucket seats and an automatic transmission called Roto-HydraMatic. Console-mounted tachometer was stylish and nearly useless.

Pontiac delivered 6,556 Grand Prix cars before the end of the 1961 calendar year, and sold 32,271 of them during 1962.

The 1963 Grand Prix was a two-door hardtop built on the Catalina's 120-inch wheelbase, but had Bonneville's finish and trim level, and a more powerful engine as standard. It had an attractive base list price of $3,489, which did not include automatic transmission ($231) or power steering ($108). No significant changes were made for the coming year.

Steve Smith wrote the report on the 1964 Grand Prix for the *Car and Driver Yearbook*. His description explains exactly what Pontiac was aiming for: "It's a handsome son-of-a-gun despite being basically only a dechromed stock Pontiac body with a concave rear window and subtle touches like grilled-over taillights and wood strips on the

Clay model and final product: 1965 Grand Prix was basically a short-wheelbase Bonneville with special front- and rear-end design. Rear-wheel spats were late addition.

Jack Humbert's Coke-bottle shape was close to its point of culmination in the 1965 Grand Prix. The car was built on a 121-inch wheelbase and carried a sticker price of $3,498. Baseline engine was a 333-hp version of the 380-cubic-inch V-8.

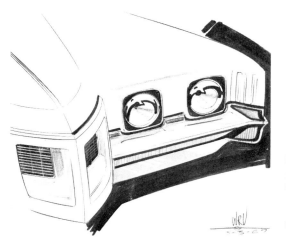

By March 1967, the Grand Prix front-end design had advanced to the stage shown on this drawing, left. The projecting centerpiece and fender tips were focal points. Grand Prix added a convertible for 1967, with concealed headlights and parking lights, chrome-plated doorsills, front bucket seats. The standard engine was a 400-cubic-inch V-8.

steering wheel and facia. The unadorned body is a marvelous understatement, the height of clean, taut line, and the fashionable wasp waist."

It had extremely impressive performance, reaching 100 mph from standstill in thirty-five seconds and covering the standing quarter-mile in 17.6 seconds with a terminal speed of 80 mph. Going from zero to sixty was a matter of 9.4 seconds. That's fast, considering the car had a curb weight of 4,125 pounds and was equipped with automatic transmission and a standard 3.08:1 axle ratio.

Driving it was not a memorable experience, however, as Smith wrote: "We were very favorably impressed with the car's tight construction, good finish, thoughtful provision for creature comfort (up to the point where it lulls the driver into thinking the car is so automatic it needs no further attention from him) and the roomy interior. We might not go along with this approach to luxurious touring—preferring smaller more nimble machinery—but the Grand Prix is certainly a superior high-quality product for people who like their pleasure big."

Smith also talked about what the car was like on the inside: "The interior is sumptuous, if a bit brassy; the clear-plastic, star-spangled steering wheel strikes a particularly garish note." It was a profitable car for Pontiac Motor Division as well as the Pontiac dealers. It had relatively low production cost, but a prestige price.

Actually it had a low base price, but then, of course, the 'stripped' Grand Prix was to be considered as just the beginning. A normally loaded version would have two-grand's worth of options, such as six-way bucket seats, power steering, power brakes, power windows, cruise control, automatic transmission, AM-FM radio with power antenna, remote-control outside mirror, Kelsey-Hayes aluminum wheels, power trunk lock, rear window defroster, tinted glass and air conditioning. From a base price of $3,500, the typical showroom Grand Prix had a sticker price in the $5,500 area. Inevitably, the base price was starting to climb, going from $3,492 in 1966 to $3,539 in 1967. That year a convertible Grand Prix was added, listed at $3,813.

The car gained some weight, so that despite increasing engine displacement, performance levels remained pretty much the same. In the Union/Pure Oil Trials, the 1968 Grand Prix completed the 25-70 mph acceleration test in 9.5 seconds but gave only 14.5 miles per gallon (largely due to lower gearing). By comparison, the heavier Bonneville took 11.9 seconds for the same acceleration test, and gave 14.8 miles per gallon in the fuel-economy test.

Tail-end design for the Grand Prix started with the basic shape of the Buick Riviera, left, using a high-faced bumper and vertical taillights. By May 1967, the tail-end design included air extractors at the backlight base, middle, which later disappeared along with the vertical taillight theme. A cleaner design with horizontal taillights and a flush, undecorated deck lid, right, evolved for the Grand Prix sometime in May 1967.

Both were below average in braking, the Bonneville taking 191.2 feet and the Grand Prix over 212 feet to come to a stop from 65 mph. Chrysler's New Yorker did it in an even 160 feet!

"Our '68 Grand Prix was a disaster," says Bill Collins. "Nobody bought it. It looked like a big fat turkey, and I would give John the credit for the idea of taking the A-body which was less expensive and building a new car on it."

Bill Collins was assistant chief engineer in charge of the body engineering group at Pontiac in 1967, and deeply involved with the new A-body cars, working in close liaison with James Lagergren who had the task of coordination between body and chassis engineering.

The new perimeter frame introduced some different engineering elements. First, the body shell came down over the frame members to form a better integrated structure. Thus the underbody and even the sheet metal contributed to the structural strength of the car. It is doubtful that this could have been achieved without prior experience with unit-body construction, such as used on the 1961-63 Tempest. Secondly, there was no metal-to-metal contact. Wide-base rubber body mounts insulated the body shell from the frame.

Proposed side treatment for the Grand Prix, dated April 1967, was the basis for the final design. Fender lines were reworked to avoid GTO-type bulges, and the simulated air extractor in the front fender skirt was not used.

Original intention was to continue the Grand Prix as a B-body car for 1969. This was the styling mockup they toyed with in January 1967. Then DeLorean had the idea for the G-body.

Apart from the use of a dual wheelbase, the 1968 Tempest was notable for going to a track of sixty inches—up two inches in front and one in the rear. The new bodies lowered the overall height by about one inch.

Front overhang increased considerably on the 1968 A-body cars, with a forward taper on both upper and lower edges ahead of the front wheels. In the side sheet metal a torpedo-like bulge extended

Jack Humbert completed most of Grand Prix design for 1969 before leaving Pontiac studio in Bill Porter's hands. Exaggerated perspective of styling sketch makes for a highly striking impression.

John DeLorean (right) and General Manufacturing Manager D. Robert Bell give their good-luck sign to the 13-millionth Pontiac, a 1969 Grand Prix, as it is shipped off from the factory.

from the front fender into the door area, oval at the top and tapering to the rear, ending in a straight horizontal accent line. The same theme was repeated for the rear fender.

Inspiration for the new Tempest grille design came from the Firebird and its construction from the B-body cars. It combined the bumper structure with a grille frame reaching up to meet the hood, just as on the full-size models. Dual headlights were enclosed in the grille frame, side by side, near the outer ends. The hood had a central bulge, shaped as a fairing for the vertical center post in the grille, which rose above the side elements of the design. Concealed wiper arms were introduced on the 1968 Tempest.

This was the A-body car that became the basis for the new Grand Prix. From the cowl back, the car was basically a LeMans coupe. A completely new and far longer front body was produced, and the combination became known as the Fisher G-body.

Although DeLorean gets credit for the idea, it stemmed from a memo written to him on April 14, 1967, by Benjamin W. Harrison, who was then in charge of the engineering department's special projects. In his memo, Ben Harrison outlined the advantages of building the next-generation Grand Prix with an A-Special body. As he remembers it, he wrote the proposal on a Friday, which meant it was on DeLorean's desk on the following Monday morning. He put his top stylists, Jack Humbert and Irvin Rybicki, to work on it the same day. Four days later, on April 21, a clay model was ready—and approved. DeLorean set his mind on getting it into production for 1969, which meant a schedule that would break records ("and backs," as one Pontiac man recalled it).

According to Ben Harrison, DeLorean called a meeting to work out the problems of developing the engineering for the car only to hear a lot of protests that it could not be done in that short a lead time. The general manager then made a short speech to the effect that the car would indeed be built for 1969-model introduction, and also that no new people would be hired to help out. "If anybody here thinks that can't be done, say so now, so that I can take you off the project," is the way he ended his talk. There were no complaints after that, and the job was done on time.

Here, Pontiac got something unique at last—a personal/specialty car at a budget price. The other divisions were caught off guard. There was nothing like it on the market. "The Grand Prix was a huge success," according to Jim Wangers. "It was supported by a popular price, but it also had a gutsy, performance-oriented image."

Bob Knickerbocker comments drily: "Pontiac's management decided we needed a specialty car in that time frame and laid out the parameters they thought it should meet, and the division accomplished that." As for how it was accomplished, let Bill Collins explain: "In the corporation's way of doing things, they only allow you so much tooling a year to work with—so you've got to figure out how the hell can I maximize the impact of my tooling? If you can get the cost down, then you can show the corporation that it makes economic sense to spend more on tooling. That's the way we got the '69 Grand Prix, which had all its own panels."

In side view, the 1969 Grand Prix was unlike anything else Detroit was building at the time. It had the fashionably long hood of the 'ponycars,' but being a larger car, it could carry a longer hood than they and still seem attractively proportioned. The windshield seems strangely upright in retrospect, for it was not inclined at an ideal angle for the car's shape, but it would have cost too much to change it. Pontiac wanted to use a maximum of A-body parts, and the A-post was part of that.

There was no real kickup in the rear fender. Instead, advantage was taken of the window frame design to pull the beltline up at its rear edge (an old Cadillac trick). The body had something of a fuselage look, with its widest point along a horizontal accent line aimed to coincide with the highest point on the wheel rims. It went through the entire skin, from the front bumper, ending at the lip around the front wheel opening and then continuing, tying the rear fender opening lip into the same design, and ending at the rear bumper.

The 1969 Grand Prix had no side glass other than the door windows. Door handles were of a new type, fitting flush with the sheet metal. The wheels were Pontiac's bolt-on design with five stylized spokes and visible wheel nuts.

In frontal aspect the car had strong Pontiac identity, with a vertical-theme split grille set in the middle of a heavy bumper. The top of the grille met the hood, and the grille extended below the bumper to give a vertical emphasis to the frontal aspect of the car. Side-by-side dual

headlights filled the panels above the bumper bar, and the fender tips carried Thunderbird-like turn signals and parking lights.

For all its length, the car had pretty restricted interior accommodations. It wasn't designed for maximum utility, and space utilization was not a point that weighed heavily in its design. At the press review, we asked John DeLorean about the reasons the Grand Prix was built that way. He grinned and said, "It illustrates our motto here at Pontiac." A pause while he pretended to wait for our guess. Then: "Put up a big front!" Jim Wangers was delighted with it: "The Grand Prix now looked like the kind of car Pontiac would build in that idiom." It was built exclusively as a two-door hardtop and had a sticker price of $3,866.

The Grand Prix was selected by GM Research engineers Arthur F. Underwood, Paul Vickers and Chuck Amann as the vehicle best suited to demonstrate a new steam engine designed to evaluate a vapor-cycle power system in a modern car fully equipped with power accessories, including air conditioning, in terms of performance, economy, reliability and passenger comfort.

The 160-hp engine was built around a 101-cubic-inch four-cylinder expander with poppet intake valves and open exhaust ports. The steam was generated in a boiler made of several sets of carbon-steel and stainless steel tubes, with an aggregate length of 430 feet. Diesel fuel or kerosene burned continuously in two turbine-type combustors. The condenser was of the plate-fin type and looked like an ordinary radiator, only three times bigger. The expander was connected to an experimental stepless toric-drive transmission. The SE–101 steam power system weighed 450 pounds more than the complete 455-cubic-inch Pontiac V–8. No doubt this experimental vehicle was built more for the purpose of demonstrating the problems of matching steam power to a modern automobile than to advance the state of the art. It remained in the research laboratories where it died a quiet death.

For 1970 the Grand Prix became available with high-performance versions of the 400- and 455-cubic-inch V-8 engines. We tested one for *Popular Science Monthly*, which included driving it through a series of performance tests at Bridgehampton race circuit on Long Island. It had bucket seats and a console-shift Turbo-HydraMatic transmission. The steering was a new variable-ratio type that gave 3.25 turns lock to lock.

Shod with 70-series Uniroyal tires, it had little or no wheelspin and good adhesion for braking. Ventilated front discs gave terrific stopping power. But the best part was in the handling. Steering response was quick and accurate, and the initial understeer was so light it seemed to be perfectly neutral. It could easily be brought to oversteer by

Pontiac Grand Prix was chosen by GM Research Staff for experimental steam power system installation in 1969. The technicians are lowering the steam generator and burner assembly into the compartment where the expander is already installed.

Grand Prix swelled in 1973, when GM went to a wider A-body. The 1974 model tries to look as crisp and different from the LeMans as possible.

applying a little too much throttle in a tight turn, letting the tail end wander out to help you get the nose pointed towards the exit from the curve. It cornered in a very flat attitude, practically without roll. It was a magnificent road car. And on the race track, it was far from silly. We got lap times down to two minutes and twelve seconds, which was five seconds faster than any other American production car we had tested there, including the Dodge Hemi-Charger, Ford Fairlane GT and other hot numbers.

No noticeable exterior changes appeared on the 1970 Grand Prix, but the 1971 model was drastically altered in frontal aspect. The grille was extended upwards into the hood and its lower edge remained below bumper level. It was also widened and filled with a new design featuring seven strong vertical bars on each side of the center divider. The bumper face was split in half horizontally, so that the upper half ran across the grille, following the pointed-nose line, while the lower half was deflected around the bottom of the grille.

This was very effective, and avoided a heavy-handed look, remaining simple, and making the most out of a few basic design

elements. At the same time, single headlights were adopted, and placed in squared-off bezels located about halfway between the grille frame and turn signal lights which remained in the fender tops. The headlamps reached up into the valley between the hood and fenders, and led to a subtle fairing that tapered off before reaching the cowl area.

That year (1970) the Grand Prix was no longer alone in its field. Bill Collins remembers: "John had gone to Chevrolet shortly after it had gone into production, and a year later he came out with the Monte Carlo." That was basically the same car, sharing the G-body, but using Chevrolet power. Not unnaturally, it cut heavily into Grand Prix sales.

Being structurally linked to the intermediates, the Grand Prix was helplessly affected by the new A-body program that the corporation had in the works, originally slated for the 1972 model year, but postponed to 1973. Before we go into that, let's bring the story up to date on the evolution of Pontiac's A-body cars.

A veritable fleet of 1968-model Tempests of different specifications was entered in the Union/Pure Oil Trials. The Tempest 1968 LeMans V-8 made the 25-70 mph acceleration run in 12.15 seconds, but returned a disappointing 16.4 miles per gallon in the fuel-economy test. The six-cylinder Tempest did much better, giving 18.6 miles per gallon, though its acceleration time was 15.8 seconds. In the 1968 Mobilgas Economy Run, a Tempest V-8 finished eighth and last in its class, at 16.9 miles per gallon, far worse than the best-placed car, a Dodge Coronet V-8, at 20.6 miles per gallon.

These poor showings caused a lot of headaches at Pontiac engineering, but improvements followed. The 1969 LeMans V-8 took 10.6 seconds for the 25-70 mph acceleration test, and returned a fuel economy of 17.8 miles per gallon. The fastest in the class was the Oldsmobile Cutlass with an acceleration time of 9.6 seconds, and the most economical was the Ford Fairlane at 19.8 miles per gallon.

The 1969 Tempest looked as if the front design from the 1968 Catalina had been transplanted on the intermediate car line. There was the same vertical centerpiece and the perimeter grille frame, forming a unit with the bumper structure. Headlights were placed side by side at the ends, and the rest of the space was filled in by a plurality of horizontal bars.

Fender lines were sharpened up for the 1970 Tempest. The accent lines above the wheel openings were blown up to look like torpedoes, especially the front one, recalling the Mercedes-Benz 190 SL of 1956. The beltline was deliberately left vague, even in the transition from door windowsill to rear fender kickup. The doorsill line was also de-emphasized, only the curved profile of the doors was there to make its optical effect and make the car seem lower from normal human eye level. Frontal aspect was improved by lowering the grille and playing down its vertical centerpiece, so that it became very close to the Buick Riviera grille of the same year, except for the middle separation.

The Tempest/LeMans ranked sixth among U.S. intermediates in 1970. Chevelle led the market, hotly chased by the Ford Fairlane. Oldsmobile F-85 and Cutlass were third, Dodge Coronet and Charger fourth, and the Buick Skylark fifth. Pontiac dropped the Tempest name plate for 1971, selling all its intermediates with the LeMans label.

The 1971 LeMans had a new front with a split grille set in a plastic nosepiece. Narrow chrome strips framed each grille element, which also had a single horizontal bar across the middle. Each grille section tapered toward the outer ends, conferring an oval look on the total package.

A protruding nose section rose into the hood and extended into a flare. The bumper was a chrome-plated bar that curved around the fender tips. It was also bent down in the middle to bare the full grille design. Dual headlights were placed side by side. In side view, the 1971 LeMans was cleaner if less spectacular than its predecessor. The accent lines above the wheel openings were reduced to gentle

creases, and a chrome molding marked the doorsill line. The beltline continued to be played down.

The T-37 was a special LeMans model in 1971 offering plenty of performance in a stripped-down package, with a lower price ($2,747 for the coupe). Failing in the market place, the T-37 was discontinued after a year, as the basic LeMans was reduced in price to $2,688 for the two-door coupe. The line also included a LeMans Sport series as well as the GTO coupe and convertible.

The Luxury LeMans was new for 1972, built as a two-door hardtop or four-door hardtop only, at prices of $3,162 and $3,285, respectively. Luxury LeMans continued with a conventional grille, using a wide split oval design with dual horizontal bars in chrome-lined frames, but the other LeMans models adopted the GTO front for 1972. Retouches in the side treatment included a revival of the heavy torpedo-like bulges in the fenders.

Who bought the LeMans? The typical private owner was thirty-eight years old, male, married, living in a suburb or small town, with an income of $12,000. Half the LeMans owners had no other car. Why did they pick the LeMans? Styling outranked value, forty-six to thirty-three percent. Driving ease was an important point, cited by twenty-seven percent. Economy and durability were taken into consideration but performance, roadholding, roominess, engineering and prestige were low-priority items.

The industry-wide swing to low-lead, low-octane fuel for the 1971-model engines necessitated a general lowering of the compression ratios, and resulted in a serious drop in power output. At this time, consumers in general could not care less whether it took twelve or fifteen seconds to go from standstill to cruising speed. Superlative acceleration was no longer an important aspect of performance.

Performance had taken on a new meaning: driveability. Cars often lacked basic driveability, a side effect of hurried development and application of emission-control devices. Engines would stall repeatedly on cold starts—when the transmission lever was first moved into drive, and again at traffic lights. To guard against this tendency, many cars came with carburetors set for an excessive fast-idle, so that there was a severe jolt through the whole car when engaging Drive, or Reverse, from Neutral.

As the nature of the Pontiac product changed, so did the buyer. The LeMans clientele of 1972 was not at all the same as it had been when DeLorean was running the division. "The thing flatly deteriorated," said Jim Wangers. "The whole car line was too closely tied into the GTO, and fell right with it. The LeMans died because the GTO died. The GTO died because performance died."

CHAPTER 14

Federal Standards

Landmark legislation on automobile safety and air pollution was ramrodded through the U.S. Congress by the Johnson administration, resulting in the Clean Air Act of 1966 and the Highway Safety Act of 1966. We call it landmark legislation because its long-term effect was to transfer certain decision-making powers over the technical specifications of automobiles, which had always been the prerogative of the industry, from Detroit to Washington, D.C.

Joe Callahan wrote in *Automotive News* in April 1966: "In the world of auto engineering, 1966 will go down in history as the first year that the federal and state governments had a significant impact on the design of automobiles. And it became increasingly clear that the government would be influencing more and more the kinds of cars Americans will be using. Although no car-design laws had yet been passed at introduction time, California was able to 'persuade' car makers to put exhaust control devices on the '66 models going into that state, and the U.S. government had 'persuaded' manufacturers to install as standard equipment a half-dozen safety items that were previously optional."

The first round of federal motor vehicle safety standards went into effect on January 1, 1968. But Pontiac had anticipated many elements of the rule-making and, in fact, gone beyond it in some areas. Included in Pontiac's safety features for the 1967 models were collapsible steering columns, dual-circuit brakes and warning lights, emergency flashers, front shoulder-belt anchors, nonreflecting wiper arms, shatterproof breakaway interior mirrors, day/night mirrors, deepdished steering wheels, nonoverriding door handles, soft window-knobs and coat hooks, folding seat latches and low-profile instrument knobs. Many of these items, which originated in the industry, were later written into the laws.

The state of California, acting on the pioneer research work of Dr. Arie J. Haagen-Smit in Los Angeles, set pollution standards for cars before the federal government did, with limits on carbon monoxide (thirty-four grams per mile) and unburned hydrocarbons (3.4 grams per mile) exhaust emmissions for 1966.

Pontiac, along with the rest of the industry, had already eliminated the major source of automotive emissions: blow-by gases escaping through the crankcase vent pipe. Positive crankcase ventilation was used on Pontiac engines destined for California from the start of the 1961 model year and became a standard feature of every Pontiac engine, beginning with the 1963 models.

Under the federal emission control standards in effect from 1967 through 1969, cars were tested in a seven-mode cycle, and limits were equivalent to 3.3 grams per mile hydrocarbons and thirty-four grams per mile carbon monoxide. That represented pollution cuts of more than half, compared with 1965-model cars.

Pontiac opened its 43,000-square-foot emissions laboratory in 1971, the first among GM's car divisions to act in anticipation of this future need.

To meet the federal and California standards, Pontiac adopted the Air Injection Reactor (AIR) system for most of its 1966-model engines to be sold in California, and standardized the AIR system for its 1967-model V-8 engines. The system had been under development at the GM Engineering Staff since 1963, and by July 1965 a total of 250 GM cars had been tested over 2½ million miles with the AIR system installed. It consisted of an engine-driven pump delivering secondary air to injectors mounted in the exhaust ports, so as to provide oxygen for post-combustion of unburned hydrocarbons in the exhaust gas.

The AIR system involved a lot of additional hardware to prevent malfunction under any circumstances, such as an anti-backfire valve and a pressure-relief valve, plus check valves to prevent damage in case of failure of the belt that drove the air pump.

The car market slipped from 9.3 million units in 1965 to nine million in 1966. The research firm Albert D. Sindlinger reported that the safety issue was a very important factor in the sales decline, since many consumers resisted paying for items they felt they did not need. Oddly, General Motors alone took the loss. Chrysler advanced and Ford's sales remained steady. Though Chevrolet received a severe setback, Pontiac seemed invulnerable, and reached a sales volume of 830,856 cars, which boosted its share of the market to 9.22 percent! Now it seemed nothing could dislodge Pontiac from third place. Pontiac executives proudly wore a gold '3' on their lapels. The stage was set for Pontiac to perpetuate its position indefinitely.

The Catalina ran fourth among full-size cars in 1966, behind the Impala, Galaxie 500 and Bel Air, while the Bonneville had it all over the Electra 225. Though the Bonneville was beaten by the Chrysler

Newport, no Ford product in its price class could compare in sales volume. The Executive name came in as an option in the Star Chief series for 1966, and the 2+2 was given up due to its poor showing in the market place. The following year the Star Chief was put to rest, its place in the lineup being filled by the Executive.

Styling was as yet unconstrained by federal regulations, and for 1966 the full-size Pontiacs had an even bolder look than the year before. The front fender edges were pulled forward, hoods extended above the headlamps, and the bumper face was countersunk to form a symmetrical lip at the bottom. The hood had no bulge but a central crease that was carried into the nosepiece of the grille. The grille design stressed its function as an air intake, and comprised four separate horizontal inserts, recessed into the sheet metal. The V-emblem was moved up to the center tip of the hood and the lettering on the hood was taken off. The upper surface of the bumper remained horizontal to let the grille make its impression without distractions from below.

Did John DeLorean personally take a hand in the styling? Jack Humbert explained: "General managers are not in the styling studio every day. He used to come down when we had something to show him. He—usually—sort of has the last word on what we finally do, or 'buy' what we're trying to 'sell' them. But our vice president here at the Design Staff usually has some power, too. Sometimes they are at odds, but things usually work out. We have day-to-day relations with engineering and whatever we need."

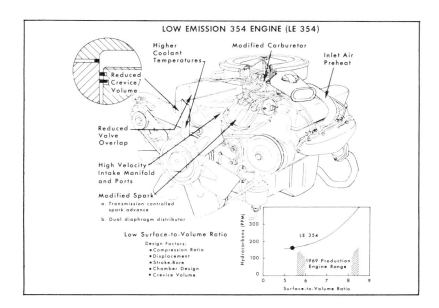

LOW EMISSION 354 ENGINE (LE 354)

Higher Coolant Temperatures

Modified Carburetor

Inlet Air Preheat

Reduced Crevice Volume

Reduced Valve Overlap

High Velocity Intake Manifold and Ports

Modified Spark
a. Transmission controlled spark advance
b. Dual diaphragm distributor

Low Surface-to-Volume Ratio

Design Factors:
● Compression Ratio
● Displacement
● Stroke-Bore
● Chamber Design
● Crevice Volume

LE 354

1969 Production Engine Range

Hydrocarbons (PPM)

Surface-to-Volume Ratio

Experimental low-emission V-8 engine built by the GM Engineering Staff was installed in a 1969 Pontiac for road testing. It represents the state of the art for its time.

F. James McDonald, left, became general manager of Pontiac in 1969. He had a strong background in manufacturing and made good at Hydra-Matic Division. Steve Malone, right, came to Pontiac in 1956 and has been chief engineer since 1965. His background was Delco and electrical engineering.

The senior-series Pontiacs were substantially redesigned for 1967, with a new front end as well as new and more subtle side treatment. The 1967 front end remains the purest and most elegant ever used by Pontiac. It was the climax of its sequence, and the pinnacle of good taste.

The bumper structure was raised to frame the two air-intake theme grille elements, and at the same time the hood lip was extended to meet the bumper in a straight horizontal line. The sheet metal extended into a tip at the center, which matched up with a protrusion in the middle of the bumper. Headlights were stacked, and bezels remained circular. The lower headlight units were inset in the bumper while the upper ones were contained in the fender top sheet metal, carrying the split-level theme through the full width of the car. The side was dominated by the gentle swell in the sheet metal that formed a rear fender line, and a straight and level accent line linking the top ends of the front and rear bumpers as they curved around at the corners.

This was the year Pontiac introduced the retracting, concealed wiper arms that sheltered below a lip on the hood when not in use. "Pontiac was one of the first cars with concealed wiper arms," says Jack Humbert. "That's no big deal—but it is rather nice they're out of the way now. And there's the antenna buried in the windshield. Pontiac led the way with that."

Technical interest in the 1967 models centered on the V-8 engines. The 389- and 421-cubic-inch units were replaced by slightly larger power units of 400- and 428-cubic-inch displacement. There was a

Computer-controlled data processing equipment facilitated emission testing for Pontiac by giving fast answers on whether or not a particular setup would meet the standards.

Pontiac engineer checks 1971 Grand Ville convertible on outdoor dynamometer in Pontiac's new emissions laboratory. Tests were automatically controlled, and could be run in all kinds of weather for mileage accumulation, durability checks and exhaust emissions analysis.

corresponding power gain, and if gasoline mileage suffered, it was not seen as a matter of great importance at the time.

In the 1967 Mobilgas Economy Run from Los Angeles to Detroit, the Pontiacs were indeed not brilliant. A Catalina came third in its class with 18.2 miles per gallon, behind a Buick LeSabre at 18.7 and an Oldsmobile Delmont at 18.5.

The 1967 Pontiac used AC-Delco's new capacitive-discharge ignition system. It was claimed to give up to 400 percent longer plug life, easier cold starting, better high-speed performance and more trouble-free operation. A three-speed column-shift synchromesh transmission was standard, with a four-speed floorshift or Turbo-HydraMatic as optional.

In 1967 the total car market, including imports, sank to less than 8.3 million units. The imports went ahead, from 7.5 to 9.4 percent, while Ford dropped four full percentage points! As for Pontiac, the division came within a fraction of taking ten percent of the market in 1967. Its cars looked great, quality was no worse than the industry average, and the division had a 'hot' image. But, as of 1979, Pontiac would not again get that close to the ten-percent mark. From 9.98 percent in 1967, its penetration slipped to 9.33 the following year.

As Dick Wright wrote in *Automotive News* in April 1967: "The safety hassle has apparently had an unusual effect on industry sales, particularly since the introduction of the 1967 models." But that was not the whole story. Faced with rising auto prices, people bought cheaper (and smaller) cars. In the 1967 model year, the industry built about twenty-five percent fewer full-size cars than in 1966. Still, Pontiac maintained its third place in 1968, when the total market rose back up to a record level of 9.4 million.

Conforming to a new and hurriedly adopted rule, the 1968 Pontiacs were equipped with buzzers that went off whenever the driver's door was opened and the key had not been removed from the ignition lock. This was more of an antitheft device than a direct safety rule, serving to remind owners that cars are more easily stolen if the keys are left in them.

Idle mixture limiter caps were added to Pontiac carburetors in 1968 and the idle-stop solenoid (to prevent running-on when the ignition was switched off) was adopted at the same time.

Lap belts for the driver and front seat passenger had been mandatory equipment since 1966. The 1968 models had to come with lap belts for all passengers, including the back seat occupants, and for the driver and front seat passenger shoulder straps also had to be fitted.

Hastily following up on the industry's lead with the collapsible steering column (which Pontiac adopted in 1967), the National Highway Traffic Safety Agency announced a new rule for 1968 that limited rearward displacement of the steering column and wheel in 30-mph frontal impact to five inches (so as to leave survival space for the driver between the wheel and the seat).

Padded steering wheel hubs and padded door posts and window pillars were standard on all Pontiacs; there was knee padding under the instrument panel and more padding on top of the instrument panel. All models had side markers and padded seat backs, and outside mirror size was increased. Pontiac had been using guard beams in the doors on the B-body cars since 1967 and the A-body cars since 1968, and in 1969 the Department of Transportation instituted a new standard making this equipment mandatory.

Effective from January 1968, Pontiac's brake systems, to conform with a new federal standard, included a split system for failsafe emergency braking, a brake-failure warning light for loss of fluid or overheating and a parking brake capable of holding the vehicle on a thirty-percent grade. Federal Motor Vehicle Safety Standard Number 205 specified that with effect from January 1, 1968, all cars must have 'improved' laminated safety-glass windshields. Pontiac had been using them for years. The exterior design of the cars still remained, by and large, an unregulated area.

The 1968-model Pontiac B-body front can be seen as a derivative of the 1967 design, but a lot of people felt that the transition was made too abruptly. The vertical element of the 1967 design was exaggerated into a protruding heavy chrome bar, integral with the bumper structure that framed the entire grillework. This centerpiece also extended into the hood at the top and below the lower grille frame at the bottom. Some said it reminded them of the Edsel. Stacked headlights were given up, and the four lamps were lined up side by side in the corners of the recessed grille, which had a tight formation of horizontal bars.

The 1968 Catalina did relatively well in the Union/Pure Oil Trials. It took 11.84 seconds to accelerate from 25 to 70 mph, and returned 15.7 miles per gallon in the fuel-economy test. In the 1968 Mobilgas Economy Run, from Los Angeles to Indianapolis, a Catalina again finished third in its class, at eighteen miles per gallon, behind a Buick LeSabre and a Dodge Polara.

Pontiac V-8 engines for 1968 were equipped with a new device that preheated the intake air. Developed by Oldsmobile and manufactured by AC, the thermostatically controlled system mixed air heated by the exhaust gas with fresh air from outside in the proportions necessary to feed air at a constant temperature of 105 degrees to the engine.

Foreign car penetration passed the magic ten-percent mark for the first time in 1968. To stem the flow of imports, Ford and Chevrolet were racing to get four-cylinder subcompacts into production. Pontiac had small-car projects, too, but they were still in the experimental stage. We shall return to take a look at them in a later chapter. Pontiac went into the 1969 model year with the intermediate-size Tempest as its smallest family car, content to leave the increasingly active compact field to Chevrolet.

In the meantime, Washington legislators were busy making new laws about auto safety and pollution. Headrests designed to meet a new federal standard were added on the 1969 Pontiacs. The ignition lock was moved from the instrument panel to the steering column and removing the key effectively locked the steering shaft so that the wheels could not be turned, and blocked the transmission linkage in Park for automatics and Reverse for manual gearboxes, so that it could not be driven away even if a thief could by-pass the ignition lock and get the car started.

No significant engineering changes were made in the 1969 Catalina, Executive and Bonneville, but a partial restyling took place. Pontiac's 1969 B-body cars had smoother front-end lines, though the vertical centerpiece remained part of the combined grille frame and bumper structure and was even extended upwards to the very tip of the hood, eliminating the ugly break in the hood-to-grille junction of the year before. The horizontal bars ran unbroken from the headlights to the narrow vertical chrome bar at the center, and curved sharply forwards to meet the bar and stress its forward-jutting aspect.

How did they perform? The Catalina was second-best in fuel economy in its class in the 1969 Union/Pure Oil Trials, for its 16.4 miles per gallon was higher than all but the Dodge Polara, which did 18.6 mpg. In return the Pontiac scored 10.4 seconds in the 25-70 mph

acceleration test, against 11.8 for the Polara. Now for the brakes—customers were entitled to a real improvement. But no, the Catalina needed an interminable 314.2 feet to come to a stop from 65 mph, mostly because of fade. The 1969 Bonneville raced through the 25-70 mph acceleration test in 8.58 seconds—about average for its class—but returned a distressing 13.9 miles per gallon. The Chrysler 300 was faster (8.2 seconds) in acceleration and still gave 15.7 miles per gallon.

In 1969 the full-size cars still held a major role in the market place, accounting for forty-seven percent of sales. The intermediates took twenty-six percent of sales, and compacts twenty percent. Specialty cars held a four percent share, and luxury cars three percent. Pontiac sales in 1969 slipped to 795,605 cars despite an overall growth in the market to 9.45 million units. Pontiac's market share declined to 8.42 percent and GM as a whole was merely treading water, not advancing. That was the last year Pontiac held third spot in the sales race. The next year was to bring a major upset.

However, it is not believed that federal standards are to blame for Pontiac's fall, though that is not to say that the new laws did not cause problems. Exhaust emission standards coming into effect for

Largest Pontiac engine ever was the 455-cubic-inch V-8 introduced in 1970. It replaced the 428 in all its applications, and disappeared at the end of the 1976 model year.

Catalina for 1970 had a vertical-theme grille that took precedence over the bumper bars for frontal display. Hood sculpturing recalled engine compartments of the thirties... side treatment perpetuated Coke-bottle shape.

1970 allowed no more than 2.2 grams per mile of hydrocarbons and no more than twenty-three grams per mile of carbon monoxide.

Pontiac's engineers coped with the new standards by making certain modifications to the Air Injection Reactor package and installing transmission-controlled spark timing, a device which was found less than ideal for driveability, and was replaced by speed-controlled spark timing on the 1972 models.

Only the GTO (and Firebirds sharing its engines) escaped the AIR system. On the GTO engines, cylinder heads were machined on all interior surfaces and had polished cylinder walls. While keeping within the prescribed emission limits, the GTO engine regained the eight to ten horsepower it usually cost to drive the air pump. But it was too costly a method for more than a small percentage of Pontiac's engines.

Evaporative controls were added to the 1970-model Pontiacs for sale in California. The system consisted of a charcoal canister connected via a plastic hose to the carburetor float bowl, and served to trap fuel vapors emanating from the carburetor when the car was parked. Also, the fuel tank contained a fill-limiter and a liquid/vapor separator with a direct connection to the charcoal canister. This system was extended to all Pontiacs in 1971 as a result of federal legislation.

What happened to Pontiac's sales in 1970 was caused by a combination of changes in both product and personnel. "We were well underway to a million-car year in 1969," says Jim Wangers, "except DeLorean left." John Z. DeLorean moved to Chevrolet as general manager on March 1, 1969, and his place at Pontiac was filled by F. James McDonald, who had been at Pontiac before, but most recently worked for a year at Chevrolet as general manufacturing manager.

DeLorean's was undoubtedly a tough act to follow. During his four years as general manager he had had his finger on Pontiac's pulse every moment of the day. Slim and six feet four inches tall, dark-haired, with a head that seemed small for his lanky frame, John DeLorean was a man of many moods. He could be patient one day, impatient the next. His impassive face was as likely to break out in a snarl as in a grin. He could be kind, and he could be intolerant. But no one questioned his mental powers.

We have seen how John Z. DeLorean was regarded as an engineer. How did his subordinates see him as a general manager? "He isn't such a great guy as he is often made out to be. DeLorean got a lot more interested in sales after he was made general manager, and then he started working on sales gimmicks," Ed Windeler reproached him. "That led to the 2+2 and things like that, the T-37 that failed. He spent too much of his time on things like that."

The 2+2 was a Catalina coupe, aiming for a sporty flavor by using the Italian way to describe the typical seating arrangement of a GT car (roomy seating for two, plus less roomy seating for two more). Steve Malone did not have much to say about it: "It was a joke, really, but we called it a 2+2. It wasn't but the name helped our image. We sold a few of them." The T-37 was a stripped-level Tempest coupe with bucket seats, based on the merchandising idea that it would find a ready market among kids that wanted a GTO but could not afford one. Very few were fooled, and the T-37 lasted only a year.

"DeLorean tried to be as demanding as Knudsen or Estes—but he didn't get the results," Windeler added. Jim Wangers, the advertising executive, takes a different view: "Everything he's credited with, he deserves. He was *that* good, believe me. DeLorean understood

marketing. He had respect for creative people, and he had respect for sales. He was very, very involved with advertising. He took a real interest in the advertising effort.

"If he had a shortcoming," admitted Wangers, "it's that he was very quick to chuck somebody. He'd meet a guy who had been with the division for twenty years or something and if the guy didn't necessarily respond as quickly as John wanted him to for a certain assignment or a certain conviction, then he'd immediately make up his mind 'this guy isn't on my team.' He'd build a team of about five or six guys, and *they* ran the division! While he was running it, it was sensational. But when he left, it started to crumble."

Steve Malone, who took over as chief engineer when DeLorean became general manager, holds a balanced view: "He had a lot of good ideas—not necessarily all his own—but he somehow knew how to put them into a context where somebody could start working on them. He's always had a lot of guys around him who helped him execute those ideas, and by the time it was done, it was done better than he could have. He had a lot of ideas that really weren't worth pursuing, and he'd get people to spend a lot of time on them, and the end result was nothing. He'd exhausted the idea, but rather than giving it up, he'd pursue it to the end. I guess I'd also have to say he's brilliant enough, and aggressive enough, and he moved up really fast, as you know."

Ed Windeler remains negative: "He came up in a good environment. I have to say that he's smart, there's no question about that. But he isn't very practical. A bit of a dreamer." Columnist Judd Arnett reported in the *Detroit Free Press* the day after Pontiac 'took the wraps off' its new general manager that he chatted with DeLorean about motivation—what got him so far in such a hurry. "I don't believe I have ever thought in terms of a job or its objectives," he replied. "The competitive drive is what brings results. You compete personally, with those around you, and with the competition." Few people, even business executives, share DeLorean's mentality of full-time competitiveness. Jim McDonald certainly did not.

No newcomer to Pontiac, Jim McDonald had been works manager of that division for three years, starting in September 1965, a time when the division was experiencing considerable manufacturing problems. He did a lot to get production straightened out, including a number of personnel changes. Pontiac was heavily stocked with manufacturing leaders who had spent lifetimes in the factory. He came in with a fresh pair of eyes, and shook everything up. His responsibility covered all manufacturing, purchasing, production control and reliability functions.

Pontiac High School cheerleaders crowd around the burgundy-colored 1970 Bonneville convertible that was the 14-millionth car with the Pontiac name plate, rolling off the home plant assembly line in December 1969.

This two-door Colonnade hardtop, a 1973 Luxury LeMans, features larger glass area and thinner corner pillars, giving improved visibility all around. A new energy-absorbing bumper system appeared on Pontiac intermediates at this time also.

When he took office as general manager, McDonald looked on Pontiac as the acknowledged styling, engineering and performance leader. But things turned sour. And it wasn't his fault. "DeLorean brought out the '69 cars and left Tom King with a lot of '68's to sell," Jim Wangers points out. McDonald no doubt looked at that as a temporary situation, and wasn't too worried. Then they showed him the 1970 models. "McDonald came in and he panicked," recalls Jim Wangers. "He panicked about the front end. The Bonneville had a 'soft' nose on it, remember? DeLorean left them with that front end on the 1970 B-car, that big square Mercedes-Benz type grille that's so popular now, but would you believe, it came under severe criticism then!"

Now, what about that front end? DeLorean had approved it. It was basically a Jack Humbert design, though in 1968 William L. Porter had taken over as chief designer in the Pontiac studio. He came from the Advanced Design studio and had formerly been in the Chevrolet studio. However, Humbert continued to exercise a great deal of influence over Pontiac styling in his new post as supervisor of the three styling studios of Buick, Oldsmobile and Pontiac.

Compared with the 1969 design, the single vertical bar that split the grille elements was spread out into a rectangular frame with the central upright divider as the boldest of the frame members. It was still slightly reminiscent of the Edsel, but also brought back memories of

prewar GM designs, such as the 1936 Cadillac, 1938 Pontiac and 1940 La Salle.

Thus the centerpiece became the grille, and the spaces on both sides of it were filled with headlamps and driving lights. The bumper bars extended from the grille frame near its lower edge, which was shaped like a broad vee. The hood had three creases, a central one running straight back to the rear end of the hood, and two diagonal ones, spreading out from the corners of the grille to simulate the the engine.

But the magic was gone, and Pontiac didn't know how to win its customers back. General Sales Manager Tom King reached the age of sixty-five in 1970 and retired, and was replaced by a former Buick man who had been working on the GM Marketing Staff for some years, Edward C. Kennard. But even he could not produce immediate results.

The market shrank in 1970, as industry sales slipped from 8.4 million to 7.1 million. And strangely, it was General Motors that took the worst beating, losing 6.7 points of its market share. GM held fifty-three percent of the U.S. car market in 1969, but that fell to 46.3 percent in 1970. Pontiac was badly hit. Calendar-year sales of the full-size Pontiac fell from 366,391 in 1969 to 248,239 in 1970, dropping the Pontiac name plate from fifth rank to ninth inside a twelve-month period. A number of embarrassed Pontiac executives had to remove their golden '3' lapel pins.

Simultaneously, new difficulties were brewing for Pontiac in the form of new auto safety and emission control standards. The 1970 limits remained in force through the 1971 model year, and then the program was cut off by a big change in test procedures for 1972. A new twenty-three-minute cycle with a more accurate constant-volume sampler was adopted.

Oxides of nitrogen emissions were not part of federal standards until 1973, but California had introduced a 4.0 grams per mile nitrogen oxides limit for 1971. This was lowered to 3.2 for 1972. The following year brought a federal nitrogen oxides standard of 3.0 grams per mile. Also for 1972, California allowed only 1.5 grams per mile unburned hydrocarbons compared with a federal limit of 3.4 grams per mile. Carbon monoxide limits were the same, thirty-nine grams per mile, for California as well as the other forty-nine states. And beginning with the 1972 models, exhaust emission systems had to be warranted for five years or 50,000 miles.

On the safety front, a long list of detail specifications was added in 1970, with an effective date of October 1, 1972. These rules laid down the master cylinder reservoir capacity, provision for visual inspection of lining thickness, and specified separate master cylinder reservoirs, covers, seals and retainers for the two separate circuits. Bumper design became subject to Federal Motor Vehicle Safety Standard Number 215 for exterior protection of safety-oriented items, beginning with the 1972 models.

Pontiac engineers found that a lot of normal development work and improvements under study had to be pushed aside to carry out all the work needed to make sure every Pontiac met every standard. In April 1971, Pontiac inaugurated a new multimillion-dollar vehicle emission-control and carburetor testing facility. However, a few minor engine changes were enough to do the emission-control job for 1972.

Pontiac put a thermospring on the carburetor to control a valve that retarded the vacuum pull-off for the choke in cold weather to assure driveability despite new automatic choke settings minimizing the duration. At the same time, Pontiac changed the way the die-cast base for the choke coil was placed on the manifold. The new version had pieces with flatter faces to assure better thermal contact.

But meeting the nitrogen oxides requirement for 1973 proved more complicated. It was done by using exhaust gas recirculation (EGR), a device that had been under development at Rochester Products Division since 1967. It consisted of a valve on the exhaust manifold admitting a certain amount of exhaust gas to a hose leading to and ducting it to a redesigned intake manifold for mixing with fresh air-fuel mixture. The metering of the desired proportion of exhaust gas was controlled by a vacuum-signal port on the carburetor throttle body.

About ten to fifteen percent of the exhaust gas, depending on conditions, was routed back through the engine, serving to reduce the combustion temperature and thereby prevent the formation of nitrogen oxides. Exhaust gas recirculation caused a drop in power output, proportional with the amount of exhaust gas recirculated, and resulted in a corresponding increase in fuel consumption.

At the same time, the automatic choke on all Pontiac V-8 engines was moved from the manifold to the carburetor, with a heat-sensing tube linking it to the heat crossover passage in the intake manifold. Camshaft timing was revised to meet emission control standards. Specific changes included revisions on the 400-cubic-inch V-8 with automatic transmission to restore driveability, and increased overlap on the 400-cubic-inch V-8's outfitted with two-barrel carburetors for improved control of nitrogen oxides formation.

The spark-timing package that year included a time delay relay, transmission control switch, thermo delay switch, and thermo override switch. A new device called a CEC valve was mounted on the carburetor, with an electro-magnetic switch having the dual function of limiting the vacuum-controlled spark advance and delaying the throttle-closing action on deceleration. It effectively eliminated the idle stop solenoid.

Because the 1973 emission control system threw a heavier load on the cooling system, Pontiac adopted a closed-system radiator cap with a separate overflow reservoir to provide constant coolant supply on demand while eliminating aeration in the coolant flow and local hotspots.

Beyond 1973 loomed the proposed standards for 1975 and 1976, setting targets that were perhaps beyond the existing technology. The cost of meeting federal standards was going up and up, even beyond the direst predictions of industry lobbyists at the start of governmental intervention. This had to be reflected in auto prices, which increased from year to year. Price was always essential to Pontiac's success. 'A lot more car for a little more money' could have been its credo. The way Pontiac coped with the profit squeeze subsequently forced the division into a reorientation of its policies, with much tighter supervision by corporate officials.

Bumpers for 1974 LeMans underwent pendulum test (top). The pendulum weighed 4,000 to 5,000 pounds according to which car was on test, swung five feet before impact, and exerted forces up to 20,000 pounds.

CHAPTER 15

Corporate Dictatorship

THROUGHOUT THE NINETEEN-SIXTIES, as each GM car division found itself adding more models, always at the low end in price and size, to defend its market share and maintain sales volume, they gradually forced themselves into a position of considerable overlap. Long gone was the rank and price-bracket order established by GM President Sloan in the mid-twenties. Now Chevrolet was competing in a price range that encompassed all of Pontiac, most of Oldsmobile and part of Buick, and reached right up to Cadillac.

Pontiac especially, and to a large extent also Buick and Oldsmobile, found it necessary to add models that could compete against Chevrolet intermediates, compacts, and so on. And due to the setup of the corporation, most of these products had to be Chevrolet-based, or they could not come into being at all.

General Motors was the last of the auto makers to leave certain manufacturing responsibilities with the car divisions. At Ford all manufacturing had been centralized since the Lincoln purchase in 1922, and at Chrysler since the Dodge purchase in 1928. But in 1971 GM moved to centralize all operations, leaving the car divisions strictly as marketing organizations.

Inevitably, this resulted in a reduced status for the divisional general managers, though they invariably had vice presidential rank. Bunkie had enjoyed a great deal of freedom and power of self-determination when he ran Pontiac. But the division's independence

was eroding. DeLorean had to be more of a team player with his colleagues at the other car divisions than did Estes. And Jim McDonald became sort of a caretaker, regarded more as the corporation's proconsul than as the local chieftain.

For a long time, McDonald had to face the inevitable comparison with his flamboyant predecessor. And DeLorean had indeed set deep marks at Pontiac in his thirteen years at the division. "A little bit of DeLorean must have rubbed off on all of us," says Russ Gee almost wistfully. And Bob Knickerbocker praised him: "DeLorean had a lot of talent and both Knudsen and Estes recognized it. All his new ideas—of course they took time. Overall, John was a combination of talents that you don't often find. He had technical ability, and he had a memory that was beyond what most of us could comprehend."

McDonald's entire background was manufacturing and administration rather than cars. A native of Saginaw, Michigan, where he first saw the light of day in 1922, Jim McDonald graduated from the GM Institute in 1944 and spent the following two years in the U.S. Navy. Returning to GM in 1946, he went to work at the Saginaw Malleable Iron plant, taking over as manager of the Central Foundry in Defiance, Ohio, in 1955. He then went to Willow Run as works manager at the Detroit Transmission Division (now HydraMatic). He remained works manager until 1963, when he was promoted to general manager.

Traffic problems inside the plant caused Pontiac to build an enclosed conveyor to freight complete cars from final assembly to final process and shipping areas. Conveyors were electric, and the system could hold 113 cars, with a delivery time of 43 minutes.

McDonald was in charge at Willow Run when the Turbo-HydraMatic was introduced. It was more trouble-free than any other unit produced there, for earlier transmissions had usually had their share of teething troubles. Design, processing, pilot production, all were carried out with the specific idea of making a quality product from the start, and production-model units were built and tested several months before they were scheduled for delivery to the car divisions. When deliveries did begin, there were no 'bugs' left in the Turbo-HydraMatic.

Both conscientious and ambitious, McDonald saw himself as an executive of presidential calibre. Realizing that the top corporate appointments are out of reach for the heads of supplier divisions, he asked for a chance to run one of the car divisions, and he went to Pontiac as works manager in 1965 with the understanding that this was to be a four-year training program before he would be considered a candidate for top spot at a car division. This program ended with a year at Chevrolet, and when DeLorean went there, McDonald succeeded him at Pontiac.

In emulation of John Z. DeLorean, who had created the Zero-Defects program. McDonald started a new quality program shortly after he arrived in the spring of 1969. The plan was called U-ADDE (you-

add). It was an acronym for Unified Assembly Development and Design Evaluation, and was administered by experts in all areas of building cars. One specialized in tooling, another in assembly methods. Others held responsibilities in processes, reliability, or inspection. One was in charge of specifications and one or more were product engineers. They worked together to pilot future models through the prototype, testing and development stages and into production.

C. L. Stevens was manager of Pontiac's assembly operations in 1969. During 1970, H.A.C. Anderson was appointed director of purchasing and production control for Pontiac and Darwin G. Simpson replaced him as director of reliability. "Cost and quality go hand in hand," Jim McDonald told Joe Callahan of *Automotive News* (July 21, 1969). "Quality doesn't cost money. It saves money. Once a part is properly designed, sloppiness in machines, tools or people becomes extremely costly. Good work results in less waste and less re-work."

A new procedure for getting cars from the drawing board to the assembly line came out of the U-ADDE program. For any new models, Pontiac built eight to ten prototype cars about eighteen to fifteen months before production was due to start. These were cobbled up by skilled craftsmen and were mockups rather than operational cars, with dummy engines and running gear. When approved, construction of a pilot series began. That would include sixty-five to seventy-five cars completed in April/May for August/September introduction. They would be built on a one-off basis but using production tooling, thus being closely representative of true specifications. U-ADDE did not replace Zero-Defects. In the long run, remnants of both programs became routine, and the labels disappeared.

But quality problems did not go away. Some defects were actually a side effect of the increasing standardization within the corporation. Callback campaigns commonly involved the products of more than one division. Without singling out Pontiac for exoneration, there is no doubt that defects in design or materials were also imported to Pontiac from other divisions.

The product planning function had been removed from the car divisions gradually, from careful beginnings in the 1930's, and transferred to a corporate office at the GM Technical Center in Warren, Michigan, which opened in 1958. After 1971 the car divisions retained only some measure of engineering responsibility in specific, assigned areas.

New-car planning, design and engineering became a corporate function, in which the car divisions played subcontracting roles. Think back to the X-100 project, which gave Pontiac, Oldsmobile and Buick its first compacts. Consider the 1964 A-body cars: one intermediate car for four divisions.

When preparations began for the 1973-model A-body cars, the divisional authority and involvement was minimal. The corporation set up an engineering task force at the Tech Center, and that's where the next LeMans came from. So it followed, with B-body, E-body, X-body cars. The makes ceased to have meaning; what counted now was the letter code for the body. An A-body car was an A-body car whether it was sold as a Buick, Chevrolet, Oldsmobile or Pontiac. The LeMans was merely Pontiac's A-body car.

This shift in divisional functions had a tremendous ripple effect within Pontiac's engineering department. In 1968 Pontiac was given corporate responsibility for vehicle handling, in coordination with the GM Engineering Staff which had an active vehicle-dynamics research program, plus Oldsmobile for steering (in consultation with

Saginaw), and Chevrolet for suspension and structures. What this boils down to, in the words of Steve Malone, is this: ''We're trying to get agreement among the divisions about the things we ought to improve.''

More and more work was being done jointly by the divisions, often under corporate direction. But each car division still had to sort out problems of its own creation and was encouraged to initiate quality improvements in various areas.

In a separate crash program, Pontiac tackled its electrical systems —not because their wiring was worse than on other cars, but because the proliferation of electrical options and equipment easily led to loss of reliability. In its studies, Pontiac set goals beyond just improved reliability. Pontiac wanted improved performance, too, and extended life, elimination of periodic maintenance, and greater serviceability. The 1972 Pontiac adopted the new Delco unitized ignition system, generators with integral rectifier and voltage regulator, and increased use of the maintenance-free Delco energizer battery.

While other GM divisions toed the line of the corporate edict that specified bias-belted tires, Pontiac was doing a lot of work with radial-ply tires, and adapting the cars' suspension systems to be fully compatible with radials.

Between 1968 and 1972 a number of Pontiac engineers retired, while those who stayed found themselves routed through seemingly aimless reassignments. John P. Charles, executive assistant chief engineer since 1961, retired in 1968. Herman Kaiser retired in 1970—he had served as assistant chief engineer at Pontiac since 1965. Kaiser was then in charge of planning, production and cost accounting.

George Roberts, who had been at Pontiac since 1938 and was Pontiac's chassis engineer, transferred to Holden's in Australia as chief engineer in 1968, and from there to Opel in Germany in 1974. Edmund L. Windeler was named assistant chief engineer in charge of administration in January 1969. That saddled him with responsibility for a million details covering every model produced by Pontiac. A tall, trim engineer, with a little brush-type moustache, Windeler always spoke and acted as a man of authority, and was a fine choice for this exposed assignment. Another assistant chief engineer, Mark Garlick, retired in 1970. He had held assistant chief engineer's rank since 1954 and most recently served as executive engineer for experimental, production and field engineering.

Pontiac also lost Albert E. Roller, who transferred to the GM Engineering Staff in 1970. Roller was born in Stuttgart, West Germany, in 1916. He came to Pontiac in 1957 as a senior project engineer, and worked in various fields. He became an assistant design engineer in

1959, and three years later was assigned to work as a transmission engineer. After a year as executive engineer for chassis, transmissions and axles since 1965, he was also given responsibility for engines. In February 1970, Malone appointed him executive engineer of advance design and design coordinator, but within four months he left Pontiac.

Clayton B. Leach, creator of the V-8 valve gear, was promoted to assistant chief engineer for power train, and F. F. Timpner was made assistant chief engineer for advanced design. Bill Collins, after a year as director of production engineering, was named assistant chief engineer for product planning, body and styling in 1967, a post he held till June 1973, when he was assigned to be chief engineer for the 1977 B-car program for the corporation.

After Collins left Pontiac for the corporate task force, John R. Seaton became chief engineer for chassis and Duane F. Miller staff engineer for body design. Leach and Windeler continued until they reached retirement age in 1976.

The year 1970 was memorable for many reasons. Among key events the arrival of the subcompacts stands out. The Gremlin arrived in March, and the Pinto and Vega in September. Their availability did not attract a lot of buyers away from Pontiac's intermediates, but they became competition for the compact Ventura II that Pontiac dealers began selling in March 1971.

The Ventura II was an X-body car, built exclusively by the GM Assembly Division. The design had been a new vehicle for 1968, replacing the Chevy II and carrying the name Nova. Two years later,

Bonneville for 1971 sported an all-new B-body with the largest windshield Pontiac had ever used. The Bonneville was built on a 126-inch wheelbase; by 1973 it was back to 124 inches.

Ventura II was a compact car added to the Pontiac range for 1971. Basically a Chevy Nova, it came with Chevrolet 250 six or 307 V-8 engine.

Oldsmobile and Buick were given their versions of the X-body car, choosing the names Omega and Apollo. Pontiac had to wait another year.

The 1971 Ventura II was built on the Nova's 111-inch wheelbase and came in two body styles, four-door sedan and two-door coupe. It was available with a 250-cubic-inch Chevrolet six or Pontiac 350-cubic-inch V-8. It had a longish hood, to provide room for the in-line six cylinder engine, and a short deck. The windshield had an unfashionably steep angle, the A-posts were thick and the roof was kind of domed, leaving an overall impression that it was a little too heavy, perhaps even clumsy. Pontiac did not have much chance to give the car any of its own styling touches. The Chevrolet grille was split into four horizontal elements, with a pointed nose of sheet metal in the middle, and that was all.

Lowest-priced 1971 Pontiac was the Ventura II coupe with the six-cylinder engine, listed at $2,458. Extra charge for a V-8 was only ninety-five dollars. The two-speed automatic transmission for either engine cost $174. The three-speed had a price of $206.

Pontiac had expected to sell 100,000 Venturas a year, but did not even reach half that figure during 1971, while Nova sales were booming. People just refused to pay a premium price for a Pontiac label, when they knew perfectly well the car was a Chevrolet through and through. Pontiac's inauspicious experience in the compact market convinced McDonald that what the division really needed was a subcompact, and they asked the corporation about getting a Pontiac version of Chevrolet's Vega.

His chief engineer, Steve Malone, wanted Pontiac to build its own subcompact, a car of his own design, with a pushrod-operated overhead-valve cast-iron engine rather than the expensive—and in fact, experimental—overhead-camshaft unlinered aluminum-block Vega power unit. But because Pontiac could not afford to tool up and produce Malone's car, the project came to nothing.

Pontiac began thinking about building its own small car as early as 1965. At that time, Ford and Chevrolet had not yet formulated their subcompact plans, but Pontiac wanted to be ready with its own minicar in case the market demanded it. And the minicar project was no ordinary car. When the Ford Pinto and Chevrolet Vega came out in 1970, they were both quite conventional in chassis layout and body design. But Pontiac's experimental engineers had other, wilder ideas.

Pontiac called it the X-4, a code name taken from the configuration of its two-stroke aircraft-type four-cylinder radial engine, a remarkably small and lightweight power unit designed by Leo Hilke. It was laid out with the four cylinders extended in X-formation from a central Scotch yoke. The four pistons worked in pairs, opposing pistons forming a pair. The two paired pistons were linked by a straight one-piece connecting rod, with a metal yoke in the middle, where it met with a similar yoke on the second rod. A plate that was part of the Scotch yoke had a small slot for holding the crankpin bearing, guiding the bearing from side to side as the pistons moved to and fro in their cylinders. This action forced the crankpin to move, thus turning the output shaft.

The X-4 engine had a cylinder displacement of about one hundred inches, developing about 75 to 80 hp. One version used twin Zenith side-draft carburetors, another had a port-type fuel injection system. The engine was air-cooled, with finned aluminum cylinders. The engine drove its cooling fan by mechanical means, an aluminum shield ducted the air to where it was needed. Dry sump lubrication was used, and since the engine ran on the two-stroke principle, cylinder lubrication was assured by adding oil to the gasoline, in a 1/25 proportion.

This engine was built as a unit with a very special HydraMatic transmission, and the whole power train was carried on the rear axle, with the engine on the forward side, tilted at a thirty-degree angle. It was so small and light that it could be carried as unsprung weight without problems. This is unusual, but not unique. In Sweden, about 1939, Volvo used a similar layout on a car with an eight-cylinder radial engine. Hot-rod constructor Don Waite bolted a Ford V-8 complete with transmission to the rear axle on a vehicle he raced in 1950. And White Trucks produced a door-to-door delivery wagon with a flat-four engine carried as a unit with the rear axle for several years in the late forties and early fifties.

On the Pontiac X-4, the axle was located by diagonal control arms and a transverse rod at the rear. The front engine mount served as the forward-end pivot point. Vertical coil springs carried the load. The front suspension had nothing unusual, looking like a scaled-down version of the Tempest front end. Tires were very small: 6.20-12.

The prototype was a stylish little coupe with a three-passenger bench seat. It had a streamlined, sloping nose with pop-up headlights and a very sharp rake on the windshield. A small trunk was provided behind the rear axle, with a lid hinged at the base of the recessed backlight, while the sail panels were stretched back along the fender tops to form a buttressed look. It was only forty-seven inches high and weighed no more than 1,500 pounds complete.

It was going into its test phase during the winter of 1969, for DeLorean was quite serious about developing the car as a basis for a future production model. But the whole project was shelved after he left. The X-4 never progressed beyond the experimental stage.

It was the last time Pontiac, entirely on its own, undertook a project involving a completely new type of car. Russ Gee explains: "At that time there was an effort made to work on things that were thought to have some feasibility for production. But in today's setup, we don't have the luxury at the division level of working too far ahead, when we do have the facilities of General Motors—research and advanced product engineering and that sort of thing—available to us."

The corporate dictatorship had taken firm control over new product planning and development, and GM displayed an incredible lack of foresight in coming out with its 1973 intermediates having a new A-body that was lower, longer and wider than the earlier version. That was the last thing Pontiac needed, having enough problems trying to sell its full-size cars in 1971 and 1972. On top of that, the B-body cars attracted public attention for a potential safety problem that GM at first did not want to recognize, but ended up in a major callback.

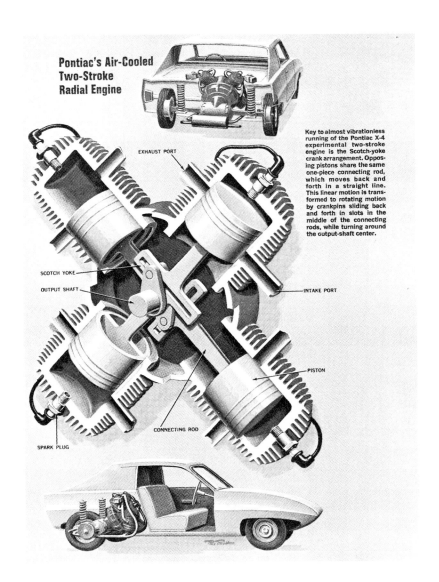

Pontiac's Air-Cooled Two-Stroke Radial Engine

Key to almost vibrationless running of the Pontiac X-4 experimental two-stroke engine is the Scotch-yoke crank arrangement. Opposing pistons share the same one-piece connecting rod, which moves back and forth in a straight line. This linear motion is transformed to rotating motion by crankpins sliding back and forth in slots in the middle of the connecting rods, while turning around the output-shaft center.

EXHAUST PORT

SCOTCH YOKE

OUTPUT SHAFT

INTAKE PORT

PISTON

CONNECTING ROD

SPARK PLUG

Pontiac's X-4 prototype minicar had a radial air-cooled engine mounted on the rear axle. Radial-four had two sets of opposed pistons with straight connecting rods and a Scotch yoke arrangement to turn the crankshaft. Real engine was, relatively, about half the size shown in these drawings.

Bonneville two-door hardtop for 1973 recaptured some of the side treatment of the 1969 Grand Prix, but carried a grille that was more reminiscent of Oldsmobile or Buick than typical of Pontiac. William L. Porter was chief designer of the Pontiac studio when it was created.

In August 1972, the National Highway Traffic Safety Administration (NHTSA) issued a consumer bulletin to warn owners of a possible steering defect on 3.5 million B- and C-body GM cars, involving the total 1971–72 model runs of the full-size Pontiac. The agency claimed that on gravel roads, stones could get trapped between the coupling at the base of the steering shaft and the frame members, jamming the steering and resulting in loss of control. Immediately General Motors went on record as saying "the conditions under which certain sized stones from gravel roads may lodge in the steering coupling are so unusual and the occurrences so rare that we don't believe this constitutes a hazard to our customers, nor a safety-related defect."

But in the NHTSA investigation that followed, no less than twenty-three cases of accidents caused by this problem came to light, and GM had to give in. Callback letters were mailed out to 3.7 million car owners in February 1973. Each car was fitted with a protective shield to keep stones from entering the space around the steering coupling. It

1974 Grand Am coupe had a special version of the A-body, with its unique front end. It was also better balanced than the contemporary Grand Prix.

Four-door Grand Am sedan for 1974 had a unique combination of ride comfort and handling precision. It was powerful, but less of a hot-rod than the GTO, and it sacrificed less soft springing to sportiness.

cost the corporation about $16 million. The 1973 models had a different design which obviated the need for a shield.

Pontiac's big news that year was the A-body cars. With the major redesign for 1973, the LeMans convertible disappeared. So did the hardtop coupe. The range included the LeMans, LeMans Sport coupe, GTO coupe, Luxury LeMans and Grand Am, plus the Safari wagon in two-and three-seat versions.

Each division had its own outer skin for the new A-body, and the Pontiac stood apart from all the others in styling. Bulging body sides were sculptured to convey the impression of separate front and rear fender lines. This was achieved by gentle curves and a total absence of horizontal striping above doorsill level. Only the windowsills marked the beltline, while the fender shapes blended smoothly into the door panels. Single headlights were set in squared-off bezels just inboard of the fender tips. Two squared-off grille elements were separated by a wide central sheet-metal protrusion that rose into the hood and flared

out towards the A-posts, giving a triangular shape to the hood design. The grilles were filled by a multitude of thin vertical bars and four thicker ones matching the chrome-plated grille frames.

We tested the 1973 LeMans Safari for *Popular Science Monthly*, and noted that it was as roomy as the full-size Pontiac wagon from 1967. There was a total of 85.1 cubic feet of cargo space, plus 5.8 cubic feet with the third seat in use, or 9.8 cubic feet in a two-seat wagon.

The Safari was powered by the two-barrel carburetor version of the 350-cubic-inch V-8, in combination with a Turbo-HydraMatic transmission and a 3.08:1 axle ratio. We found it would go from standstill to 60 mph in 10.8 seconds, and to 80 mph in 20.5 seconds. Speeding up from 25 to 70 mph was a matter of 12.3 seconds (with kick-down to Low range).

In our handling tests, the LeMans wagon was faster than its rivals (which were tested at the same time, under identical conditions). The Pontiac felt and acted like a passenger car throughout, while the AMC Matador oversteered, the Dodge Coronet Crestwood was balked by power steering pump catch and the Mercury Montego Villager suffered from excessive understeer.

The most memorable model that came out of Pontiac's 1973-model A-car program was the Grand Am. The two-door was, without doubt, a Grand Touring coupe, and the four-door could be called a Grand

Touring sedan. They had tremendous power (400- or 455-cubic-inch V-8's), and suspension modifications that stressed roadholding and steering precision without sacrificing ride comfort. It had the same soft springs as the Luxury LeMans, but specially calibrated shock absorbers and reinforced stabilizer bars. Also, it had wider rims and tires.

William T. Collins was in charge of the engineering team that developed the Grand Am. He saw this assignment as a way to build the car he personally would most like to drive, using the main components of the Pontiac LeMans and a certain amount of special parts and equipment. "I felt that we needed to get back to a *road* kind of car for the guy who really likes automobiles and likes to drive," said Collins.

"I have never quite understood the Woodward Avenue dragstrip macho kind of cars. In all cars that I have worked on—including the GTO's—I always tried to have a little bit of sophistication in the handling and suspension areas—more than you would need to go out to a red light and run away from somebody."

Bill Collins is a tall and athletic-looking man, but professes to be no sportsman at all. Unlike DeLorean, he does not play golf. We asked him what he did with his evenings and weekends, and got a frank but brief explanation: "I work overtime a lot."

The Grand Am had its own front end built around a plastic bumper consisting of a straight bar running the full width of the body plus a soft nose cone that the Pontiac engineers disrespectfully referred to as a 'rubber ducky.' The Grand Am grille design consisted of six vertical-theme grille inserts, separated by the plastic bumper frame in their clusters, and divided into two sets of three. The whole front end was obviously inspired by the 1953-54 Studebaker with its notable backwards slope—then unique, attractive and aerodynamically advantageous. The standard LeMans single-headlight arrangement was used, with very subtle side decor. A thin chrome molding marked the wheel opening profiles and tied them together below doorsill level. The windshield was framed in chrome, but the side windows had black frames.

Keeping the cost under control was perhaps the most difficult challenge. "We were able to take some parts off the Grand Prix," explained Collins, "such as the instrument panel, and on the exterior, we were able to give the car enough frontal distinction so that the car had a personality apart from the LeMans series. I think we sold about 40,000 the first year—damn nice volume for a first year out," Collins went on, "but the sales guys struggled with the concept. They didn't know what it was—or how to sell it. They got confused between a bunch of luxury stuff that looks like a showroom and the image the car can get

with the people that drive it. It died after I left. I still have my '75 silver four-door which I love dearly."

Collins left Pontiac in 1974 and General Motors two years later. "I was voted by all the chief engineers to run the '77 B-car program. I started that and set up the project center." McDonald left Pontiac at the end of September 1972, to take over as general manager of Chevrolet. Two years later, he was named executive vice president in charge of the U.S. and Canadian automotive operations of General Motors.

It had become tradition by now that whenever Chevrolet needed a new general manager, they took the top man at Pontiac. Promotion to general manager of Pontiac began to be seen as a stepping stone to running Chevrolet, and after that, General Motors. Thus, the next man to be appointed to head Pontiac had to be aware of the boundless opportunities implicit in the promotion. The corporation's choice was Martin J. Caserio. As a young man Caserio had taken no particular interest in cars, and his first job was as a metal research engineer at AC Spark Plug in Flint. He stayed at AC for twenty-one years, rising through the ranks from chief metallurgist via the positions of process and development, military contracts engineer and assistant chief engineer, to take over as chief engineer of AC Automotive products in 1953.

A native of Laurium, Michigan, Caserio was a youthful fifty-six when he came to Pontiac. His schooling was capped by graduation from the Michigan College of Mining and Technology (now Michigan Technological University) in Houghton with a B.S. degree in metallurgical engineering in 1936. During his career at AC, he began to acquire more and more managerial duties while doing less and less engineering. His responsibilities expanded to include equipment sales, reliability and quality control in 1956.

After a year of running the AC plant in Milwaukee, he was offered the top job at Delco Radio Division (now Delco Electronics) at Kokomo, Indiana. He took it, and stayed with Delco for six years, but returned to Flint in 1964 as general manager of AC Spark Plug Division. That brought him election as a vice president of General Motors and membership of the corporation's administration committee. He was regarded as a potential chief executive officer. His next promotion followed in 1966, when Calvin J. Werner left GMC Truck and Coach to take over as general manager of Cadillac. Caserio was picked to lead the truck division and he moved from Flint to Bloomfield Hills, between Pontiac and Detroit. He did well at GMC. The truck business was good, and GMC (in close collaboration with Chevrolet) prospered. On the same date Caserio took office at Pontiac Motor Division, John

Newly appointed general manager of Pontiac, Martin J. Caserio, greeted the 16-millionth Pontiac with a 55-pound lollipop in the company of the 16-year-old daughter of an employee, on November 26, 1972. Car was a 1973 Catalina. Caserio came up through AC Spark Plug and successfully ran GMC Truck and Coach Division before taking charge of Pontiac.

Z. DeLorean was named group executive in charge of the Car and Truck group.

After three years at Chevrolet, DeLorean regained responsibility for Pontiac at a higher level, just as the division went into its period of Caserio management.

A blue four-door Catalina built in Pontiac on November 27, 1972, was the division's sixteen-millionth car. On that occasion, General Manager Caserio pointed out that it took ten years to build the first million Pontiacs and only sixteen months to build the newest million. Half of all Pontiacs built by that time had been produced since 1962.

At this time, the share of Pontiac cars built in Pontiac was diminishing, as smaller models built elsewhere were in greater demand. In 1972 the home plant accounted for forty-one percent of Pontiac car production, but the number fell to 35.2 percent in 1974.

The Pontiac range of models included A-body, B-body, F-body, G-body and X-body cars, with the addition of the H-body and HS-body cars on the horizon. How many were true Pontiacs? The G-body (Grand Prix) was a Pontiac creation. The 1971 B-body and 1973 A-body cars were corporate projects. The F-body and X-body cars had been developed at Chevrolet.

We asked Jack N. Humbert if it was more difficult for Pontiac to obtain some styling individuality in view of all the commonality with the other GM makes forced on the division. "No," said Humbert, "I don't think so, necessarily. It's somewhat more difficult. There is a lot more sharing going on. But that's not what I see as the main problem. I think the problem now is to make it fresh enough every year to see a change."

As for engineering individuality, Steve Malone stresses Pontiac's leadership in its assigned field: "I'd like to think that Pontiac probably has the most responsive and precise handling of any GM cars. Primarily because we insist on having tight control over steering response, no delay in the driver input to the car, and like to have a relatively quick-steering car, contrary to the philosophy of some of the other divisions. We have a reputation for handling and we're trying to keep it." Malone went on, "We have a record of originating more specialty cars, such as the Firebird Trans Am, the Grand Prix. We've had some that we're not too proud of—such as the Judge—and some other price-leader kind of cars that were not too successful, like the T-37."

Here, it's important to distinguish between engineering and packaging. The Judge and the T-37 were mere packaging variations on the A-body, while the Trans Am and Grand Prix involved a considerable engineering effort. The conclusion seems to be that Pontiac is very good at engineering and very poor at packaging.

But Jim Wangers disagrees, hinting at a certain amount of bluff in the Pontiac marketing policy: "Pontiac is a promotion. And when they start taking that thing seriously, that's when they got trouble." On another occasion, Wangers told us: "Who buys a Pontiac? It's a snob who won't buy a Chevy because it's too common for him."

And trouble was to hit hard at Pontiac while Caserio was in charge. It had nothing to do with taking the job or the car too seriously. It had everything to do with the fuel crisis. And that was destined to turn the whole auto industry upside down.

CHAPTER 16

Fuel Crisis to CAFE

CAFE IS AN ACRONYM that signifies Corporate Average Fuel Economy, and what it means in practice is that by 1985 the cars built by a manufacturer must reach 27.5 miles per gallon as a sales-weighted average in a specific test. That does not mean that all cars must give 27.5 mpg.

CAFE rules are based on the amount of fuel consumed by a fleet of cars representing the maker's actual product mix in retail trade over a given number of miles. The formula is so arranged that if Pontiac has two models, one giving 10 mpg and another giving 30 mpg, the average fleet economy is 15 mpg—not the 20 mpg that would appear to be the answer.

Congress passed the CAFE act in November 1976, and Brock Adams, Secretary of the Department of Transportation, announced the CAFE rules in July 1977. A graduated timetable was set, fixing the CAFE at 18 mpg for 1978, rising to 20 mpg in 1980, 22 in 1981 and 24 in 1982. After an average of 26 mpg in 1983 and 27 the following year, it reaches its final ceiling of 27.5 mpg in 1985. In the 1975 model year, General Motors, including Pontiac, had a CAFE of 15.7 mpg, an improvement of 3.5 mpg over the 1972 models, but still far short of the goals for 1978 and beyond.

This legislation came about as a direct result of the fuel crisis in 1973/74, after which fuel conservation became a major national goal. When the Arabs turned off the tap in October 1973, domestic refinery capacity was inadequate to handle the national demand for gasoline, and many car owners in the country suffered the dreary experience of waiting in line to fill up—sometimes for hours.

Even before there was any fuel-economy legislation, people started clamoring for smaller cars. Big cars were a glut on the market, and both of Pontiac's main lines, the A-body and B-body cars, were indeed big. It wasn't just car size that bothered the customers. It was lack of driveability, and low efficiency in engines of all sizes. Pontiac's emission-control systems for 1973 were severely detrimental to fuel economy, with a combination of exhaust gas recirculation, preheated air, secondary air injection, hot-air choke and transmission-controlled spark timing.

As the law stood in 1973, the Federal emission standards for 1976 included a requirement for nitrogen oxides control with a maximum limit of 0.4 grams per mile. At the end of 1973, the EPA was having second thoughts about nitrogen oxides control, and asked Congress for a thirteen-year program of progressively stricter limits, starting with 2.0 grams per mile for the 1977 through 1981 model years, 1.0 from 1982 to 1989, and 0.4 from 1990 onwards.

Safety rules were blamed for some of the weight increase on recent models, such as the 1973 bumper standards, requiring that cars must have no damage to safety-related items after one 5 mph front and one 2.5 mph rear barrier impact. A pendulum test with angled impacts was

1975 Grand Prix boasted new front end but remained otherwise unchanged. It was about to become Pontiac's best-selling series.

added the following year, using a pendulum equal to the weight of the car, with requirements now raised to 5 mph at the rear end as well.

Front and rear bumpers with gas-filled cylinders to act as self-restoring energy absorbers were adopted for the B-body and A-body Pontiacs in the 1973 model year. The Ventura and Firebird had rigid bumper mounting systems that were not self-restoring on barrier impacts. What hurt Pontiac's cost picture most was not the setting of such standards, but the fact that progressively more demanding bumper standards forced Pontiac to design new bumper systems each year for the period 1973 to 1977.

For 1974 the use of energy-absorbing self-restoring bumpers was extended to include the Ventura, while the Firebird models were given cast urethane front and rear bumper systems. The front impact bar was

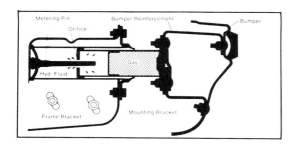
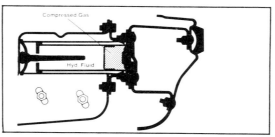
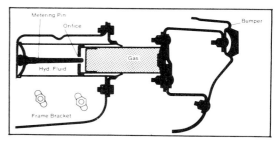

The 1974 bumper systems for Pontiac B-body cars contained hydraulic energy-absorbers that allowed the bumper mounting system to retract about four inches under impact. This was used on both front and rear bumpers.

Intermediate LeMans was regarded as a gas-guzzler during the 1973-74 fuel crisis. It was too heavy to gain economy with six-cylinder engines and needed a V-8 for normal performance. Sales went down.

Grand Ville for 1974 was built on a 124-inch wheelbase and weighed 4,655 pounds. Bumper systems with hydraulic energy-absorbing cylinders added up to 150 pounds per car.

a low-density urethane foam cast over a stamped high-strength steel retainer, with a box-section reinforcement that was bolted on behind the retainer. The rear impact bar was a low-density flexible urethane foam casting bonded to an E-shaped high-strength aluminum reinforcement structure. All the work on the bumpers and new safety

devices came to be the responsibility of Byron L. Warner, who was named chief engineer for body and design in June 1974, after many years of working with men like Kaiser, Miller, Timpner and Lagergren.

Other safety items caused both expense and annoyance to the car buyers. The 1974 models had to be equipped with a seat belt interlock device, so that the car could not be started unless the driver and front passenger had buckled their belt locks. This proved to be a real headache for lots of people, and their protest was loud enough to bring about the cancellation of the interlock rule in time for the 1975 models.

Beginning with cars built after September 1, 1974, brake systems had to conform to a set of arbitrary performance tests established by the NHTSA. A total of seventeen tests included 2½-mph blows at each end to test the parking pawl in the transmission system. After warming up the brakes, the car had to make six stops from 30 mph within a fifty-four-foot distance with a pedal pressure not exceeding 150 pounds, and then another six stops from 60 mph within 216 feet at a pedal pressure not exceeding 120 pounds.

After burnishing the brakes, another series of stops were to be made under the same conditions, but with distances shortened to forty-nine feet from 30 mph and 194 feet from 60 mph. Finally, the car must pass a test of stopping from 80 mph within 383 feet at a pedal pressure not exceeding 150 pounds, and stop from within 4 to 8 mph of its top speed in a closely defined distance, also without pedal pressure exceeding 150 pounds.

Other tests specified maximum distances and pedal pressures for cars with partial brake failure (half the hydraulic system inoperative, or power brake booster disconnected). Most cars could meet these standards without further modification, but Pontiac had to undertake a vast test program to make sure that every car, with any combination of factory-installed options, did in fact meet them. And wherever there was doubt, higher braking capacity was added.

Front disc brakes had become optional on the 1967 Pontiac and Tempest, but only 1.7 percent of Pontiac buyers bought them while 2.4 percent of Tempest buyers did. Most big Pontiacs were sold with power brakes—ninety-nine percent in 1967. A new type of single-piston floating-caliper disc brake was adopted for the 1969 Pontiac, Grand Prix and Firebird—but still only as optional equipment.

That meant higher prices. And prices were all-important. After a period of inflation came a dollar devaluation, then a floating dollar, then more inflation. And it was very much on people's minds that federal standards were costing them a lot of money as well as wasting energy. Under popular pressure, Congress began deferring the effective dates on some of its legislation. But it turned out to be a trade-off. The slackening of the rules and timetables for safety and pollution control was followed by CAFE.

What happened to Pontiac in the middle of all this? Its sales just crumbled. Sales were off by more than one third from 1973 to 1974, and fell still lower in 1975. Sales of the full-size Pontiac were cut by more than half, from 316,778 cars in 1973 to a mere 154,780 cars in the 1974 calendar year.

The division was not equipped to respond rapidly to the sudden change in demand. Pontiac could not independently make the A-body and B-body cars smaller. Any major change—and a major change was what was needed—could only be made by the corporation, involving all divisions using those bodies. Nor could much be done about the product mix. F-body and X-body cars could not be produced in the plants that had excess A-body and B-body capacity. Pontiac was stuck with having to try and sell what it could make—or get from the GM Assembly Division.

All GM car divisions were dogged by quality problems and NHTSA-ordered callbacks. In December 1973, consumer advocate Ralph Nader alerted the National Highway Traffic Safety Administration to a potential safety defect in the steering systems of the 1974-model GM A-, B- and C-body cars. The problem was described as a risk that the nuts holding the front suspension members on their mounts could work loose, which in turn could lead to breakage of a shaft that is part of an assembly that keeps the front wheels in proper alignment. Fracture of this shaft would result in one of the wheels going sharply out of line, accompanied by a pull in the steering wheel to one side or the other. This forced GM to call back 843,000 cars, including about 172,000 Pontiac intermediates and full-size cars and station wagons. The problem was cured by fitting special lock nuts (or welding the old nuts in place).

The Environmental Protection Agency also had callback power in case cars tested failed to meet the standards they were guaranteed for. As late as October 1976 the Environmental Protection Agency ordered General Motors to call back 330,000 1974-model Pontiacs equipped with 350- and 400-cubic-inch V-8 engines using two-barrel carburetors to check for defective thermal vacuum valves controlling the volume of exhaust gas. In January 1977 the same check had to be made on a further 195,000 Pontiacs from 1974 having four-barrel engines.

Action came fast in all legal matters; more slowly in the problems of downsizing the cars. The B-body cars dated from 1971 and were not to be renewed until 1977. Some realignment was made in the model lineup during the period immediately preceding the fuel crisis. The Grand Ville had been introduced in 1970 as a 1971 model, as a replacement for the Bonneville Brougham, and nearly 2,000 of them were sold before the end of the calendar year. The Grand Ville continued through the 1975 model year.

Catalina prices for 1971 started at $3,405 for the four-door sedan. That price did not include items that the vast majority of buyers specified, such as automatic transmission ($190) and power steering ($126). But ventilated front-disc brakes with power assist had at last been standardized. For 1972, power steering and automatic transmission were also made standard on the B-body Pontiacs. Base price for the four-door Catalina went to $3,713, while Bonneville prices started at $4,169. Further increases followed inexorably in 1973, 1974, 1975 and 1976.

The corporation agreed to let Pontiac have the subcompact H-body car for 1975, giving birth to the Astre. The 1975 Pontiac Astre was nothing but a Vega sports coupe outfitted with a Pontiac-type front end consisting of a plastic panel with a small split-grille design giving the impression of a family relationship with the Firebird. The sloping hood line helped reinforce this idea, but a massive bumper did a lot to destroy it, especially in view of the car's small overall dimensions.

Astre was offered in two levels, Custom and SJ. In addition to the hatchback coupe, the Astre was also built as a two-door wagon. It was powered by Chevrolet's aluminum-block overhead-camshaft 140-cubic-inch engine, coupled with three-speed or four-speed synchromesh floorshift transmission or a small three-speed Turbo-HydraMatic.

Testing the 1975 Astre wagon for *Popular Science* magazine, Jim Dunne noted that the car took 19.7 seconds for the 0-to-60 mph acceleration run, and thirty-eight seconds to reach 80 mph from standstill. Speeding up from 25 to 70 mph took 26.8 seconds. Driven around the Bridgehampton race circuit at a constant speed of 45 mph the Astre returned fuel economy of 23.9 mpg. Speeding up to a 60 mph average—which involves hard cornering, and with a low-powered car of this type, a high proportion of full-throttle driving—pushed the fuel economy back to 18.6 mpg.

Thinking the subcompact was the answer to the slack in sales, Pontiac scheduled 100,000 Astre sales for the 1975 model year, including 10,000 SJ models. After October introduction, only 5,662 Astre cars were delivered up to the end of the 1974 calendar year, which was an ill omen for its sales potential. Pontiac sold a little more than 50,000 Astre cars during the 1975 calendar year. This figure shrank to just over 40,000 during 1976, and less than 30,000 in 1977.

The Astre was discontinued at the end of the 1977 model year, though it was not without offspring. Starting with the 1976 model year, Pontiac was given an HS-body car, which was sold as the Sunbird. It was a Pontiac edition of the Chevrolet Monza notchback coupe, using the same Vega engine as the Astre. Nearly 50,000 Sunbirds were sold in 1976. For 1977 the Sunbird received Pontiac's own 151-cubic-inch four-cylinder engine, and its fuel economy (EPA tested) went up from 28 to 30 mpg.

From 1974 to 1975 the Federal standards demanded a reduction in unburned hydrocarbons from 3.4 to 1.5 grams per mile and in carbon monoxide from thirty-nine to fifteen grams per mile. At the same time, California standards demanded a reduction in hydrocarbons from 3.2 to 0.9 grams per mile, and from thirty-nine to nine grams per mile carbon monoxide.

Between 1963 and 1969 General Motors Engineering and Research Staff made and tested a number of experimental cars equipped with emission-control devices, including manifold reactors, catalytic converters, fuel injection, retarded spark timing and exhaust gas recirculation.

By mid-year 1969 the catalytic converter had emerged as the type of device offering the greatest potential for meeting future emission control standards.

It was in November 1969 that GM President Ed Cole was invited by Dr. Lee Du Bridge, science advisor to President Nixon, to come to the White House for a review, with other industry leaders, of the proposed standards for 1971, 1975 and 1980. At this meeting, Cole stated that GM believed it was technically possible to develop systems that could meet the 1975 standards, but that more time was needed to engineer these systems and prove their durability.

AC Spark Plug Division became the lead division for catalyst development, working in liaison with all the car divisions and GM Engineering Staff. Between 1970 and 1973 AC tested over 1,000 different catalysts submitted by sixty different suppliers. Oldsmobile was placed in charge of developing the total converter system.

Catalytic converters came into use on the 1975-model Pontiac engines. They increased the cost of the car by $150 but permitted some gain in fuel economy and driveability (because some of the earlier emission control systems could be discarded). The catalysts have a higher capacity for cleaning the exhaust gases, so that the engineers were able to let the engines run more efficiently—and therefore with higher pollutant levels—while still meeting the standards.

But Pontiac found that its engines still needed AIR, EGR and a retarded spark. And, naturally, the evaporative control system as well as positive crankcase ventilation remained in use.

The GM catalytic converter was developed by a product engineering task force directed by Thomas E. Hustead, and was put in production by AC Spark Plug Division in April 1974 after 886 test cars using the system had completed some 14.5 million miles.

Pontiac cars equipped with the 400- and 455-cubic-inch V-8's used Model 260 and vehicles powered by the 350-cubic-inch V-8's used the smaller Model 175. Six-cylinder engine exhaust systems carried a still smaller Model 135 catalytic converter.

All used similar pellets of 0.111-inch diameter coated with a thin layer of 1.4 grams of platinum and palladium. These noble metals are the catalysts that assure the chemical clean-up process. The catalysts were wrapped in thin aluminum sheet and placed inside a container

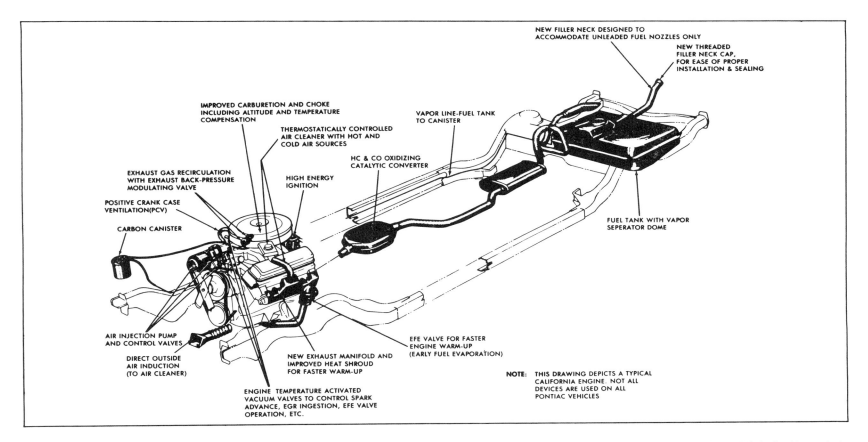

NEW FILLER NECK DESIGNED TO
ACCOMMODATE UNLEADED FUEL NOZZLES ONLY

NEW THREADED
FILLER NECK CAP,
FOR EASE OF PROPER
INSTALLATION & SEALING

IMPROVED CARBURETION AND CHOKE
INCLUDING ALTITUDE AND TEMPERATURE
COMPENSATION

THERMOSTATICALLY CONTROLLED
AIR CLEANER WITH HOT AND
COLD AIR SOURCES

VAPOR LINE-FUEL TANK
TO CANISTER

HC & CO OXIDIZING
CATALYTIC CONVERTER

EXHAUST GAS RECIRCULATION
WITH EXHAUST BACK-PRESSURE
MODULATING VALVE

HIGH ENERGY
IGNITION

POSITIVE CRANK CASE
VENTILATION(PCV)

CARBON CANISTER

FUEL TANK WITH VAPOR
SEPERATOR DOME

AIR INJECTION PUMP
AND CONTROL VALVES

DIRECT OUTSIDE
AIR INDUCTION
(TO AIR CLEANER)

NEW EXHAUST MANIFOLD AND
IMPROVED HEAT SHROUD
FOR FASTER WARM-UP

EFE VALVE FOR FASTER
ENGINE WARM-UP
(EARLY FUEL EVAPORATION)

ENGINE TEMPERATURE ACTIVATED
VACUUM VALVES TO CONTROL SPARK
ADVANCE, EGR INGESTION, EFE VALVE
OPERATION, ETC.

NOTE: THIS DRAWING DEPICTS A TYPICAL
CALIFORNIA ENGINE. NOT ALL
DEVICES ARE USED ON ALL
PONTIAC VEHICLES

Engines were supposed to be able to run more efficiently ('dirtier') with catalytic converters, but the 1975 Pontiac emission control system still involved low compression, exhaust gas recirculation and preheated intake air.

with ports at both ends and a layer of thermofix insulation all around. The outer casing was made of 6125-M stainless steel containing eleven percent chrome but no nickel, with sheet metal stampings only 0.05-inch thick.

Pontiac's 1975-model engines were given the benefit of the Delco high-energy ignition system which had the coil built into the upper part of the distributor, and a magnetic-pulse generator with an integrated-circuit electronic control unit built into the lower deck.

In 1975, there was a backlash from the market's earlier abrupt turn to smaller cars. But not only did customers now demand large size, they also wanted performance, luxury and styling. That year the Grand Prix became Pontiac's best-selling car. We tested one that came

equipped with the 455-cubic-inch V-8 engine with four-barrel carburetor and had a 2.56:1 axle ratio. On dry, level ground it went from standstill to 60 mph in twelve seconds flat, and reached 80 mph in under twenty-one seconds. Two years later, the 455-cubic-inch engine was discontinued, leaving the 400 as Pontiac's largest-displacement power plant. Its days, too, were numbered, as the down-sizing program progressed.

Pontiac Catalina for 1974 included a so-called hardtop where the door glass was extended towards a B-post that was moved back towards the C-post. A 400-cubic-inch V-8 was standard equipment.

Grand Prix for 1974 seems oddly dis-proportioned, with heavy front over-hang and angular greenhouse lines.

New A-body cars had to wait for the 1978 model year, due to the long lead time necessary for development and tooling for completely new cars. For Pontiac, that meant trying to engineer maximum economy into the existing LeMans, all-new in October 1972.

"How much gas can you save with a six?" "How much performance do you give up?" Those were the questions a lot of car owners asked us in the fuel-crisis winter of 1973-74. We went out and tested sixes versus V-8's from all American auto makers, including two 1974 Pontiac LeMans two-door sedans. The difference in fuel economy, as measured by running around Bridgehampton race circuit at a constant 60 mph, was only 6.25 percent. Under other test conditions, the difference might be much greater. At lower speeds, the six-cylinder engine had a stronger advantage. In heavy traffic, with frequent stops and lots of idling, it really saved fuel. But on country roads, expressways and turnpikes, it didn't save enough gasoline to make up for the performance loss. The Pontiac six was nearly thirty percent slower in acceleration than its V-8 stablemate, zero-to-sixty mph acceleration taking 18.8 seconds with the six, compared to 13.5 seconds with the V-8.

The baseline V-8 was equipped with a two-barrel carburetor, while the six had a single-barrel carburetor. That meant the six ran with restricted breathing, so that the cylinders didn't get properly filled up with fresh mixture. Lower volumetric efficiency is a definite block to good performance, and its benefits to fuel economy have not been proved. But the six had certain characteristics that made it more economical under certain conditions. The Chevrolet six was a long-stroke unit, with low-overlap valve timing, that generated its peak torque at a low-low speed of 1600 rpm—far below the modern V-8. Consequently, the six was better suited to both slow driving and manual transmissions. The six had adequate torque for city/suburban driving without ever exceeding 2000 rpm. But the fuel savings in cars of this weight class were not important enough to make up for the lack of power. Substantial fuel economy gains could only be obtained by taking weight out of the cars, which meant, in the first move, smaller size. The 1978 'intermediates' were designed to be smaller and lighter than the compacts with which they would have to coexist for a number of years.

As for the compact Ventura (X-body), it would have been reasonable to expect soaring demand, but instead sales fell lower and lower, year after year. Here was the right size car, light enough to use an economical six-cylinder engine without the drawbacks encountered in the LeMans. The X-body was certainly the most sensible and rational design in the entire corporation during 1974. And as a Chevrolet Nova it was a success, but as a Pontiac Ventura it was a disappointment.

Another disappointment was that Pontiac's smaller models were no more secure from quality problems and safety defects than the larger ones. In May 1975, Pontiac dealers were instructed to call back about 5,000 Venturas for checking a possible carburetor defect that would prevent the engines from idling properly. Some cases of broken carburetor throttle cable housings had been reported to cause a bend in the cable that would prevent the throttle from returning to idle position when the accelerator pedal was released.

The Firebird was involved in a 1975 callback for checking a possible defect in the steering system. A total of 3,100 cars (Firebird, Camaro, Nova, Buick Apollo and Skylark) were said to be affected. The Firebirds were checked for having been assembled with insufficient torque on the mounting nuts and bolts of the steering shaft clamp.

But while Chevrolet later had to recall about 31,000 Camaros to check for faulty fan blades in the air-conditioning unit, the Firebird was not involved. The Camaro trouble stemmed from an engine resonance problem that was unique to Chevrolet's 350-cubic-inch V-8.

In February 1975, General Motors called back 220,000 1975-model intermediates, including about 55,000 Pontiac LeMans to check for a possible defect in the rear wheel bearings. Field reports indicated that some 4,500 side thrust plates that are part of the bearings had been incorrectly machined and installed in cars built between mid-September and mid-November of 1974. Rear wheel bearing failure can, of course, result in loss of the wheel. After one minor accident had been reported, a full callback was made to find and rectify the defective cars.

In December 1975, General Motors called back 39,000 cars for checking on the proportioning valve in the hydraulic lines to the rear wheel brakes. About 10,000 Pontiac cars were involved, including LeMans, Catalina, Bonneville and Grand Ville. If the valve was defective, there would be the risk of total failure in the rear wheel brakes.

In February 1976, about 20,000 Pontiac Sunbirds were called back for inspection of the front brakes. Apparently repeated hard braking could dislodge the disc brake pads in their calipers and cause a loss of front braking action. The problem affected a total of 34,000 vehicles (Chevrolet Monza, Buick Skyhawk and Oldsmobile Starfire in addition to the Pontiac), and to find them, over 100,000 cars had to be brought in.

In May 1977, about 600,000 1976-model Pontiacs were called back for installation of a special filter in the vacuum line between the engine and the power brake booster because of a loss-of-power-assist condition occurring in sub-zero temperatures, due to condensation of gasoline vapor in the intake manifold.

In September 1977, about 32,000 GM compacts were called back for a check on their rear axle shafts. There was a risk that the shafts had a flaw that could cause them to break. This involved about 6,000 Pontiac Ventura and Phoenix cars, made late in the 1977 model year or early in the 1978 run.

In January 1978, it was discovered that about 200 GM cars had been assembled with incorrectly machined parts on the steering shaft—threatening a loss of steering. To find them, GM had to call back some 22,000 vehicles, including Pontiac Sunbirds, Chevrolet Monzas, Buick Skyhawks, Oldsmobile Starfires, and GMC motor-home chassis.

The total cost of these callbacks to Pontiac has never been released, and how far it set back the timetable for the corporation's downsizing programs can only be guessed at. Still, new-car projects were rammed through all divisions on a crash schedule; there were also several significant changes in personnel at Pontiac, and at the corporation. A Pontiac veteran and an engineer, James G. Vorhes, had replaced Ed Kennard as general sales manager of Pontiac in 1973. Jim Vorhes had become director of parts and service for Pontiac in 1967 after many years in field service with Pontiac. A native of Pontiac, born in 1923, he attended Michigan College of Mining and Technology and in 1947 joined Pontiac Motor Division as a clerk in the service department.

During his years in the New York zone office, where we first met him in the early 1960's, he gave an impression of machine-like efficiency and infallible accuracy, at the same time being friendly and helpful. In those days, Pontiac test cars were always impeccably prepared and ready on time. He took charge of Pontiac's sales department when it was in a crisis, and saw it through to better days. He left Pontiac in 1977, when the corporation promoted him to vice president for consumer relations and service staff.

Pontiac scheduled only 475,000 cars for the 1975 model year. They were built and sold, and Pontiac, despite lower volume, improved its position during 1975. The GM share of industry sales went ahead as its volume grew from just under 3.7 million to 3.75 million cars while industry sales took a step back from 7.5 to 7.05 million units.

In October 1974, Pete Estes became president of General Motors. By that time, it had become obvious that Caserio did not provide the leadership that was needed for Pontiac Motor Division to get back out of the slump. Estes knew whom he wanted in charge at Pontiac. He had worked closely with Alex Mair at Chevrolet; Mair already had his office in Pontiac, Michigan, as general manager of GMC since 1972, and in Pete's judgment he had the talent, drive and the will to succeed where Caserio had floundered.

The problem was how to ease Caserio out of his position without demoting him. He did not deserve a demotion. He had worked extremely hard, and took his duties so seriously that his time at Pontiac had aged him severely. Estes saw no better way than to create a whole new vice presidency, which meant revamping the corporate organizational chart and creating a whole new group, combining the AC, Delco and Packard Cable divisions under joint authority. On October 1, 1975, Caserio was named vice president in charge of this

The 1976 Bonneville was in the last generation of what was traditionally full-size cars at Pontiac. The line had undergone a minimum of modifications (and minimum investment) since it was doomed by the fuel crisis and coming energy problems.

Ventura SJ for 1976 received a split grille to give it Pontiac identity. Glass was stretched into the roof structure to give impression of a lowered beltline without going to the cost of new dies for either roof or basic underbody.

new electrical components group, and Alex Mair took over as general manager of Pontiac.

On taking office, Alex Mair predicted that the division's sales in 1976 would reach 700,000 cars. He beat that figure by 6,000 cars. Alex Mair is a dynamic individual with an easy smile and an assertive voice, of medium height and build. He spent thirty-three years at Chevrolet engineering before being appointed to run GMC, having started work at Chevrolet in 1939 as a GM Institute student. He served in the U.S. Navy during World War II, and returned to the Chevrolet drafting department in the spring of 1946. After a series of assignments as project engineer, senior engineer and design engineer, he was promoted to staff engineer in 1954. He became engineering director for Chevrolet in 1966, a year after Estes took over as general manager of that division. "Mair has done a pretty good job of making a comeback for Pontiac," says Jim Wangers. "He understands it—what it is and what makes it work. He's savvy."

Chevrolet, Buick and Oldsmobile needed new A-body and B-body cars just as badly as did Pontiac, and the corporation set about to renew them. Priority was given to the larger cars, however, reasoning

that they were a bigger problem and must be replaced first. The idea behind the 1977 B-body project was to create a car of X-body exterior dimensions, with more interior room than in the 1976 Catalina.

The 1977 Catalina turned out to be both longer and heavier than the Ventura, but it was a lot shorter and lighter than the Catalina from the year before. Overall length was trimmed by more than a foot, and wheelbase was shortened by 7.5 inches. It was also 3.5 inches narrower. The four-door Catalina was 738 pounds lighter than its 1976 counterpart. Yet interior space and trunk capacity were actually increased. Instead of a big V-8, the standard engine was a Buick-built 231-cubic-inch V-6. The Bonneville was powered by Pontiac's new 301-cubic-inch V-8 engine, designed by Tom Davis. The X-body car, however, got last priority for full renewal, and the corporation voted a very modest budget to update it for the 1975–80 period.

In contrast with Ford Motor Company, which went to enormous expenses to develop and tool up for its 1974 super-compacts Granada and Monarch, GM stuck to a tight budget for its 1975 compacts. No big investments were made. And yet the changes in the Ventura were so thorough and so well worked out that it felt like a newer car than the all-new Ford products.

On the Ventura, only the outer sheet metal was new for 1975. The old underbody structure was the same, and the seating dimensions practically unchanged. It was a masterpiece of low-budget retooling for maximum effect. The car lost much of its dumpy looks, and began to look bright and modern. Very obvious, even radical, changes were achieved with very minor revisions in design and tooling. For instance, it looked as if the beltline had been lowered. But no, there was no

Experimental Phoenix weighed 700 pounds less than a 1975-model Ventura coupe of identical overall dimensions, greatly due to material changes. Fixed hood on Phoenix experimental car, middle, gave birth to service access hatch. Nonopening hood was of lightweight construction, and eliminated hinges and spring-counterbalancing. Cast thermoplastic wheels, right, were a feature of the experimental Phoenix. In addition to overall weight saving, plastic wheels cut unsprung weight to improve ride and handling.

change there. Instead, the designers had carved away at the roof to make room for taller windows. That's the way the effect was produced. Windshield and backlight bases were not moved, yet the hood looked shorter and the car better balanced.

For 1975 the Ventura came in three trim levels: plain Ventura, Ventura Custom and Ventura SJ. Each series had the same three body styles: sedan, coupe and hatchback. Underneath, the Firebird front suspension was adopted, to replace the former Nova front-end assembly. This suspension had different geometry that gave higher directional stability, yet faster steering response. A torsion spring was built into the steering linkage to provide more positive returnability (self-centering action), and the steering linkage was moved ahead of the front wheel axis. Steel-belted radial-ply tires were standardized and the suspension systems retuned for radials.

The new Ventura continued using the Chevrolet six as standard, while making a new 260-cubic-inch V-8 made by Oldsmobile optional. Pontiac lowered the axle ratios to cover a longer distance in relation to engine rpm, and HydraMatic engineers adopted lower blade angles on the stator members on the torque converter to reduce hydraulic friction and power loss.

Pontiac had a 95,000-unit sales target for the 1975-model Ventura, with an expected 14,500 with SJ specifications. Incredibly, it missed by about half.

Since the current X-body car still had five years of production life in it, Steve Malone and his assistants went to work to try and establish the limits for improving the car by substitutions of components and

materials that would not greatly affect tooling and production cost. The result was the experimental Phoenix, unveiled as the 1976 Ventura was introduced. It was basically a 1975 Ventura two-door coupe, but weighed 700 pounds less than the original vehicle. It had a new four-cylinder engine which was still on the secret list at the time, designed at Pontiac by John M. Sawruk.

It had a new lightweight Turbo-HydraMatic transmission that was under development for coming generations of four- and six-cylinder engines. A lighter-gauge steel stub frame was used, with associated chassis changes. In combination, these alterations saved about 300 pounds. Another 400 pounds were saved by using plastic components wherever practical.

Joshua R. Madden, materials development engineer at Pontiac, chose plastic for the bumpers, fenders, wheels and fuel tank. But he did not stop there. The side impact beams in the doors, usually made of steel, were changed to a high-modulus plastic with fiberglass reinforcement. The hood was a thin-gauge steel stamping combined with a sheet-molding-compound plastic base. the deck lid was of similar construction. The hood was permanently closed to save the

B-body cars were downsized for 1977. The 1978 Bonneville has saved more than 100 pounds from the 3,704-pound '77 model that was more than 700 pounds lighter than the last of the big ones.

The 1977 Grand Prix was the last of the long-hood versions. The car was downsized the following year, along with the A-body 'intermediates' which became smaller and lighter than what were traditionally called 'compacts.'

weight of the hinge mechanisms, and instead had a plastic access door in the middle. The cowl vent was made of injection-molded polyester. All in all, the Phoenix contained more than twenty-five new applications of plastic materials, quite apart from the many uses that were already becoming commonplace.

In mid-year 1977, Pontiac added a super-deluxe model in the Ventura series which was called Phoenix. It became known as project Phoenix in the styling studio, partly after the location of the GM desert proving grounds near Phoenix, Arizona, and partly to invoke the legend of the Egyptian bird that is consumed in flames but rises from the ashes. For the 1978 model year, the Ventura name was dropped in favor of Phoenix. This name will surely be continued when the next-generation X-body cars go into production in 1980—an all-new creation on a 102-inch wheelbase, with front-wheel drive.

Some of the weight-saving advances from the Phoenix prototype may appear on future production models, but they came too late to help the 1978-model A-body program, instituted in 1974 to create a true family-type economy car. "We had its forerunner in 1972 or 1973," said Russ Gee. R. E. Denzer was then in charge of the advanced engineering group at Pontiac, having come into that post in 1967.

It had a 250-cubic-inch all-aluminum V-8 engine, and the whole vehicle weighed no more than 3,500 pounds. "It was then proposed as the next generation GM intermediate, but we could never sell it downtown," said Russ Gee. "Then the corporation came up with the new A-body car for 1978, and it was almost a dead ringer," continued Gee, "except it didn't have an aluminum engine. They never got approval for tooling up to make an aluminum engine."

On the corporate engineering level, Edward Mertz, formerly of Chevrolet, was head of the A-body project. Wilson West, assistant chief engineer of Fisher Body, was his division's top man on the A-body design and engineering.

The 1978 LeMans models were eight to seventeen inches shorter and between 530 and 925 pounds lighter than the respective 1977 models. They receded to a common 108.1-inch wheelbase for all models which included two-doors, four-doors and station wagons. The Grand Prix became a special coupe using the basic A-body, striking the G-body from the active list. The individual styling touches of the Grand Prix were made by Irv Rybicki, who had replaced Bill Mitchell as director of the GM Design Staff in 1976, but Chuck Jordan is credited with the Pontiac LeMans styling. He had also played a major role in designing the 1977 B-body cars.

The Grand Am was revived for 1977 (having been discontinued at the end of the 1975 model year) with its own frontal appearance and higher-grade interior, but otherwise retaining its usual relationship to the LeMans. "There were a lot of letters that came in when it was dropped," said Bill Collins, "so the sales people said 'gee, there must

be something there, so let's do another one!' Now it's back in the 1978 line, but I don't think it quite comes up to the original concept."

Pontiac's 1978-model sales set an all-time record for the division, with deliveries of 870,000 cars, neatly topping the old mark of 867,000 set in 1968, but falling short of Mair's target of 950,000 units. He confidently forecast the same number in 1979. Taking GM Assembly Division into account, a million Pontiacs a year is a possibility. But with six product lines, the mix is vitally important for the production flow. No one appreciates this more than Donald G. Upton, who became general manufacturing manager of Pontiac in April 1977. Upton succeeded D. Robert Bell, who had held that post for nine years. Bell was promoted to director of automotive manufacturing resources utilization for General Motors in North America, reporting directly to Executive Vice President F. James McDonald. In September 1977, McDonald took Pontiac's foundry away from the division and placed it under GM's Central Foundry, for more efficient coordination with the production of castings for the other divisions.

In November 1978, Pontiac lost its general manager when Alex Mair was appointed GM group executive in charge of the recently formed technical staffs group. Now both Alex Mair and Jim McDonald are well placed for moving into the president's chair when Pete Estes retires. Mair's place at Pontiac was taken by Robert C. Stempel.

Like Pete Estes, Bob Stempel is basically an Oldsmobile engineer who made good. Stempel joined Oldsmobile in 1958 as a senior detailer in the chassis design department and went through a number of assignments of growing importance and rank, becoming senior designer in 1962, transmission design engineer in 1964, motor engineer in 1969 and assistant chief engineer in 1972.

Ed Cole, then president of General Motors, made Stempel his special assistant in 1973, and on Cole's retirement in September 1974, Stempel went to Chevrolet as chief engineer for engines and components. A year later he received the title of director of engineering for Chevrolet and remained there until his promotion to Pontiac.

Native of Trenton, New Jersey, Bob Stempel graduated from Worcester Polytechnic Institute at the age of twenty-two in 1955. He also holds a master's degree in business administration from Michigan State University and a doctor of engineering degree from Worcester Polytechnic conferred in 1977.

Steve Malone remains in overall charge of Pontiac's engineering. "Steve has been chief engineer ever since DeLorean was chief engineer," says Bill Collins. "That's too long. He has no more enthusiasm. Pontiac needs new thinking." Is there much a chief engineer can do today, under the corporate dictatorship? "Look at what Reuss has done at Buick in just a couple of years," argues Collins. "Yes, you can still have a dynamic division today, even with all the government and corporate restrictions."

When Ed Windeler retired in 1976, Russell F. Gee was promoted to assistant chief engineer for power train and chassis. He started at

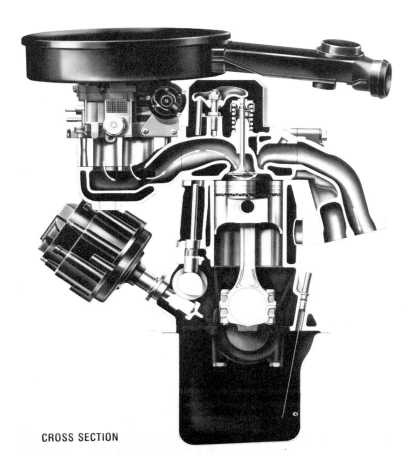

CROSS SECTION

Cross section of Pontiac's own four-cylinder engine for the 1979 Sunbird shows big bore and short stroke (four inches by three inches) and a simple OHV valve train. Pontiac now supplies this engine to other divisions, including Chevrolet, whose aluminum-block Vega SOHC design was scrapped.

Back to square one—compare the 1978 Grand Am with the 1961 Tempest, and see history take a turn toward the orthodox. The two are the same size, but it's the newer one that's purely conventional.

Pontiac in 1953 as test and development engineer. At first he worked mainly on tires and brakes. After about a year, he was transferred to engines. In 1956 he was assigned to take charge of Pontiac's test car fleet at the desert proving grounds. After his return to Pontiac a few years later he had a hand in every major power train development.

Russ Gee is one who misses the 'old days,' as he thinks of the years when he worked under John DeLorean. "At that time, the chief engineer had more time to spend with staff engineers. Now he sits in meetings and flies to Washington, D.C.," he complained. But he still identified with Pontiac when this interview was done. "We have a stronger team," he said. "We seem to be able to pull together better than some other divisions." But when the opportunity came, he accepted the chance to go to Chevrolet.

The man behind the latest A-body cars, Edward H. Mertz, joined Pontiac as assistant chief engineer in December 1977. He had first come to GM in 1956 as a college student trainee with Chevrolet's engineering center.

What can we expect future Pontiacs to be? "I think performance is still our niche today," said Russ Gee, "but by that I mean total car performance, not just stoplight acceleration. I think we excel particularly in the area of ride and handling. I see Pontiac as having the edge there. Pontiac also has a lead position in emission-control systems. We developed the EFP valve that controls heat to the crossover, the exhaust gas channel below the carburetor. Pontiac had the first modern emissions lab. Cadillac now has one, too, and Oldsmobile is building one."

Sunbird Formula for 1979 was intended to project the Firebird image into lower price brackets, and is doing it successfully. Its styling evolved under the direction of John R. Schinella.

Towards the end of 1977 Mair told *Automotive News* that the division has an active diesel program, based on the four-cylinder 151-cubic-inch engine, and that by 1985, Pontiac may feature front-wheel drive on about one-third of its car lines.

With regard to Pontiac's position in the market, Bill Collins remarked: "Our notch in this corporation is to be a step above Chevrolet, in terms of price—and value for money—and yet not get too high up, where we're treading in Buick's and Oldsmobile's back yard. We have managed to stay clear of Chevrolet, with slightly higher prices. But we've got some cars that are getting into Buick's domain —and I don't know if that's where we should be. It leads to an awful product spread.

"Some day, sooner or later," he went on, "this corporation will find itself with complete overlap or the corporation is going to have to ask each division to reduce its lineup and narrow it down to keep within a specific slot in the market. I don't know which. For Pontiac," Collins states, "it's a constant battle to keep in the proper slot and maintain position. It's a competitive market, and if we can sell cars and make money by going up against Buick and Oldsmobile we'd be silly not to do it—because they've got cars going down into our class."

Grand Am for 1979 is part of the corporate A-body line of cars, but represents Pontiac ideas in equipment, dynamic behavior and performance. Frontal treatment evolved under the direction of Terry Henline.

Does Pontiac make money? "The exact profit margin for each of GM's five automobile divisions is a secret as well guarded as the ingredients of Coca-Cola," said Bradford Snell, counsel to the Senate subcommittee on antitrust and monopoly, as quoted in the *New York Times*, March 24, 1974.

What is certain is that the principles laid down by Alfred P. Sloan in the early 1920's, assigning a specific price bracket to each make of car, have been abandoned by the chairmen and presidents who have run the corporation since his retirement. A return to these principles would be very difficult, because each division (except Cadillac) now has a dealer organization that has become used to offering an extremely wide price range. If Pontiac dealers are restricted to one or two car sizes and a narrow band of retail prices, some of them are sure to protest that their business is being hurt. And they may have a strong case, depending on how the corporation goes about realigning the divisional product mix.

Another future possibility that would deeply affect Pontiac's operations is the threat of government intervention to break up

General Motors. Such moves by consumer activists and anti-big-business politicians surface from time to time. The Federal Trade Commission has not closed its dossier on taking anti-trust action against GM.

Could Pontiac survive on its own? Certainly not as a marketing outfit for a range of unified products. And if it were to take control of its manufacturing and assembly operations, production would become more specialized, which in turn means higher cost. That goes straight against economic sense. But the whole issue is political, and politics do not always make sense. Whatever happens, Pontiac enthusiasts everywhere will hope and pray that the make will continue to exist and that the cars bearing the Pontiac name will be spectacular in looks, dramatic in performance, original in engineering and flawless in quality.

Appendix I
Pontiac Models and Body Styles

Year	4d-sdn	4d-htp	2d-sdn	2d-htp	2d-cpe	Conver-tible	Hatch-back	Wagon	Van	TOTAL
1946	3	0	3	0	0	1	0	1	1	9
1947	3	0	3	0	0	2	0	2	1	11
1948	3	0	3	0	0	3	0	4	1	15
1949	3	0	2	0	2	1	0	2	1	11
1950	3	0	1	1	3	1	0	1	1	11
1951	2	0	2	1	3	2	0	2	1	13
1952	2	0	2	1	3	1	0	2	1	12
1953	2	0	2	2	0	1	0	3	1	11
1954	3	0	2	2	0	1	0	3	0	11
1955	4	0	2	2	0	1	0	3	0	12
1956	3	3	1	3	0	1	0	4	0	15
1957	4	3	1	3	0	2	0	4	0	17
1958	3	3	1	4	0	2	0	3	0	16
1959	2	3	2	2	0	2	0	2	0	13
1960	2	4	2	3	0	2	0	2	0	15
1961	4	4	4	3	0	2	0	4	0	21
1962	4	4	4	3	0	3	0	4	0	22
1963	4	3	4	3	0	3	0	4	0	21
1964	4	3	4	4	0	4	0	5	0	24
1965	5	3	4	5	0	4	0	5	0	26
1966	4	5	5	8	0	6	0	5	0	33
1967	4	5	5	8	0	7	0	8	0	37
1968	5	5	1	8	3	6	0	7	0	35
1969	5	5	0	8	3	6	0	7	0	34
1970	5	5	0	11	3	4	0	7	0	35
1971	6	6	0	13	3	4	0	6	0	38
1972	4	6	0	17	2	3	0	6	0	38
1973	7	3	8	7	4	1	2	6	0	38
1974	7	3	8	4	3	1	3	8	0	37
1975	7	2	9	5	3	1	6	11	0	44
1976	5	2	11	2	5	0	3	5	0	33
1977	8	2	9	0	7	0	4	5	0	35
1978	8	0	10	0	7	0	2	5	0	32

Appendix II
Pontiac Engines

Years made	Cylinders	Bore x stroke	Displacement	Valves
1946–1954	L-6	3.56 x 4.00	239.2	SV
1946–1950	L-8	3.25 x 3.75	248.9	SV
1951–1954	L-8	3.375 x 3.75	268.4	SV
1955	V-8	3.75 x 3.25	287.2	OHV
1956	V-8	3.94 x 3.25	316.6	OHV
1957	V-8	3.94 x 3.56	347	OHV
1958	V-8	4.06 x 3.56	370	OHV
1959–1966	V-8	4.06 x 3.75	389	OHV
1961–1966	V-8	4.09 x 4.00	421	OHV
1967–1969	V-8	4.12 x 4.00	428	OHV
1970–1976	V-8	4.15 x 4.21	455	OHV
1961–1963	L-4	4.06 x 3.75	194.5	OHV
1964–1965	L-6	3.75 x 3.25	215	OHV
1961–1962	V-8 (Buick)	3.50 x 2.80	215	OHV
1963	V-8	3.78 x 3.75	326 (336)	OHV
1964–1967	V-8	3.72 x 3.75	326	OHV
1966–1967	L-6	3.875 x 3.25	230	SOHC
1968–1969	L-6	3.875 x 3.53	250	SOHC
1970–1976	L-6 (Chev)	3.875 x 3.53	250	OHV
1971–1972	V-8 (Chev)	3.875 x 3.25	307	OHV
1967–1979	V-8	4.12 x 3.75	400	OHV
1968–1977	V-8	3.875 x 3.75	350	OHV
1975–1977	L-4 (Chev)	3.50 x 3.625	140	SOHC
1975–1976	V-8 (Olds)	3.50 x 3.385	260	OHV
1975 to date	V-8 (Buick)	3.80 x 3.85	350	OHV
1976 to date	V-6 (Buick)	3.80 x 3.40	231	OHV
1977 to date	L-4	4.00 x 3.01	151	OHV
1977 to date	V-8 (Chev)	3.74 x 3.48	305	OHV
1977 to date	V-8	4.00 x 3.01	301	OHV
1977 to date	V-8 (Chev)	4.00 x 3.48	350	OHV
1977 to date	V-8 (Olds)	4.06 x 3.385	350	OHV
1977 to date	V-8 (Olds)	4.35 x 3.385	403	OHV

Appendix III
U.S. Pontiac Calendar Year Registrations

YEAR	TORPEDO	STREAMLINER	STAR CHIEF	BONNEVILLE	CHIEFTAIN	TOTAL
1940	Incl. in Streamliner	235,815				235,815
1941	"	286,123				286,123
1946	"	113,109				113,109
1947	"	206,411				206,411
1948	"	228,939				228,939
1949	Disc.	Incl. in Chieftain			321,033	321,033
1950	"	"			440,528	440,528
1951		"			337,821	337,821
1952		Disc.			266,351	266,351
1953					385,692	385,692
1954			358,167		Incl. in Star Chief	358,167
1955			530,007		"	530,007
1956			358,668		"	358,668
1957			319,719	Incl. in Star Chief	"	319,719
1958			229,740	"	"	229,740

YEAR	STAR CHIEF	CATALINA	VENTURA	EXECUTIVE	BONNEVILLE	GRAND PRIX	TEMPEST	FIREBIRD	SAFARI	TOTAL
1959	63,573	200,339			78,592				39,633	382,137
1960	43,113	173,492	52,899		81,881		12,335		35,926	399,646
1961	32,540	128,199			71,575	6,556	110,188		23,813	372,871
1962	40,429	181,023			98,101	38,686	138,144		32,271	528,654
1963	40,927	211,897			108,445	72,642	139,313		33,567	606,791
1964	34,410	214,564			106,919	58,933	240,524		32,552	687,902
1965	35,214	242,348			136,777	56,810	313,495		46,804	831,448
1966	Disc.	216,821		43,706	122,270	40,173	363,256		44,630	830,856
1967		221,353		35,468	96,722	39,690	296,598	94,730	49,585	834,146
1968		231,997		29,749	92,336	49,259	329,199	92,498	52,344	877,382
1969		206,324		24,512	85,485	92,834	274,001	58,859	53,590	795,605

YEAR	CATALINA	BONNEVILLE	EXECUTIVE	GRAND VILLE	GRAND PRIX	SAFARI	LE MANS	FIREBIRD	VENTURA & PHOENIX	ASTRE	SUNBIRD	TOTAL
1970	149,971	49,348	14,680	1,986	50,329	33,854	188,263	56,284				544,715
1971	191,060	40,636	535	59,215	71,059	39,058	176,556	53,345	48,633			680,097
1972	198,170	37,104		63,678	96,716	41,937	187,128	21,864	66,178			712,775
1973	174,129	39,363		60,006	144,666	40,800	222,070	50,793	75,719			807,546
1974	92,412	20,434		31,461	81,547	18,797	129,922	65,303	59,280	4,925		504,081
1975	53,775	17,611		24,739	94,363	14,805	90,418	77,607	49,943	51,536	3,345	478,142
1976	62,319	57,370			233,052	19,834	86,687	99,590	59,138	40,101	48,369	706,460
1977	52,560	113,211			234,629	29,488	70,562	135,263	70,347	28,759	59,351	794,170
1978*	55,000	120,000			175,000	25,000	100,000	165,000	45,000	1,299	75,000	691,299

* Estimated

Appendix IV
Pontiac Model Year Output

YEAR	TORPEDO	STREAMLINER	CHIEFTAIN	STAR CHIEF	BONNEVILLE	TOTAL
1940	31,224	185,777				217,001
1941	181,247	148,814				330,061
1942	44,307	39,248				83,555
1946	44,909	92,731				137,640
1947	101,940	128,660				230,600
1948	84,562	160,857				245,419
1949	Disc.	incl. in Chieftain	304,819			304,819
1950		"	446,429			446,429
1951		"	370,159			370,159
1952		Disc.	271,373			271,373
1953			418,619			418,619
1954			172,656	115,088		287,744
1955			354,466	199,624		554,090
1956			184,232	221,498		405,730
1957			162,575	171,466		334,041
1958			124,685	73,019	19,599	217,303

YEAR	STAR CHIEF	BONNEVILLE	CATALINA	VENTURA	EXECUTIVE	GRAND PRIX	TEMPEST	FIREBIRD	TOTAL
1959	68,815	82,944	231,561						383,320
1960	43,691	85,814	210,934	56,277					396,716
1961	29,581	69,708	113,354	27,209			100,783		340,635
1962	41,642	102,249	204,654	Disc.		30,195	143,193		521,933
1963	40,757	110,316	234,549			72,959	131,490		590,071
1964	Disc.	120,259	257,768		37,653	63,810	235,126		715,261
1965		134,020	271,058		31,315	57,681	307,181		801,255
1966		135,401	254,310		45,212	36,757	359,098		831,331
1967		102,996	240,750		46,987	42,981	301,069	82,560	817,826
1968		104,436	276,182		44,635	31,711	346,406	107,112	910,977
1969		96,315	246,596		39,061	112,486	287,915	87,708	870,528

YEAR	CATALINA	BONNEVILLE	GRAND PRIX	EXECUTIVE	GRAND VILLE	LE MANS	FIREBIRD	VENTURA PHOENIX	ASTRE	SUNBIRD	TOTAL
1970	223,380	82,031	65,750	32,426		213,239	48,739				618,204
1971	173,489	41,269	58,325	Disc.	46,330	165,638	53,124	48,484			536,047
1972	228,262	50,293	91,961		63,411	169,993	29,951	72,787			638,773
1973	237,065	46,898	153,899		90,172	248,785	46,313	96,500			919,872
1974	110,599	20,560	99,817		44,494	129,105	73,729	81,799			560,216
1975	70,998	27,815	86,582		27,682	97,058	84,063	66,554	64,601		525,413
1976	72,745	64,471	228,091		Disc.	96,229	110,775	74,116	50,384	24,803	729,137
1977	74,736	133,184	288,430			69,944	155,736	90,764	32,788	7,014	850,428
1978*	60,000	108,000	262,000			100,000	170,000	75,000	Disc.	65,000	840,000

* Estimated

Appendix V
Pontiac Engine Specifications

Year	Compr. ratio	Carb.	Hp @ rpm	Torque @ rpm	Remarks
239.2 cid in-line six					
1946	6.5	1–1V	93.5 @ 3400	186 @ 1400	
1947	6.5	1–1V	93.5 @ 3400	186 @ 1400	
1948	6.5	1–1V	90 @ 3400	178 @ 1200	
1949	6.5	1–1V	90 @ 3400	178 @ 1200	Synchromesh
1949	7.5	1–1V	93 @ 3400	183 @ 1200	HydraMatic
1950	6.5	1–1V	90 @ 3400	178 @ 1200	Synchromesh
1950	7.5	1–1V	93 @ 3400	183 @ 1200	HydraMatic
1951	6.5	1–1V	90 @ 3400	191 @ 1200	Synchromesh
1951	7.5	1–1V	96 @ 3400	195 @ 1200	HydraMatic
1952	6.8	1–1V	100 @ 3400	189 @ 1400	Synchromesh
1952	7.7	1–1V	102 @ 3400	194 @ 1400	HydraMatic
1953	7.0	1–1V	115 @ 3800	193 @ 2000	Synchromesh
1953	7.7	1–1V	118 @ 3800	197 @ 2000	HydraMatic
1954	7.0	1–1V	115 @ 3800	193 @ 2000	Synchromesh
1954	7.7	1–1V	118 @ 3800	197 @ 2000	Hydramatic
248.9 cid in-line eight					
1946	6.5	1–1V	107.5 @ 3700	192 @ 2100	
1947	6.5	1–1V	107.5 @ 3700	192 @ 2100	
1948	6.5	1–1V	103 @ 3700	188 @ 2000	
1949	6.5	1–1V	104 @ 3800	190 @ 2200	Synchromesh
1949	7.5	1–1V	106 @ 3800	194 @ 2200	HydraMatic
1950	6.5	1–1V	108 @ 3600	208 @ 2000	Synchromesh
1950	7.5	1–1V	113 @ 3600	214 @ 2000	HydraMatic
268.4 cid in-line eight					
1951	6.5	1–1V	116 @ 3600	220 @ 2000	Synchromesh
1951	7.5	1–1V	120 @ 3600	225 @ 2000	HydraMatic
1952	6.8	1–1V	118 @ 3600	222 @ 2200	Synchromesh
1952	7.7	1–1V	122 @ 3600	227 @ 2200	HydraMatic
1953	6.8	1–2V	122 @ 3600	222 @ 2200	Synchromesh
1953	7.7	1–2V	127 @ 3800	227 @ 2200	HydraMatic
1954	6.8	1–2V	122 @ 3800	226 @ 2200	Synchromesh
1954	7.7	1–2V	127 @ 3800	234 @ 2200	HydraMatic
287 cid V–8					
1955	8.0	1–2V	180 @ 4600	264 @ 2400	
1955	8.0	1–4V	200 @ 4600	264 @ 2400	
1955	7.4	1–2V	173 @ 4400	256 @ 2400	synchromesh only
317 cid V–8					
1956	8.0	1–2V	202 @ 4600	294 @ 2600	synchromesh
1956	8.9	1–2V	205 @ 4600	294 @ 2600	860 and 870 with HydraMatic
1956	8.9	1–4V	227 @ 4800	312 @ 3000	Star Chief with HydraMatic

347 cid V-8

1957	8.5	1-2V	227 @ 4800	306 @ 2400	Chieftain with synchromesh
1957	8.5	1-4V	244 @ 4800	316 @ 2800	Super Chief and Star Chief with synchromesh
1957	10.0	1-2V	252 @ 4600	354 @ 2400	Chieftain with HydraMatic
1957	10.0	1-4V	270 @ 4800	359 @ 2800	Super Chief and Star Chief with HydraMatic

370 cid V-8

1957	10.0	FI	310 @ 4800	400 @ 3400	std in Bonneville only
1958	8.6	1-2V	240 @ 4500	354 @ 2600	std in Chieftain and Super Chief
1958	8.6	1-4V	255 @ 4500	360 @ 2600	std in Star Chief and Bonneville
1958	10.0	1-2V	270 @ 4600	388 @ 2800	opt in Super Chief with HydraMatic
1958	10.0	1-4V	285 @ 4800	395 @ 2800	opt in Bonneville with HydraMatic
1958	10.5	3-2V	300 @ 4600	400 @ 3000	optional for all models
1958	10.5	FI	310 @ 4800	400 @ 3400	optional for all models

389 cid V-8

1959	8.6	1-2V	245 @ 4200	392 @ 2000	std in Catalina and Star Chief with synchromesh
1959	8.6	1-4V	260 @ 4200	400 @ 2800	std in Bonneville; opt. Star Chief and Catalina with synchromesh
1959	8.6	1-2V	215 @ 3600	290 @ 2000	opt on all models with HydraMatic
1959	10.0	1-2V	280 @ 4400	408 @ 2800	opt in Catalina and Star Chief with HydraMatic
1959	10.0	1-4V	300 @ 4600	420 @ 2800	opt in Bonneville, Star Chief and Catalina with HydraMatic
1959	10.5	3-2V	315 @ 4600	425 @ 3200	opt on all models (any transmission)
1959	10.5	1-4V	330 @ 4800	420 @ 2800	opt on all models (any transmission)
1959	10.5	3-2V	345 @ 4800	425 @ 3200	opt on all models (any transmission)
1960	8.6	1-2V	215 @ 3600	290 @ 2000	std in Catalina, Ventura and Star Chief with synchromesh; std in all models with HydraMatic
1960	8.6	1-4V	281 @ 4400	407 @ 2800	std in Bonneville with synchromesh
1960	10.25	1-2V	283 @ 4400	413 @ 2800	opt in Catalina, Ventura and Star Chief with HydraMatic
1960	10.25	1-4V	303 @ 4600	425 @ 2800	opt in Bonneville with HydraMatic
1960	10.75	3-2V	318 @ 4600	430 @ 3200	opt on all models
1961	8.6	1-2V	215 @ 3600	290 @ 2000	std on Catalina, Ventura and Star Chief with synchromesh
1961	8.6	1-2V	230 @ 4000	380 @ 2000	opt on all models with HydraMatic
1961	8.6	1-4V	235 @ 3600	402 @ 2000	std on Bonneville, opt on all other models with synchromesh
1961	10.25	1-2V	267 @ 4200	405 @ 2400	opt on Catalina and Ventura with HydraMatic
1961	10.25	1-2V	283 @ 4400	413 @ 2800	opt in Star Chief with HydraMatic
1961	10.25	1-4V	303 @ 4600	425 @ 2800	opt in Bonneville with HydraMatic
1961	10.25	1-4V	287 @ 4400	416 @ 2400	opt in Catalina with HydraMatic
1961	10.75	3-2V	318 @ 4600	430 @ 3200	opt in all models (any transmission)
1961	10.75	1-4V	333 @ 4800	425 @ 2800	opt in all models (any transmission)
1961	10.75	3-2V	348 @ 4800	430 @ 3200	opt in all models (any transmission)
1962	8.6	1-2V	215 @ 3600	290 @ 2000	std on Catalina and Star Chief with synchromesh
1962	8.6	1-4V	235 @ 3600	402 @ 2000	std on Bonneville with synchromesh; opt on all other models
1962	8.6	1-2V	230 @ 4000	380 @ 2000	opt on all models with HydraMatic
1962	10.25	1-2V	267 @ 4200	405 @ 2400	opt on Catalina with HydraMatic
1962	10.25	1-2V	283 @ 4400	413 @ 2400	opt on Star Chief with HydraMatic
1962	10.25	1-4V	305 @ 4600	425 @ 2800	std on Bonneville and Grand Prix with HydraMatic; opt for Catalina and Star Chief with HydraMatic
1962	10.75	3-2V	318 @ 4600	430 @ 3200	opt on all models (any transmission)
1962	10.75	1-4V	333 @ 4800	425 @ 2800	opt on all models (any transmission)

Year	Compr. ratio	Carb.	Hp @ rpm	Torque @ rpm	Remarks
1962	10.75	3-2V	348 @ 4800	430 @ 3200	opt on all models (any transmission)
1962	10.75	1-4V	385 @ 5200		Super Duty opt for 2-door Catalina only
1963	8.6	1-2V	215 @ 3600	394 @ 2000	std on Catalina and Star Chief with synchromesh
1963	8.6	1-4V	235 @ 3600	407 @ 2000	std on Bonneville with synchromesh; opt on all other models
1963	8.6	1-2V	230 @ 4000	386 @ 2000	opt on all models with HydraMatic
1963	10.25	1-4V	303 @ 4600	430 @ 2800	std on Bonneville and Grand Prix with HydraMatic; opt on all other models (any transmission)
1963	10.25	1-2V	267 @ 4200	410 @ 2400	std on Catalina with HydraMatic
1963	10.25	1-2V	283 @ 4400	418 @ 2800	std on Star Chief with HydraMatic
1963	10.25	3-2V	313 @ 4600	430 @ 3200	opt on all models (any transmission)
1964	8.6	1-2V	230 @ 4000	386 @ 2000	opt on all models with HydraMatic
1964	8.6	1-2V	235 @ 4000	386 @ 2000	std on Catalina and Star Chief with synchromesh
1964	8.6	1-4V	255 @ 4000	407 @ 2000	standard on Bonneville with synchromesh; opt on all other models
1964	10.5	1-4V	306 @ 4800	420 @ 2800	opt on all B-body models
1964	10.5	1-2V	267 @ 4200	410 @ 2400	std on Catalina with HydraMatic
1964	10.5	1-2V	283 @ 4400	418 @ 2800	std on Star Chief with HydraMatic
1964	10.5	1-4V	303 @ 4600	430 @ 2800	std on Bonneville and Grand Prix with HydraMatic
1964	10.75	3-2V	330 @ 4600	430 @ 3200	opt on all B-body models
1964	10.75	1-4V	325 @ 4800	428 @ 3200	std on GTO
1964	10.75	3-2V	348 @ 4900	428 @ 3600	opt on GTO
1965	8.6	1-2V	256 @ 4600	388 @ 2400	std on all B-body models
1965	10.5	1-2V	290 @ 4600	418 @ 2400	opt on all B-body models
1965	10.5	1-4V	333 @ 5000	429 @ 3200	opt on all B-body models
1965	10.5	1-4V	325 @ 4800	429 @ 2800	opt on all B-body models
1965	10.75	1-4V	335 @ 5000	431 @ 3200	std on GTO
1965	10.75	1-4V	338 @ 4800	433 @ 3600	opt on all B-body models
1965	10.75	3-2V	360 @ 5200	424 @ 3600	opt on GTO
1966	8.6	1-2V	256 @ 4600	388 @ 2400	std on Catalina with synchromesh; opt on all models with HydraMatic
1966	10.5	1-4V	325 @ 4800	429 @ 2800	std on Bonneville and Grand Prix with HydraMatic; opt on all other B-body models except 2+2
1966	10.5	1-4V	333 @ 5000	429 @ 3200	std on Bonneville and Grand Prix with synchromesh; opt on all other B-body models except 2+2
1966	10.5	1-4V	290 @ 4600	418 @ 2400	std on Catalina, Star Chief and Executive with HydraMatic
1966	10.5	1-4V	338 @ 4600	459 @ 2800	std on 2+2 with HydraMatic; opt on all other B-body models (any transmission)
1966	10.75	1-4V	335 @ 5000	431 @ 3200	std on GTO
1966	10.75	3-2V	360 @ 5200	424 @ 3600	opt on GTO
1966	10.75	3-2V	356 @ 4800	459 @ 3200	opt on all B-body models (any transmission)
1966	10.75	3-2V	376 @ 5000	461 @ 3600	opt on all B-body models (any transmission)
194.5 cid four					
1961	8.6	1-1V	110 @ 3800	190 @ 2000	std on Tempest with synchromesh
1961	8.6	1-1V	130 @ 4400	195 @ 2200	std on Tempest with automatic transmission
1961	10.25	1-1V	120 @ 3800	202 @ 2000	opt on Tempest with synchromesh
1961	10.25	1-1V	140 @ 4400	207 @ 2200	opt on Tempest with automatic transmission
1961	10.25	1-4V	155 @ 4800	215 @ 2800	opt on Tempest (any transmission)

1962	8.6	1-1V	110 @ 3800	190 @ 2000	std on Tempest with synchromesh
1962	8.6	1-1V	115 @ 4000	195 @ 2200	std on Tempest with automatic transmission
1962	10.25	1-1V	120 @ 3800	202 @ 2000	opt on Tempest with synchromesh
1962	10.25	1-1V	140 @ 4400	207 @ 2200	opt on Tempest with automatic transmission
1962	10.25	1-4V	166 @ 4800	215 @ 2800	opt on Tempest (any transmission)
1963	8.6	1-1V	115 @ 4000	195 @ 2200	std on Tempest (any transmission)
1963	10.25	1-1V	120 @ 3800	202 @ 2000	opt on Tempest with synchromesh
1963	10.25	1-1V	140 @ 4400	207 @ 2200	opt on Tempest with automatic transmission
1963	10.25	1-4V	166 @ 4800	215 @ 2800	opt on Tempest (any transmission)

215 cid V-8 (Buick)

1961	8.8	1-2V	155 @ 4600	220 @ 2400	opt in Tempest
1962	11.0	1-4V	190 @ 4800	235 @ 3000	opt in Tempest

326 cid V-8

1963	10.25	1-2V	260 @ 4800	352 @ 2800	opt in Tempest and LeMans
1964	8.6	1-2V	250 @ 4600	333 @ 2800	opt in Tempest and LeMans
1964	10.5	1-4V	280 @ 4800	355 @ 3200	opt in Tempest and LeMans
1965	9.2	1-2V	250 @ 4600	333 @ 2800	opt in Tempest and LeMans
1965	10.5	1-4V	285 @ 5000	359 @ 3200	opt in Tempest and LeMans
1966	9.2	1-2V	250 @ 4600	333 @ 2800	opt in Tempest and LeMans
1966	10.5	1-4V	285 @ 5000	359 @ 3200	opt in Tempest and LeMans
1967	9.2	1-2V	250 @ 4600	333 @ 2800	opt in Tempest, LeMans, Firebird
1967	10.5	1-4V	285 @ 5000	359 @ 3200	opt in Tempest, LeMans, Firebird HO

215 cid six

1964	8.6	1-1V	140 @ 4200	206 @ 2000	std in Tempest and LeMans
1965	8.6	1-1V	140 @ 4200	206 @ 2000	std in Tempest and LeMans

230 cid six

1966	9.0	1-2V	165 @ 4700	216 @ 2600	std in Tempest and LeMans
1966	10.5	1-4V	207 @ 5200	228 @ 3800	opt in Tempest and LeMans
1967	9.0	1-2V	165 @ 4700	216 @ 2600	std in Tempest and Firebird
1967	10.5	1-4V	215 @ 5200	240 @ 3800	opt in Tempest; std in Firebird Sprint

250 cid six

1968	9.0	1-2V	175 @ 4800	240 @ 2600	std in Tempest, LeMans, Firebird
1968	10.5	1-4V	215 @ 5200	255 @ 3800	opt in Tempest and LeMans; std in Firebird Sprint
1969	9.0	1-2V	175 @ 4800	240 @ 2600	std in Tempest, LeMans, Firebird
1969	10.5	1-4V	230 @ 5400	260 @ 3600	opt in Tempest and LeMans; std in Firebird Sprint
1969	10.5	1-4V	215 @ 5200	255 @ 3800	opt in Tempest and LeMans

250 cid six (Chevrolet)

1970	8.5	1-1V	155 @ 4200	235 @ 1600	std in Firebird and LeMans
1971	8.5	1-1V	145 @ 4200	230 @ 1600	std in LeMans, Firebird, Ventura
1972	8.5	1-1V	110 @ 3800	185 @ 1600	std in LeMans, Firebird, Ventura
1973	8.2	1-1V	110 @ 3600	175 @ 1600	std in LeMans, Firebird, Ventura
1974	8.2	1-1V	110 @ 3600	175 @ 1600	std in LeMans, Firebird, Ventura
1975	8.25	1-1V	105 @ 3800	185 @ 1600	std in LeMans, Grand LeMans, Ventura, Firebird and Firebird Esprit
1976	8.3	1-1V	110 @ 3600	185 @ 1200	std in LeMans, Grand LeMans, Ventura, Firebird and Firebird Esprit

421 cid V-8

1961	11.0	2-4V	405 @ 5600	425 @ 4400	Super Duty—opt in Catalina 2-door only
1962	11.0	2-4V	405 @ 5600	425 @ 4400	Super Duty—opt in Catalina 2-door only
1963	10.75	1-4V	353 @ 5000	455 @ 3400	opt in all B-body models (any transmission)
1963	10.75	3-2V	370 @ 5200	460 @ 3800	opt in all B-body models (any transmission)

Year	Compr. ratio	Carb.	Hp @ rpm	Torque @ rpm	Remarks
1963	12.0	1-4V	390 @ 5800	425 @ 3600	Super Duty—opt in Catalina 2-door only
1963	12.0	2-4V	405 @ 5600	425 @ 4400	Super Duty—opt in Catalina 2-door only
1963	13.0	2-4V	410 @ 5600	435 @ 4400	Super Duty—opt in Catalina 2-door only
1964	10.5	1-4V	320 @ 4400	455 @ 2800	opt in all B-body models
1964	10.75	3-2V	370 @ 5200	460 @ 3800	opt in all B-body models
1964	10.75	3-2V	350 @ 4600	454 @ 3200	opt in all B-body models
1965	10.5	1-4V	338 @ 4600	459 @ 2800	opt in all B-body models
1965	10.75	3-2V	356 @ 4800	459 @ 3200	opt in all B-body models
1965	10.75	3-2V	376 @ 5000	461 @ 3600	opt in all B-body models
1966	10.5	1-4V	338 @ 4600	459 @ 2800	std on 2+2, opt on all other B-body models
1966	10.75	3-2V	356 @ 4800	459 @ 3200	opt on all B-body models
1966	10.75	3-2V	376 @ 5000	461 @ 3600	opt in all B-body models

428 cid V-8

Year	Compr. ratio	Carb.	Hp @ rpm	Torque @ rpm	Remarks
1967	10.5	1-4V	360 @ 4600	472 @ 3200	opt on Catalina, Executive, Bonneville, Grand Prix
1967	10.75	1-4V	376 @ 5100	462 @ 3400	opt on Catalina, Executive, Bonneville, Grand Prix
1968	10.5	1-4V	375 @ 4800	472 @ 3200	opt on Catalina, Executive, Bonneville, Grand Prix
1968	10.75	1-4V	390 @ 5200	465 @ 3400	opt on Catalina, Executive, Bonneville, Grand Prix
1969	10.5	1-4V	360 @ 4600	472 @ 3200	std on Bonneville
1969	10.5	1-4V	370 @ 4800	472 @ 3200	opt on Grand Prix
1969	10.75	1-4V	390 @ 5200	465 @ 3400	opt on Catalina, Executive, Bonneville, Grand Prix

350 cid V-8

Year	Compr. ratio	Carb.	Hp @ rpm	Torque @ rpm	Remarks
1968	9.2	1-2V	265 @ 4600	355 @ 2800	opt in Tempest, LeMans, Firebird
1968	10.5	1-4V	320 @ 5100	380 @ 3200	opt in Tempest; std in Firebird HO
1969	9.2	1-2V	265 @ 4600	355 @ 2800	opt in Tempest, LeMans, Firebird
1969	10.5	1-4V	325 @ 5100	380 @ 3200	std in Firebird HO
1969	10.5	1-4V	330 @ 5100	380 @ 3200	opt in Tempest and LeMans
1970	8.8	1-2V	255 @ 4600	355 @ 2800	opt in LeMans and Firebird; std in Catalina and Firebird Esprit
1971	8.0	1-2V	250 @ 4400	350 @ 2400	std in Firebird Esprit and Catalina; opt in LeMans
1972	8.0	1-2V	160 @ 4400	270 @ 2000	std in Luxury LeMans and Firebird Esprit; opt in Ventura, Firebird and LeMans
1972	8.0	1-2V	175 @ 4400	275 @ 2000	opt in LeMans and Firebird; std in Firebird Formula 350
1973	7.6	1-2V	150 @ 4000	270 @ 2000	std in Catalina, Luxury LeMans, Firebird Esprit; opt in Ventura, LeMans, Firebird
1973	7.6	1-2V	175 @ 4400	280 @ 2400	opt in Ventura, LeMans, Catalina; std in Firebird Formula 350
1974	7.6	1-2V	170 @ 4000	280 @ 2400	std in Firebird Formula 350; opt in Ventura; LeMans, Firebird
1974	7.6	1-2V	155 @ 3600	275 @ 2400	std in Luxury LeMans, Firebird Esprit; opt in Ventura, LeMans, Firebird
1974	7.6	1-4V	170 @ 4000	290 @ 2400	opt in Ventura and LeMans
1974	7.6	1-4V	200 @ 4400	295 @ 2800	std in GTO, opt in Ventura and LeMans
1975	7.6	1-2V	155 @ 4000	280 @ 2000	opt in Firebird and LeMans
1975	7.6	1-4V	175 @ 4000	280 @ 2000	std in Firebird Formula 350; opt in Firebird and LeMans
1976	7.6	1-2V	160 @ 4000	280 @ 2000	std in Firebird Formula 350 and Grand Prix; opt in LeMans
1976	7.6	1-4V	165 @ 4000	260 @ 2400	std in Grand Prix SJ, opt in LeMans and Firebird
1977	7.6	1-4V	170 @ 4000	280 @ 1800	opt in Firebird, LeMans, Catalina, Bonneville, Grand Prix

350 cid V–8 (Buick)

1975	8.0	1–2V	145 @ 3200	270 @ 2000	opt in Ventura
1975	8.0	1–4V	165 @ 3800	260 @ 2200	opt in Ventura
1976	8.0	1–2V	140 @ 3200	280 @ 1600	opt in Ventura
1976	8.0	1–4V	155 @ 3400	280 @ 1800	opt in Ventura
1978	8.0	1–4V	155 @ 3400	280 @ 1800	opt in Catalina, Bonneville, and B-body station wagons

350 cid V–8 (Oldsmobile)

1977	8.0	1–4V	170 @ 3800	275 @ 2000	opt in Ventura, Phoenix, Firebird (Calif.), LeMans, Grand Prix, Catalina, Bonneville
1978	7.9	1–4V	170 @ 3800	275 @ 2000	opt in Catalina and Bonneville

350 cid V-8 (Chevrolet)

1977	8.5	1–4V	170 @ 3800	270 @ 2400	opt in Ventura and Phoenix
1978	8.2	1–4V	160 @ 3800	260 @ 2400	opt in Phoenix and Firebird

140 cid in-line four (Chevrolet)

1975	8.0	1–1V	78 @ 4200	120 @ 2000	std in Astre
1975	8.0	1–2V	87 @ 4400	122 @ 2800	opt in Astre, std in Astre SJ and GT
1976	7.9	1–1V	70 @ 4400	107 @ 2400	std in Astre and Sunbird
1976	7.9	1–2V	84 @ 4400	113 @ 3200	opt in Astre and Sunbird
1977	8.0	1–2V	84 @ 4400	117 @ 2400	std in Astre, opt in Sunbird

400 cid V-8

1967	8.6	1–2V	255 @ 4400	397 @ 2400	opt in GTO with Turbo-HydraMatic
1967	8.6	1–2V	265 @ 4600	397 @ 2400	std in Catalina and Executive with synchromesh; opt in all B-body models (any transmission)
1967	10.5	1–2V	290 @ 4600	428 @ 2500	std in Catalina and Executive with Turbo-HydraMatic; opt in other B-body models
1967	10.5	1–4V	350 @ 5000	440 @ 3200	std in Grand Prix
1967	10.75	1–4V	325 @ 4800	410 @ 3400	std in Firebird Formula 400
1967	10.75	1–4V	325 @ 5200	410 @ 3600	opt in Firebird Formula 400
1967	10.5	1–4V	325 @ 4800	445 @ 2900	std in Bonneville with Turbo-HydraMatic; opt in other B-body models with THM
1967	10.5	1–4V	333 @ 5000	445 @ 3000	std in Bonneville with synchromesh; opt in Catalina and Executive with synchromesh
1967	10.75	1–4V	335 @ 5000	441 @ 3400	std in GTO
1967	10.75	1–4V	360 @ 5100	438 @ 3600	opt in GTO
1967	10.75	1–4V	360 @ 5400	438 @ 3800	opt in GTO
1968	8.6	1–2V	265 @ 4600	397 @ 2400	opt in GTO and B-body models with Turbo-HydraMatic
1968	10.5	1–2V	290 @ 4600	428 @ 2500	std in Catalina and Executive
1968	10.5	1–4V	350 @ 5000	445 @ 3000	std in Grand Prix
1968	10.5	1–4V	340 @ 4800	445 @ 2900	std in Bonneville; opt in other B-body models
1968	10.75	1–4V	330 @ 4800	430 @ 3300	std in Firebird Formula 400
1968	10.75	1–4V	335 @ 5000	430 @ 3400	opt in Firebird Formula 400
1968	10.75	1–4V	350 @ 5000	445 @ 3000	std in GTO
1968	10.75	1–4V	360 @ 5100	445 @ 3600	opt in GTO (ram air)
1968	10.75	1–4V	366 @ 5400	445 @ 3800	opt in GTO (ram air II)
1969	8.6	1–2V	265 @ 4600	397 @ 2400	opt in Catalina, Executive and GTO
1969	10.5	1–2V	290 @ 4600	428 @ 2500	std in Catalina and Executive
1969	10.5	1–4V	350 @ 5000	445 @ 3000	std in Grand Prix
1969	10.75	1–4V	330 @ 4800	430 @ 3300	std in Firebird Formula 400
1969	10.75	1–4V	335 @ 5000	430 @ 3400	opt in Firebird Formula 400, std in Trans Am
1969	10.75	1–4V	345 @ 5400	430 @ 3700	opt in Firebird Formula 400 and Trans Am
1969	10.75	1–4V	350 @ 5000	445 @ 3000	std in GTO

Year	Compr. ratio	Carb.	Hp @ rpm	Torque @ rpm	Remarks
1969	10.75	1–4V	366 @ 5100	445 @ 3600	opt in GTO
1969	10.75	1–4V	370 @ 5500	445 @ 3900	opt in GTO
1970	8.6	1–2V	265 @ 4600	397 @ 2400	opt in all B-body models, Grand Prix, LeMans, Firebird Esprit
1970	10.0	1–2V	290 @ 4600	428 @ 2500	std in Executive and Safari, opt in Catalina
1970	10.0	1–4V	330 @ 4800	445 @ 2900	opt in all B-body models and LeMans
1970	10.25	1–4V	330 @ 4800	430 @ 3000	std in Firebird Formula 400
1970	10.25	1–4V	350 @ 5000	445 @ 3000	std in Grand Prix and GTO
1970	10.5	1–4V	345 @ 5000	430 @ 3400	std in Trans Am, opt in Formula 400
1970	10.5	1–4V	366 @ 5100	445 @ 3600	opt in GTO
1970	10.5	1–4V	370 @ 5500	445 @ 3900	opt in GTO, Trans Am and Formula 400
1971	8.2	1–2V	265 @ 4400	400 @ 2400	opt in Catalina, LeMans, Firebird Esprit; std in Catalina Brougham
1971	8.2	1–4V	300 @ 4800	400 @ 2400	std in GTO
1971	8.2	1–4V	300 @ 4800	400 @ 3600	std in Grand Prix, Firebird Formula 400; opt in LeMans and Catalina
1972	8.2	1–2V	200 @ 4000	325 @ 2400	opt in LeMans and Catalina
1972	8.2	1–4V	200 @ 4000	295 @ 2800	opt in LeMans and Catalina
1972	8.2	1–4V	250 @ 4400	325 @ 3200	std in Grand Prix, GTO, Formula 400; opt in LeMans and Catalina
1973	8.0	1–2V	170 @ 3600	320 @ 2000	std in Grand Am, Safari, Bonneville; opt in LeMans, Catalina, Firebird Esprit
1973	8.0	1–2V	185 @ 4000	320 @ 2400	opt in LeMans, Grand Am, Catalina
1973	8.0	1–4V	200 @ 4000	310 @ 2400	std in Grand Safari; opt in Catalina and Bonneville
1973	8.0	1–4V	230 @ 4400	325 @ 3200	std in GTO, Grand Prix; opt in LeMans, Grand Am, Formula 400, Catalina, Bonneville
1974	8.0	1–2V	175 @ 3600	315 @ 2000	std in Grand Am, Catalina, Bonneville, Safari; opt in LeMans and Firebird Esprit
1974	8.0	1–2V	190 @ 4000	330 @ 2400	opt in LeMans, Grand Am, Firebird Esprit and Formula 400
1974	8.0	1–4V	200 @ 4000	320 @ 2400	opt on Catalina and Bonneville
1974	8.0	1–4V	225 @ 4000	330 @ 2800	std on Grand Prix and Trans Am; opt on Formula 400, LeMans, Grand Am
1975	7.6	1–2V	170 @ 4000	305 @ 2000	std on Catalina, Bonneville, Grand Am; opt Grand Ville
1975	7.6	1–4V	185 @ 3600	310 @ 1600	std on Grand Ville, Grand Prix, Trans Am; opt on Formula 400, LeMans, Catalina, Bonneville
1976	7.6	1–2V	170 @ 4000	310 @ 1600	std in Catalina, Bonneville; opt in LeMans and Grand Prix
1976	7.6	1–4V	185 @ 3600	310 @ 1600	std in Grand Prix SJ, Bonneville Brougham, and Trans Am; opt in Catalina, Bonneville, Grand Prix, LeMans, and Firebird
1977	7.6	1–4V	180 @ 3600	325 @ 1600	std in Trans Am; opt in Formula 400, Grand Prix, LeMans, Catalina, Bonneville
1977	8.0	1–4V	200 @ 3600	325 @ 2400	opt in Firebird, Trans Am and Formula 400
1978	7.7	1–4V	180 @ 3600	325 @ 1600	std in Trans Am; opt in Formula 400, Catalina and Bonneville
1978	8.1	1–4V	220 @ 4000	320 @ 2800	opt in Firebird Formula 400 and Trans Am

455 cid V–8

1970	10.0	1–4V	360 @ 4300	500 @ 2700	std in Bonneville; opt in Catalina, Executive
1970	10.25	1–4V	360 @ 4600	500 @ 3100	opt on GTO
1970	10.25	1–4V	370 @ 4600	500 @ 3100	opt in Grand Prix, Catalina, Bonneville
1971	8.2	1–2V	280 @ 4400	455 @ 2000	std in Bonneville; opt in Catalina
1971	8.2	1–4V	325 @ 4400	455 @ 3200	std in Grand Ville; opt in Firebird Formula 455, LeMans, GTO, Catalina, Bonneville
1971	8.4	1–4V	335 @ 4800	480 @ 3600	std on Trans Am; opt in GTO and LeMans
1972	8.2	1–2V	185 @ 4000	350 @ 2000	std on Bonneville; opt in Catalina
1972	8.2	1–2V	200 @ 4000	370 @ 2000	opt on Catalina, Bonneville
1972	8.2	1–4V	220 @ 3600	350 @ 2400	std on Grand Ville; opt in Catalina, Bonneville
1972	8.2	1–4V	230 @ 4400	360 @ 2800	opt on LeMans and GTO
1972	8.2	1–4V	250 @ 3600	375 @ 2400	opt on LeMans, GTO, Grand Prix, Catalina, Bonneville, Grand Ville
1972	8.4	1–4V	300 @ 4000	415 @ 3200	std on Trans Am; opt on LeMans, GTO, Firebird Formula 455
1973	8.0	1–4V	215 @ 3600	350 @ 2400	std in Grand Ville; opt in Catalina, Bonneville
1973	8.0	1–4V	250 @ 4000	370 @ 2800	std in Trans Am; opt in Grand Prix, Grand Ville, Catalina, Bonneville, GTO, LeMans, Formula 455
1973	8.4	1–4V	290 @ 4000	390 @ 3600	opt in Trans Am, Formula 455
1974	8.0	1–4V	215 @ 3600	355 @ 2400	std in Grand Ville; opt in Catalina, Bonneville
1974	8.0	1–4V	250 @ 4000	370 @ 2800	opt in Grand Am, Grand Prix, Grand Ville, Catalina, Bonneville, LeMans, Firebird Formula 455, Trans Am
1974	8.4	1–4V	290 @ 4000	390 @ 3600	opt in Trans Am, Formula 455
1975	7.6	1–4V	200 @ 3500	330 @ 2000	opt in Grand Am, Grand Prix, Catalina, Bonneville, Grand Ville and Trans Am
1976	7.6	1–4V	200 @ 3500	330 @ 2000	opt in Catalina, Bonneville, Grand Prix, LeMans, Trans Am; std in B-body station wagons

307 cid V–8 (Chevrolet)

1971	8.5	1–2V	200 @ 4600	300 @ 2400	opt in Ventura
1972	8.5	1–2V	130 @ 4400	230 @ 2400	opt in Ventura

260 cid V–8 (Oldsmobile)

1975	8.0	1–2V	110 @ 3400	205 @ 1600	opt in Ventura
1976	7.5	1–2V	110 @ 3400	205 @ 1600	opt in Ventura and LeMans

231 cid V–6 (Buick)

1976	8.0	1–2V	105 @ 3400	185 @ 2000	opt in Sunbird
1977	8.0	1–2V	105 @ 3200	185 @ 2000	std in Ventura, Phoenix, Firebird, LeMans and Catalina; opt in Sunbird
1978	8.0	1–2V	105 @ 3400	185 @ 2000	std in Firebird, Phoenix, LeMans, Catalina and Grand Prix, opt in Sunbird

305 cid V–8 (Chevrolet)

1977	8.5	1–2V	145 @ 3800	245 @ 2400	opt in Firebird, Ventura, Phoenix
1978	8.4	1–2V	145 @ 3800	245 @ 2400	opt in Firebird, Phoenix, Sunbird, Grand Am, LeMans, Grand Prix

151 cid four

1977	8.3	1–2V	88 @ 4400	128 @ 2400	std in Astre wagon and hatchback, std in Sunbird; opt in Ventura and Phoenix
1978	8.3	1–2V	85 @ 4400	123 @ 2800	std in Sunbird; opt in Phoenix

Year	Compr. ratio	Carb.	Hp @ rpm	Torque @ rpm	Remarks
301 cid V–8					
1977	8.2	1–2V	135 @ 4000	235 @ 2000	std in Firebird Formula with synchromesh
1977	8.2	1–2V	135 @ 4000	245 @ 2000	std in Bonneville, Grand Prix; opt in Catalina, Ventura, Firebird Esprit and Formula
1978	8.2	1–2V	140 @ 3600	235 @ 2000	std in Bonneville, Grand Am, Grand Prix LJ; opt in Catalina and Grand Prix
1978	8.2	1–4V	150 @ 4000	240 @ 2000	opt in Grand Am; std in Grand Prix SJ
403 cid V–8 (Oldsmobile)					
1977	8.0	1–4V	185 @ 3600	320 @ 2200	opt in Trans Am and Formula, LeMans, Grand Prix, Catalina and Bonneville
1978	7.9	1–4V	185 @ 3600	320 @ 2200	opt in Catalina, Bonneville, Firebird Formula and Trans Am

NOTES ON ENGINE SPECIFICATIONS

Horsepower: The industry switched from SAE gross to SAE net hp at the start of the 1972 model year.
Pontiac adopted catalytic converters for all engines at the start of the 1975 model year.

SV = side valves   OHV = overhead valves   SOHC = single overhead camshaft

Displacement is indicated in cubic inches.
Torque is measured in pounds-feet.

Carburetors: V = venturi (throat or barrel).
1–4V means single four-barrel.   3–2V means triple two-barrel.

Appendix VI
NASCAR Pontiac Victories

Courtesy of the National Association of Stock Car Auto Racing, Daytona Beach, Fla.

Date	Race Winner	Year of Car	Location	Date	Race Winner	Year of Car	Location
1958 Season:				August 27	Junior Johnson	1960	So. Boston, Va.
February 23	Paul Goldsmith	1958	Daytona Beach, Fla.	September 10	Joe Weatherly	1961	Richmond, Va.
July 25	Cotton Owens	1957	Rochester, N.Y.	September 17	David Pearson	1961	Atlanta, Ga.
September 28	Joe Eubanks	1957	Hillsboro, N.C.	September 24	Joe Weatherly	1961	Martinsville, Va.
				October 15	Joe Weatherly	1961	Charlotte, N.C.
1959 Season:				October 22	Joe Weatherly	1961	Bristol, Tenn.
July 4	Fireball Roberts	1959	Daytona Beach, Fla.	October 28	Junior Johnson	1961	Greenville, S.C.
				October 29	Joe Weatherly	1961	Hillsboro, N.C.
1960 Season:							
February 12 – (1)	Fireball Roberts	1960	Daytona Beach, Fla.				
– (2)	Fireball Roberts	1960	Daytona Beach, Fla.	**1962 Season:**			
July 4	Jack Smith	1960	Daytona Beach, Fla.	November 5, 1961	Jack Smith	1961	Concord, N.C.
July 31	Fireball Roberts	1960	Atlanta, Ga.	February 16 – (1)	Fireball Roberts	1962	Daytona Beach, Fla.
August 16	Cotton Owens	1960	Spartanburg, S.C.	– (2)	Joe Weatherly	1962	Daytona Beach, Fla.
September 5	Buck Baker	1960	Darlington, S.C.	February 18	Fireball Roberts	1962	Daytona Beach, Fla.
October 30	Bobby Johns	1960	Atlanta, Ga.	February 25	Joe Weatherly	1961	Concord, N.C.
				March 4	Joe Weatherly	1961	Weaverville, N.C.
1961 Season:				March 17	Jack Smith	1962	Savannah, Ga.
February 24 – (1)	Fireball Roberts	1961	Daytona Beach, Fla.	April 21	Jack Smith	1961	Myrtle Beach, S.C.
– (2)	Joe Weatherly	1961	Daytona Beach, Fla.	April 29	Bobby Johns	1962	Bristol, Tenn.
February 26	Marvin Panch	1960	Daytona Beach, Fla.	May 4	Jim Pardue	1962	Richmond, Va.
March 4	Cotton Owens	1960	Spartanburg, S.C.	May 5	Jack Smith	1961	Hickory, N.C.
March 12	Fireball Roberts	1961	Hanford, Calif.	May 6	Joe Weatherly	1961	Concord, N.C.
March 26	Bob Burdick	1961	Atlanta, Ga.	June 16	Johnny Allen	1961	Winston-Salem, N.C.
April 2	Cotton Owens	1960	Hillsboro, N.C.	June 19	Joe Weatherly	1961	Augusta, Ga.
April 20	Cotton Owens	1960	Columbia, S.C.	June 22	Jim Paschal	1962	Richmond, Va.
April 22	Junior Johnson	1961	Hickory, N.C.	July 4	Fireball Roberts	1962	Daytona Beach, Fla.
April 30	Junior Johnson	1961	Martinsville, Va.	July 13	Jack Smith	1961	Asheville, N.C.
May 21	Joe Weatherly	1961	Charlotte, N.C.	July 17	Joe Weatherly	1961	Augusta, Ga.
May 28	David Pearson	1961	Charlotte, N.C.	July 20	Joe Weatherly	1961	Savannah, Ga.
June 2	Jim Paschal	1961	Spartanburg, S.C.	August 3	Joe Weatherly	1961	Chattanooga, Tenn.
June 8	Jack Smith	1961	Greenville, S.C.	September 9	Joe Weatherly	1962	Richmond, Va.
June 24	Junior Johnson	1960	Roanoke, Va.	October 14	Junior Johnson	1962	Charlotte, N.C.
July 4	David Pearson	1961	Daytona Beach, Fla.				
July 20	Cotton Owens	1960	Columbia, S.C.	**1963 Season:**			
July 22	Joe Weatherly	1961	Myrtle Beach, S.C.	April 7	Joe Weatherly	1963	Richmond, Va.
July 30	Jack Smith	1961	Bristol, Tenn.	April 13	Buck Baker	1963	Greenville, S.C.
August 6	Jim Paschal	1961	Nashville, Tenn.	May 11	Joe Weatherly	1963	Darlington, S.C.
August 13	Junior Johnson	1960	Weaverville, N.C.	October 27	Joe Weatherly	1963	Hillsboro, N.C.
August 18	Junior Johnson	1960	Richmond, Va.				

Appendix VII
Pontiac Literature 1946–1974
Compiled by Jeffrey I. Godshall and Autoenthusiasts International

1946:
Folder, 8½ x 5½, full-line, color, 5-46
Folder, 10 x 7, Streamliners, color, 8-45

1947:
Folder, 11 x 6½, full-line, color
Folder, 11 x 6½, full-line, color, 11-47

1948:
Folder, 11 x 6½, full-line, color
Catalog, 9 x 6, HydraMatic, b&w&red, 12p.
Catalog, 9 x 6, access., b&w&grey&yellow, 16p.
Catalog, 7½ x 5½, Body by Fisher, b&w&brown, 12p.

1949:
Folder, 11½ x 7½, full-line, color
Folder, 12 x 7, Wood wagon, color, 3-49
Folder, 11 x 7, Sedan-Delivery, color, 5-49
Mailer/Folder, 10½ x 7, *Life* ad reprint, color
Catalog, 8½ x 11, access., b&w&buff with color covers, 24p.

1950:
Folder, 11½ x 10, full-line, color, red car on cover
Folder, 11½ x 10, full-line, color, white car on cover
Folder, 11 x 8½, Catalina, color
Catalog, 8½ x 11, access., blue&b&w with color cover, 24p.
Folder, 11½ x 9, wagon, color
Folder, 4 x 4½, ". . . with HydraMatic," b&w&brown& grey

1951:
Folder, 8 x 11, full-line, color, 10-50
Folder, 11½ x 9, Catalina, color, 11-50
Folder, 8 x 10½, partial full-line, color
Folder, 4 x 8½, access./prices, green&white
Catalog, 8½ x 11, access., b&w&blue with color covers, 24p. plus covers
Folder, 5 x 8½, access., red&grey&white

1952:
Folder, 11 x 11, full-line, color, 10-51
Folder, 8 x 10½, full-line, color
Folder, 12 x 8½, Catalina, color, 1-52
Catalog, 10 x 8, Dual-Range transmission, red& blue&white, 8p.
Folder, 6 x 9, access., b&w&red
Catalog, 9 x 6, Dual-Range transmission, red&blue& white, 8p.
Catalog, 8½ x 11, access., 2-color, 24p.
Folder, 5 x 7, "You're Invited," color

1953:
Catalog, 11 x 14½, full-line, color, 8p.
Folder, 12 x 11½, full-line, color, 11-52
Folder, 11 x 10½, wagon, color, 5-53
Folder, 7 x 4½, prices, b&w&red
Folder, 3½ x 8½, prices, blue&white
Catalog, 11 x 14½, full-line, color, 8p., 3-53
Catalog, 5 x 7, Body by Fisher, b&w, 24p.
Folder, 11 x 14, full-line, color
Folder, 7 x 4, prices, b&w&blue

1954:
Catalog, 12½ x 10½, full-line, color, 24p., 11-53
Catalog, 11 x 14, full-line, color, 8p., 11-53
Catalog, 11 x 14, full-line, color, 8p., 5-54
Folder, 9 x 6½, access., brown&white
Postcards, 5½ x 3½, assorted models (10), color
Folder, 9 x 5½, Bonneville/Strato Streak show cars and production models, b&w
Card, 7 x 5, Strato Streak show car, b&w
Folder, 10 x 6, Bonneville/Strato Streak show cars and production models, color
Folder, 7 x 4, prices, b&w&yellow

1955:
Catalog, 11½ x 11, full-line, color, 28p., 11-54
Catalog, 11½ x 8, Safari/wagons, color, 8p., 2-55
Folder, 8 x 6, V-8, color, 10-54
Catalog, 6½ x 9, access., b&w&gold, 16p.
Folder, 8 x 4, "New From Ground Up," color
Folder, 10 x 6, Safari/Strato Star show car, color
Catalog/Folder, 11 x 14, full-line, color, 8p., 10-54
Catalog/Folder, 11 x 14, full-line, color, 8p., 1-55
Catalog/Folder, 11 x 14, full-line, color, 8p., 7-55
Postcard, 8 x 5, 860 2-door, color
Folder, 6½ x 4, "Colony" wagon, color

1956:
Catalog, 12½ x 12, full-line, color, 28p., 10-55
Catalog/Folder, 11½ x 14, full-line, color, 12p., 10-55
Catalog/Folder, 11½ x 14, full-line, color, 12p., 1-56
Postcards, 5½ x 3½, assorted models (2), color
Catalog, 6½ x 9, access., b&w&orange, 20p.
Folder, 10 x 7, Club de Mer show car, color
Booklet, 4½ x 8½, Harrison AC, b&w&blue

1957:
Catalog, 11½ x 11, full-line, color 28p.
Catalog, 8 x 5, access., b&w&chartreuse, 20p.

Catalog 11 x 5, Safaris, color, 12p.
Folder, 12 x 5½, Bonneville/4-door Safari show cars, color
Folder, 8½ x 4½, colors (Star Chief convertible/ sedan, Super Chief and Chieftain), color
Folder, 8½ x 4½, colors (Star Chief Catalina, custom sedan, Safari)
Catalog/Folder, 5 x 3, full-line, color, 8p.
Folder, 12 x 6, full-line, color

1958:
Catalog, 10½ x 12½, full-line, color, 28p.
Folder, 8½ x 4, full-line, color
Catalog, 14 x 5, access., b&w&blue, 16p.
Postcards, 5½ x 3½, Chieftain 4-door hardtop, 2- door sedan, convertible
Catalog, 10½ x 12½, full-line, 28p.

1959:
Catalog, 12 x 10½, full-line, color, 28p.
Catalog, 11 x 8½, full-line, color, 16p.
Catalog, 6 x 4, access., b&w&gold, 16p.
Catalog, 3½ x 2, full-line, color, 20p.

1960:
Catalog, 12 x 10½, full-line, color, 28p., 9-59
Catalog, 11 x 8½, full-line, color, 16p., 9-59
Catalog, 11 x 8½, full-line, color, 16p., rev. 1-60
Folder, 4 x 8½, prices, b&w
Folder, 6 x 9, "What's New?," b&w&yellow
Folder, 10 x 8½, fleet cars, 2-color

1961:
Catalog, 11 x 14, Tempest, b&w, 16p. plus tissue sheets
Catalog, 11 x 8½, full-size, color, 16p. ("Litho USA" —left side)
Catalog, 8 x 11, Tempest, b&w, 16p.
Folder, 8½ x 5½, access., b&w&orange
Folder, 6 x 11, Tempest (with coupe), color
Folder, 6 x 9, Tempest access., b&w&brown& orange
Booklet, 8½ x 11, *Motor Life* Tempest Report, b&w with color covers, 6p.
Catalog, 12 x 10½, full-size, color, 28p.
Catalog, 3½ x 2, full-size, color, 20p.
Booklet, 8½ x 11, SAE Tempest paper, b&w, 44p. plus covers
Postcards, 5½ x 3, assorted models (6), color

Catalog, 11 x 8½, full-size, color, 16p., revised ("Litho USA"—right side)
Folder, 8½ x 11, "What's New . . . Pontiac," b&w&red
Booklet, 4 x 6½, Pontiac Accessorizer, orange
Booklet, 4 x 6½, Pontiac Accessorizer, orange, Revised 1-1-61
Booklet, 4 x 6½, Tempest Accessorizer, orange
Folder, 11 x 7½, "Hot Topic," b&w
Booklet, 6 x 9½, *Popular Science* Tempest Report, b&w with color gate fold covers, 4p., 9-60

1962:
Catalog, 12 x 7, full-line, color 16p.
Folder, 7 x 9, access., b&w&blue
Folder, 7 x 10, access., b&w&red
Catalog, 8½ x 9½, Tempest, color, 16p.
Catalog, 10½ x 12, Tempest, color, 16p.
Catalog, 8½ x 11, "Royal Pontiac Story," brown& white, 20p.
Catalog, 15 x 8½, full-line, color, 28p.
Portfolio, 10 x 12, Superior Ambulance/Hearse, color (2 folders, 2 sheets)

1963:
Catalog, 12 x 12, Tempest, color, 16p. plus tissue sheets
Catalog, 8 x 8, Tempest, color, 12p.
Catalog, 8½ x 11, access., b&w&gold&orange, 24p.
Catalog, 15 x 8, regular line, color, 32p. plus covers
Catalog, 12 x 7, regular line, color, 16p.

1964:
Catalog, 11½ x 12½, Tempest, color, 20p.
Catalog, 7½ x 8, Tempest, color, 16p.
Catalog, 7½ x 8, GTO, color, 8p.
Catalog, 8½ x 11, access., b&w&blue, 24p.
Catalog, 11 x 9, Pontiac, color, 16p.
Catalog, 13 x 11, Pontiac, color, 24p. plus covers
Catalog, 8½ x 11, Trailer Towing, b&w&blue, 12p., SP-1703, 11-63
Folder, 9 x 4, full-line, b&w&blue, SP-1539, 9-63
Catalog, 11 x 9, Superior Funeral Cars, color, 12p.
Sheet, 8½ x 11, Superior Funeral Cars, b&w
Sheet, 11 x 9, Limousine/Sedan, b&w
Folder, 9 x 4, "64 Wide-Tracks," b&w&blue, SP-1539, 9-63
Portfolio, 10 x 17, "Fleet Story," including production information guide, accessory catalog and sheet (8½ x 11, Taxi, b&w)
Folder, 8½ x 11, Police, b&w, SP-1686, 10-63
Folder, 6½ x 3, colors, color, SP-1548, 8-63

1965:
Portfolio, 12 x 12, "Fleet Owner's Choice," b&w& red&blue cover, 2 b&w plates, mailer envelope
Sheet, 8½ x 11, Tempest/Pontiac Taxi, b&w
Folder, 8½ x 11, Tempest/Pontiac Police, b&w, SP-1926, 9-64

Catalog, 12 x 10, Performance Cars, color, 16p.
Catalog, 11 x 12, full-line, color, 8p. (newspaper supplement)
Catalog, 11 x 14, full-line, 48p. plus covers
Catalog, 8½ x 11, Trailer Towing, b&w&green, 16p., SP-1932, 11-64
Folder, 8½ x 11, Embassy Limousine (Superior), color, (folder 1)
Catalog, 11½ x 9, Superior Coaches, color, 12p. with foldout
Catalog, 14 x 11, Grand Prix, color, 8p.
Folder, 10 x 10, Wagons, color
Catalog, 8 x 11, accessories, b&w&gold with color covers, 32p.
Folder, 9 x 4, full-line, b&w&red, SP-1934, 8-64
Magazine, 8½ x 11, "Safari" 1965 introduction, color, 24p.
Catalog, 8 x 10½, full-line, color, 48p. plus covers
Folder, 4 x 7, Pontiac/Tempest prices, b&w (Toledo)
Catalog, 8½ x 11, Trailer-Towing Options, b&w& green, 16p., SP-1932, 11-64
Catalog, 8½ x 5½, air conditioning, color, 8p., SP-2092

1966:
Folder, 4 x 9, full-line, b&w&red&purple, SP-2089
Catalog, 10½ x 10½, Performance Cars, color, 20p.
Catalog, 8½ x 10½, full-line, color, 52p. plus covers
Catalog, 8½ x 10½, access., b&w with color covers, 48p.
Folder, 10 x 10, Wagons, b&w
Folder, 13½ x 10½, Grand Prix, color,
Folder, 6½ x 3, colors and interiors, color, SP-2127, 8-65
Folder, 8½ x 11, Catalina "Enforcer," b&w, SP-2080
Catalog, 10½ x 13, full-line, color, 52p. plus covers
Card, 9 x 6, Superior Ambulance, color
Catalog, 11½ x 9, Superior Coaches, color, 4p. plus insert pages
Catalog, 8½ x 11, Pontiac Trailer-Towing, b&w& green&blue&grey, 16p., SP-2079
Booklet, 7 x 3½, Dealer-Installed Access., b&w, 22p. plus cover, 9785254 (revised 3-66)
Magazine, 8½ x 11, Safari with 1966 introduction
Mailer/Folder, 11 x 7½, Catalina, color

1967:
Catalog, 9 x 12, Superior Coaches, color, 8p. with foldout
Catalog, 11 x 12, full-line (including Firebird), color, 8p. (newspaper insert)
Folder, 3½ x 7, Space-Saver Spare (Firebird), b&w& green
Catalog, 8½ x 12, Firebird, color, 8p. with foldouts
Catalog, 10½ x 13, full-line (no Firebird), color, 52p. plus covers

Catalog, 10½ x 12, Firebird, color, 8p. (newspaper insert)
Folder, 8½ x 11, "How to Buy GTO," b&w (reprint- "Super Stock")
Magazine, 8½ x 11, "Safari" 1967 introduction, color, 24p.
Catalog, 8 x 16, Performance Cars, color, 24p.
Mailer/Folder, 9 x 6, Catalina, color
Catalog, 8½ x 10½, access., b&w with color covers, 56p., DM-18197
Catalog, 8½ x 10, full-line (no Firebird), color, 52p. plus covers
Catalog, 7 x 3½, Colors/Interiors, color, 16p. with foldout, SP-2329, R8-66
Catalog, 8½ x 11, Trailer Towing, b&w&green, 12p., SP-2492
Catalog, 9 x 6, Air Conditioning, color 8p., SP-2454
Folder, 8½ x 10½, access., Firebird, b&w
Catalog, 12 x 10½, Grand Prix, color, 8p.
Catalog, 11 x 9, Wagons, color, 16p.
Catalog, 7 x 3½, full-line (no Firebird), b&w, 16p.
Catalog, 10½ x 12½, full-line (no Firebird), color, 16p.
Folder, 6 x 6, Firebird Innovation, color
Booklet, 4 x 7, access. prices, black&cream, 28p. SP-2563
Magazine, 8½ x 11, "Safari" Jan-Feb 1967, color (Firebird issue)
Booklet, 3½ x 7, Dealer-Installed Access., b&w& blue, 30p. plus cover, 9788694, SP-2439, revised 10-66

1968:
Magazine, 8 x 11, *Motor Trend* "Car of the Year," color, 24p.
Catalog, 8½ x 11, Trailer Towing, b&w&brown, 12p. SP-2821, 10-67
Catalog, 10½ x 11, full-line, color, 56p.
Catalog, 10½ x 11, full-line, color, 24p.
Catalog, 11 x 9, full-line, color, 8p. (newspaper insert)
Card, 9 x 4, Bonneville Brougham, color
Catalog, 8½ x 5, "10 Ways . . . ," color, 12p.
Catalog, 8 x 10½, access., color and b&w, 32p.
Catalog, 10 x 10, Grand Prix, color, 12p.
Catalog, 9 x 9, Wagons, color, 16p.
Catalog, 11 x 11, Firebird, 12p.
Catalog, 11 x 11, Performance Cars, color, 24p.
Folder, 7 x 3½, colors/interiors, color, SP-2724, revised 8-67, updated 9-67
Folder, 6 x 9, Air Conditioning, color, SP-2819

1969:
Catalog, 7 x 3½, full-line, b&w, 16p., SP-2594
Mailer/Catalog, 9 x 9, "Great Break-Away Sale," color, 8p., SP-3033

Ad, 15½ x 11, Firebird Trans Am, color
Sheet, 8½ x 11, Firebird Trans Am Specs, black&
  green
Card, 7½ x 3, GTO "Judge," color
Catalog, 8½ x 11, Trailer-Towing, b&w&gold&
  green, 12p., SP-3005
Mailer/Folder, 9½ x 7½, "8 Great Ways," color, SP-
  3000
Sheet, 8½ x 11, Judge Specs, black&pink
Catalog, 11 x 9, Wagons, color, 16p.
Catalog, 10 x 13, Grand Prix, color, 16p. plus covers
Catalog, 8 x 8, Air Conditioning, color, 8p., SP-2676
Catalog, 10½ x 11, full-line, color, 28p.
Catalog, 9 x 12, Performance Cars, color, 20p. plus
  foldouts
Catalog, 8½ x 11, access., part color, 28p., 9-68
Catalog, 9 x 10½, Firebird, color, 12p. (also without
  1969 imprint on car), 3-69
Catalog, 10½ x 13, full-line, color, 52p. plus covers
Catalog, 8½ x 11, "Join Great Break-Away," color,
  16p., SP-3000
Catalog, 8½ x 11, *Car Life* Engine Award, b&w with
  color covers, 20p.

1970:
Booklet, 10 x 11½, "Fleet Buyer's Guide," b&w&
  color, 38p. plus accessory catalog and order
  sheets, SP-3104
Catalog, 7 x 3½, colors/interiors, color, 16p. plus
  foldout, SP-3109, 8-1-69
Catalog, 10 x 8, "Take A Good Look . . . Inside,"
  color, 12p., SP-3130
Catalog, 8½ x 11, access., part color, 28p., DM-
  27225, 9-69
Catalog, 9 x 12, full-line (no Firebird), color, 52p.
  plus covers, DM-27229, 9-69
Catalog, 10 x 13, Grand Prix, color, 12p. plus covers,
  9-69
Catalog, 9 x 11, 1969 Firebird, color, 12p., 3-69
Catalog, 10 x 5, Air Conditioning, color, 8p., SP-
  3122
Catalog, 9 x 11, Wagons, color, 16p., 9-69
Catalog, 8½ x 11, Trailer Towing, color, 12p., SP-
  3123
Sheet, 8½ x 11, Trailer-Towing Prices, black&gold,
  SP-3325
Catalog, 8½ x 10½, full-line, Preview for Pontiac
  Owners (no Firebird), color, 20p.
Catalog, 11 x 9, 1970 Firebird, color, 20p., DM-
  27291, 2-70
Catalog, 8½ x 11, Royal Bobcat, b&w with color
  covers, 32p. with foldout
Card, 9 x 4, Bonneville 2-door hardtop, color
Folder, 4 x 8½, Pocket Facts—Catalina, b&w&green,
  4657, 11-69

Folder, 4 x 8½, Pocket Facts—Tempest, blue, 4686-
  1169
Catalog, 10 x 10, Performance Cars, color, 32p.,
  DM-27228, 9-69
Sheet, 8½ x 11, Tempest GT-37, b&w
Folder, 11 x 7, T-37 Tempest and LeMans Catalina,
  color, SP-3348
Card, 8½ x 4½, T-37, color, SP-3456
Postcards, 5½ x 3, assorted models (3), color
Folder, 8 x 5, Hurst SSJ Grand Prix, b&w&gold
Folder, 11 x 8½, Hurst SSJ Grand Prix, b&w&gold
Catalog, 10½ x 11, full-line (no Firebird), color, 24p.,
  11-69
Catalog, 10½ x 11, full-line (no Firebird), color, 24p.,
  9-69
Folder, 8½ x 4, Firebird Bumper, b&w
Magazine, 8½ x 11, "Safari" June 1970, color, 24p.
  (also September 1969 introduction)

1971:
Folder, 11 x 8½, SSJ Hurst, color
Mailer/Catalog, 10½ x 13, Ventura II (also LeMans
  T-37), color, 8p., SP-3720
Catalog, 10½ x 11, full-line, color, 24p., DM-29134,
  11-70
Catalog, 10½ x 11, full-line, color, 24p. with purple
  cover, DM-29103, 8-70
Catalog, 10½ x 11, full-line, color, 24p. with brown
  cover
Folder, 9 x 8, Ventura II, color
Catalog, 9 x 11, Wagons, color, 16p., DM-29107,
  8-70
Catalog, 11 x 11, Performance Cars, color, 28p.,
  DM-29104, 8-70
Catalog, 8½ x 11, Trailer-Towing, color, SP-3523
Catalog, 8 x 11, access., b&w with brown covers,
  24p., DM-29101
Catalog, 12 x 10½, full-line, color, 56p. with covers,
  DM-29106, 8-70
Booklet, 3½ x 7, colors/interiors, color, 18p., SP-
  3503

1972:
Folder, 11 x 8½, SSJ Hurst, color
Catalog, 10½ x 8, full-line, color, 32p., DM-26627,
  8-71
Catalog, 7 x 3½, colors/interiors, color, 18p. with
  foldout, SP-3756
Catalog, 8½ x 11, access., b&w with brown&black
  covers, 24p., DM-26630
Catalog, 11½ x 10½, full-line, color, 56p. plus covers,
  DM-26626, 8-71
Mailer/Catalog, 10½ x 8½, full-line with correction
  note, color, 32p., SP-3931, 8-71
Catalog, 8 x 11, Trailer-Towing, color, 8p., T-1972,
  8-71

1973:
Catalog, 8½ x 11, access., b&w&blue, 24p., BH-
  46839
Folder, 12 x 10, access., color
Folder, 12 x 10, Grand Ville
Folder, 12 x 10, Bonneville
Folder, 12 x 10, Catalina
Folder, 12 x 10, Safari
Folder, 12 x 10, Grand Prix
Folder, 12 x 10, Grand Am
Folder, 12 x 10, Luxury LeMans
Folder, 12 x 10, LeMans Sport Coupe
Folder, 12 x 10, LeMans
Folder, 12 x 10, Firebird
Folder, 12 x 10, Ventura
Catalog, 10 x 12, full-line, color, 16p., BH-46836,
  8-72
Catalog, 10 x 12, full-line, color, 16p., 8-72
Catalog, 10 x 12, full-line, color, 16p., BH-46836,
  8-72, revised 10-72
(Also white folder for above literature)
Catalog, 8½ x 11, Trailer-Towing, color, 8p. with
  black&yellow insert sheet, T-1973, 8-72
Sheet, 10 x 10½, Specifications, b&w
Catalog, 4 x 8, colors/interiors, color, 22p., SP-
  30642, 7-72
Mailer/Folder, 8½ x 6, "If You Own . . . ," color, SP-
  3964
Mailer/Folder, 10½ x 6, "Drive the Greatest," color,
  SP-3964

1974:
Sheet, 8½ x 11, Catalina "Elegante," b&w&red
Catalog, 10½ x 8, full-line, color, 16p.
Catalog, 8½ x 11, access., b&w, 24p., BH-40957
Catalog, 12 x 10½, full-line, color, 28p.
Folder, 12 x 10, Grand Ville, color
Folder, 12 x 10, Bonneville
Folder, 12 x 10, Catalina
Folder, 12 x 10, Safari
Folder, 12 x 10, Grand Am
Folder, 12 x 10, Grand Prix
Folder, 12 x 10, LeMans
Folder, 12 x 10, Luxury LeMans
Folder, 12 x 10, Ventura
Folder, 12 x 10, GTO
Folder, 12 x 10, Firebird
Catalog, 4 x 9, colors/interiors, color, 26p., SP-
  41009, 8-73
Catalog, 8½ x 11, Trailer-Towing, b&w&green, color
  cover, 8p., SP-41059

Index